A Ⅰ

D0525116

DK READERS is a compelling programme for beginning readers, designed in conjunction with leading literacy experts.

Beautiful illustrations and superb full-colour photographs combine with engaging, easy-to-read stories to offer a fresh approach to each subject in the series. Each DK READER is guaranteed to capture a child's interest while developing his or her reading skills, general knowledge and love of reading.

The four levels of DK READERS are aimed at different reading abilities, enabling you to choose the books that are exactly right for your child:

Level 1 – Beginning to read
Level 2 – Beginning to read alone
Level 3 – Reading alone
Level 4 – Proficient readers

The "normal" age at which a child begins to read can be anywhere from three to eight years old, so these levels are only a general guideline.

No matter which level you select, you can be sure that you are helping your child learn to read, then read to learn!

LONDON, NEW YORK, MELBOURNE,
MUNICH AND DELHI

Editor Kate Phelps
Designer Sooz Bellerby
Series Editor Alastair Dougall
Production Nicola Torode
Picture Researcher Jo de Gray
Picture Library Rose Horridge

06 07 10 9 8 7 6 5 4 3
First published in Great Britain in 2003 by Dorling Kindersley
Limited, 80 Strand, London WC2R ORL
A Penguin Company

Page design copyright © 2003 Dorling Kindersley Limited.

ISBN 1-4053-0193-7

Colour reproduction by Media Development and Printing Ltd, UK
Printed and bound in China by L Rex Printing Co., Ltd.

The publisher thanks the following for their kind permission
to reproduce their photographs:
c=centre; t=top; b=below; l=left; r=right

Cover Anglo Australian Observatory; 5 NASA: bc; 9 NASA: c; 11
NASA: bc; 13 NASA: tc; 15 NASA: tr; 18 London Planetarium: tl; 19
NASA: c, SPL: Novosti tr; 20 NASA: bc; 21 NASA/JPL; 23 SPL: Science,
Industry & Business Library/New York Public Library br; 24 London
Planetarium: tl; 25 NASA: br, NASA/JPL: tc; 27 NASA, NASA/JPL tc;
29 SPL: George Bernard tr; 31 NASA: tc; 33 NASA/JPL: tc; 35 Anglo
Australian Observatory: cb, Anglo Australian Observatory: tc; 37 NASA:
tc; 40 SPL: Space Telescope Science Institute tl; 41 NASA: tc; 43 NASA:
JPL tc, SPL: David Parker cr, SPL: Victor Habbick Visions bc; 44 SPL:
Mark Garlick bc; 47 NASA: bc.

All other photographs © Dorling Kindersley.
For further imformation see: www.dkimages.com

Dorling Kindersley would like to thank the following artists for their
contribution to this book: Marlo Alquiza, Jon Bogdanove, John Byrne,
James Calafiore, Andrew Chiu, John Dell, Dale Eaglesham,
George Freeman, Ron Frenz, Dick Giordano, Tom Grummet,
Andrew Hennessy, John Holdredge, Stuart Immonen, Georges Jeanty,
Dave Johnson, Jeff Johnson, Andy Lanning, Doug Mahnke, Jason Martin,
Kenny Martinez, José Marzan, John McCrea, Ed McGuinness,
Mark McKenna, Mike McKone, Jaime Mendoza, Mark Millar,
Paul Neary, Tom Nguyen, Jerry Ordway, Howard Porter, Pablo Raimondi,
Rodney Ramos, Cliff Rathburn, Darick Robertson, Denis Rodier,
Hanibal Rodriguez, Duncan Rouleau, Paul Ryan, Joe Shuster,
Bill Sienkiewicz, Cam Smith, Dexter Vines, Mike Wieringo,
Anthony Williams, Walden Wong

Discover more at
www.dk.com

Contents

 SUPERMAN'S GUIDE TO THE

Written by Jackie Gaff
Superman created by Jerry Siegel and Joe Shuster

Amazing space

Welcome on board, Earthling, for the trip of a lifetime. Launch yourself into space and fly with me, Superman, on a sensational exploration of the Universe!

Prepare yourself for a long flight, because the Universe is unbelievably big – if it were the size of the Pacific Ocean, the Sun would be smaller than a grain of sand!

We're going everywhere, so hang on tight. The Universe is space and everything in it—you, your friends, your family and everything else on planet Earth. It's the Earth itself and the other planets, plus Earth's moon and all the other planets' moons. Our star, the

Comic debut
The Man of Steel made his first appearance in *Action Comics* in June 1938. Also making their debuts were Clark Kent and Lois Lane.

Sun and all the stars you can see in the night sky are part of the Universe, too. Don't forget, there are billions and billions more stars you can't see because they are too far away.

Are you ready for the journey of a lifetime? Up, up, and away!

Several hundred never-before-seen galaxies are visible in this view of the Universe, taken by the Hubble Space Telescope. Hubble is a satellite telescope that orbits Earth.

"S" symbol
Superman's emblem has its origins in a Native American blanket that belonged to the Kents' ancestors. The "S" represents a snake.

Time travel
The deeper we look into space, the farther back we look in time. This is because starlight takes time to cross the vast distances of space to reach our eyes.

Family circle

The planet Earth belongs to a family of nine planets that travel around a star, the Sun. From nearest to farthest from the Sun, the nine planets are: Mercury, Venus, Earth, Mars, Jupiter, Saturn, Uranus, Neptune and Pluto. The Sun together with the planets, their moons and all the other space bodies that travel around the Sun make up the Solar System – "solar" means "of the Sun".

Narrow escape
Just seconds before a cataclysmic explosion destroyed their home planet of Krypton, Superman's parents, Jor-El and Lara Lor-Van, launched their baby in a spacecraft towards Earth.

The path of a space body around the Sun is called an orbit. Each of the nine planets orbits the Sun at a different speed, and the planets are all travelling incredibly quickly – Earth, for instance, is speeding around the Sun at almost 110,000 km/h (68,500 mph). The time that Earth takes for a single orbit is called a year.

This illustration shows from left to right: Pluto, Neptune, Uranus, Saturn, Jupiter, Mars, the Moon, Earth, Venus and Mercury. Below them glows the hot surface of the Sun. The planets are shown roughly to scale. A comet streaks through the sky between Mars and Jupiter.

But that's not the only way the planets are moving. Each planet is also rotating, or turning around. The planets rotate at different speeds, and as each one turns around, different areas move into and out of the Sun's heat and light. The areas facing the Sun have daylight, while those facing away have the darkness of night. A day is the time from sunrise to sunrise, and on Earth, it lasts 24 hours.

Happy landing
The superbaby's spacecraft fell to Earth near Smallville, in Kansas, USA, where it was found by Martha and Jonathan Kent. They decided to raise the boy as their own son.

The living planet

Earth is unique – the only planet in the Solar System known to have living things. The chief reason why life on Earth is possible is that it is the only planet to have liquid water on its surface. There are millions of different creatures and plants on Earth, but they all have one thing in common. None would survive without water. Earth is in the Sun's life zone – just the right distance away for liquid water and, therefore, life to be possible. All Earth's water would have boiled away if it were too close to the Sun's heat. If it were too far away from the Sun, the water would be locked away as ice.

There is another reason why life exists on Earth – its atmosphere, the skin of gases around it. This protects Earth from the Sun's harmful rays and contains the gases that most animals and plants need to breathe.

Ocean king Superman's fellow JLA member, Aquaman, safeguards Earth's oceans from his home city of Poseidonis, deep beneath the Atlantic waves.

Earth looks blue from space because nearly three-quarters of its surface is covered by vast oceans of liquid water. In the lowest layer of the atmosphere, winds blow clouds and weather around the planet.

EARTH: VITAL STATISTICS
Diameter: 12,756 km (7,926 miles)
Average surface temperature: 15°C (59°F)
Length of a day (sunrise to sunrise): 24 Earth hours
Length of a year: 365.25 Earth days
Distance from the Sun: 150 million km (93 million miles)

The Moon

Earth's nearest neighbour in space is the Moon, and it's the only place beyond Earth that humans have visited. The first men to walk on the Moon were American astronauts Neil Armstrong and Buzz Aldrin, on 21 July 1969. Only 10 other men have been lucky enough to follow in their footsteps, the last in 1972.

Moons are space bodies that orbit a planet, and most of the planets have them. Earth only has

Sea of Serenity

Lunar world
The surface of the Moon is pocked with craters, caused by space rocks bombarding it. There are also mountain ranges and wide plains known as "seas".

Heavenly HQ
The HQ of Earth's super-powered protectors, the JLA, is a fortress on the Moon. It's called the Watchtower and is in the Sea of Serenity.

one, but the record-holder, Jupiter, has an astonishing 60 or more of them!

The Moon is roughly a quarter the size of Earth and about 384,500 km (239,000 miles) away. Its orbit of Earth takes just over 27 days.

League matters
The JLA meets on the Moon to discuss any threats to Earth.

Buzz Aldrin walks on the Moon in July 1969 during the first-ever Moon landing. The photograph was taken by fellow astronaut Neil Armstrong.

HOW MANY MOONS?

Mercury	0
Venus	0
Earth	1
Mars	2
Jupiter	60
Saturn	31
Uranus	21
Neptune	11
Pluto	1

Hot stuff

At 109 times the size of Earth, the Sun is unimaginably huge. It is also immensely hot.

Even the coolest part, its surface, is 5,500°C (9,900°F) – hot enough not just to melt iron, but to make it boil away in a puff of gas.

Unlike the planets, whose cores are made of rock or metal, stars are made only of gas. The Sun is fuelled by hydrogen gas, as are most other stars. It's like a gigantic power station, generating enormous amounts of heat and light.

All this energy is produced in the Sun's centre, or core, where temperatures reach an astonishing 15 million°C (27 million°F). Conditions in the core are so extreme that atoms of hydrogen gas join together to form helium gas. This process is called nuclear fusion,

Sun lover
Superman's superpowers are fuelled by the effect of the Sun's rays on his Kryptonian body cells.

Tyrant sun
The JLA fought and conquered Solaris, an evil artificial star from a future time.

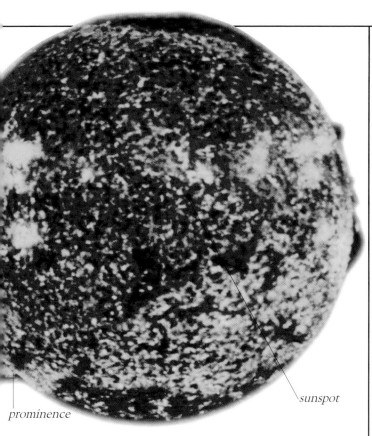

prominence

sunspot

Just one square cm (0.15 square inches) of the Sun's surface shines as brightly as 230,000 candles.

and it generates all the energy the Sun needs to keep shining.

The Sun's surface is dotted with dark patches called sunspots. These areas are about 1,500°C (2,700°F) cooler than the rest of the Sun's surface. Prominences are gigantic fountains of glowing gas that shoot out into space from the surface of the Sun.

Golden globe
The Sun's surface is called the photosphere. The core is where the Sun's energy is produced.

core

photosphere

13

Invisible glue

An invisible force keeps things on Earth and stops them from floating off into space. It's called gravity, and it's so powerful that to escape its pull and blast off into space, rockets have to travel at over 11 km (7 miles) per second!

Everything in the Universe has gravity, however, not just Earth. Gravity is the invisible glue that holds the Universe together.

An object's mass is the amount of matter, or material, it is made of, and the greater an object's mass, the stronger its gravity.

Earth's gravity not only keeps people's feet on the ground, but it also holds the Moon in

Superlight flight
As Earth's gravity is weaker than that of Superman's home planet, Krypton, its pulling effect on Superman's Kryptonian body is weaker. That's one reason why he's able to fly.

Superman didn't realise he could fly until his late teens, when his dog Rusty accidentally knocked him into a deep ravine.

orbit around Earth. At 28 times the strength of Earth's, the Sun's gravity is powerful enough to hold all the other space bodies in

the Solar System in orbit around it.

When a spacecraft orbits Earth, it is actually falling towards the planet's surface, pulled by its gravity. The spacecraft manages to stay out in orbit because it's travelling so fast that it only falls as much as Earth's surface curves beneath it.

Floating feeling
The astronauts in and around an orbiting spacecraft are falling, too. This makes them float about and seem weightless.

SURFACE GRAVITY
(in comparison to Earth, which = 1)

Sun	28
Mercury	0.38
Venus	0.91
Earth	1
Mars	0.38
Jupiter	2.36
Saturn	0.92
Uranus	0.89
Neptune	1.12
Pluto	0.06

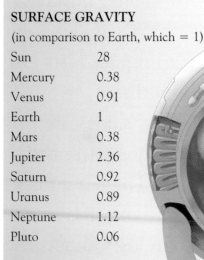

Gravity beaters
Kryptonian scientists invented an anti-gravity generator to lift and propel their futuristic flyer pods.

Mysterious Mercury

The closest planet to the Sun, Mercury is only slightly larger than our Moon. It looks similar to the Moon, too, with its surface pockmarked by thousands of craters made by space rocks crashing into the planet.

Mercury has almost no atmosphere. That means that there's nothing to protect it from the Sun's fierce heat during the daytime or to hold in warmth after darkness falls. And a day is very very long on Mercury. Sunrise to sunrise lasts just under six Earth months.

Although Mercury's days are long, its year is the shortest in the entire Solar System. The planet is so close to the Sun, and orbiting so quickly, that its year lasts about three Earth months.

Breath of air
There's no air in space, and although Superman can hold his breath for a super-long time, for extra-long journeys he sometimes wears a high-tech oxygen mask.

Brainy back-up
Superman's oxygen mask was invented by technological genius Professor Emil Hamilton.

Almost everything we know about Mercury came from the US spacecraft *Mariner 10*, which flew past the planet in the 1970s and took close-up photographs.

core   mantle   crust

Mercury's cratered surface.

The rocky planets
Mercury, Venus, Earth and Mars are mainly made of rock and metal. Each has an outer layer called a crust that is solid rock. A layer of molten rock, called the mantle, is underneath. The rocky planets' cores are made of solid metal.

MERCURY: VITAL STATISTICS
Diameter: 4,879 km (3,032 miles)
Average surface temperature: 167°C (333°F)
Length of a day (sunrise to sunrise): 176 Earth days
Length of a year: 88 Earth days
Distance from the Sun: 58 million km (36 million miles)

US spacecraft Mariner 10.

Venomous Venus

Venus is almost the same size as Earth.

Armour plating
When the going gets tough, JLA ally John Henry Irons (Steel) protects his body by donning super-strong armour.

Landing on Venus would be like touching down in hell! It may not be the closest planet to the Sun, but it's the hottest place in the Solar System, with temperatures soaring as high as 475°C (900°F) – the Sahara Desert, the hottest place on Earth, only reaches about 66°C (150°F).

Venus gets so hot because, unlike Mercury, it has an atmosphere. This is mainly made of a gas called carbon dioxide that acts like a big heavy blanket, trapping in heat and turning the planet into an oven.

But that's not all. Venus's clouds are made of deadly sulphuric acid, while its atmosphere pushes down on the planet's surface with 92 times the pressure of Earth's. This means that anything unlucky enough to land on its surface would be crushed within minutes!

The planet Venus is the brightest object in the night sky after the Moon, and it is clearly visible from Earth with the naked eye. It's best seen just after sunset (look to the west) or before dawn (look to the east).

Venus is covered in volcanoes, some of which are higher than Mount Everest. Scientists aren't sure whether the volcanoes are still active.

VENUS: VITAL STATISTICS
Diameter: 12,104 km (7,521 miles)
Average surface temperature: 464°C (867°F)
Length of a day (sunrise to sunrise): 117 Earth days
Length of a year: 225 Earth days
Distance from the Sun: 108 million km (67 million miles)

Space invaders
A series of Soviet *Venera* spacecraft visited Venus and sent robot landers to its surface in the 1960s to 1980s.

Man of Steel
Superman's Kryptonian body is protected by an invisible force field. Even bullets just bounce off him.

Mars, the red planet

For centuries, people thought that life might exist on Mars. As recently as the last century, science-fiction writers were populating it with little green men.

Humans got their first chance to investigate the planet's surface in 1976, when two US *Viking* spacecrafts sent down robot landers. Then, in 1997, the US *Pathfinder* mission used a robot buggy called *Sojourner* to rove across the landscape analysing the rock.

Martian Manhunter
Superman's fellow JLA member, the green-skinned J'onn J'onzz, is the sole survivor of a plague that wiped out the rest of his kind.

This robot buggy, called Sojourner, *was sent to explore the surface of Mars.*

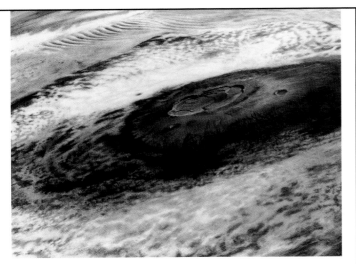

The biggest Martian volcano, Olympus Mons, is the largest in the Solar System. At 27 km (16 miles) high, it's three times taller than Mount Everest!

Mission to Mars
Scientists hope to send human explorers to Mars one day. It'll take them a long time to get there, though—the one-way trip takes at least six months.

No signs of life have been discovered, although scientists hope that future missions may yet find traces of tiny bacteria or algae. This is because there is evidence that liquid water once flowed across the Martian landscape. None remains today, but Mars still has some frozen water in its polar regions.

MARS: VITAL STATISTICS
Diameter: 6,794 km (4,222 miles)
Average surface temperature: –65°C (–85°F)
Length of a day (sunrise to sunrise): 25 Earth hours
Length of a year: 1.9 Earth years
Distance from the Sun: 228 million km (142 million miles)

Alien alert
The White Martians are an evil race, determined to conquer Earth.

Astonishing asteroids

Orbiting the Sun between Mars and Jupiter is a belt of billions of chunks of space rock. The smallest are just a few metres (feet) wide, but, at 930 km (580 miles) across, the largest, Ceres, is about a quarter the size of the Moon. These space rocks are called asteroids.

Most, but not all, asteroids lie in this belt. Some have broken free and follow their own individual orbits around the Sun. Sometimes their orbits bring them close to Earth, and scientists call these rogue rocks Near Earth Asteroids (NEAs for short).

From time to time, Earth is hit by an NEA.

Hot stuff
When an asteroid threatened Earth, Superman and Green Lantern used their superpowers to blast the rock into oblivion.

When the JLA defeated the General, they teleported the monster to a rock in the Asteroid Belt.

Most are small and plunge harmlessly into the ocean, but scientists are using space telescopes to keep an eye out for any dangerously large ones. If a big NEA is found to be heading for Earth, scientists hope to use missiles or lasers to push the NEA off course long before it hits, so don't panic!

Some asteroids contain huge amounts of valuable metals, such as iron, nickel, cobalt and copper. One day it may be possible to send spacecraft to NEAs to mine these precious materials.

Shooting stars
Earth is under constant bombardment from space dust and pebbles. Most of this space rubble burns up in the atmosphere, creating streaks of light as it falls. These are meteors, or shooting stars.

Gigantic Jupiter

The fifth planet from the Sun, Jupiter, is the biggest in the Solar System – more than two and half times as massive as all the other planets combined!

Jupiter is the record holder in more ways than one, because it also has the greatest number of moons. Most of its 60 moons are tiny, but its largest moon, Ganymede, is the biggest moon in the Solar System.

At a massive 5,268 km (3,272 miles) across, it's larger than the planet Mercury.

Jupiter is also the fastest-spinning of all the planets, rotating once every 10 Earth hours. It is Jupiter's speed that pulls its clouds out into the bands that pattern its surface.

The beautiful patterns on Jupiter's surface are created by swirling bands of clouds.

Secret hero
Daily Planet reporter Clark Kent hides a secret. He is really the Man of Steel, ready when duty calls to transform into Superman!

Watery worlds
Jupiter's two largest moons, Ganymede and Callisto, seem to have a solid crust of rock and ice, while its fourth largest, Europa, is covered in cracked ice.

Jupiter's Great Red Spot is a storm three times as big as Earth that has been raging for more than 300 years.

There's no way that we could land on Jupiter to explore it, though, because it doesn't have a solid crust. Along with Saturn, Uranus and Neptune, Jupiter's outer layer is a gassy atmosphere, with liquid gas beneath and a small rocky core.

World of lava
Jupiter's third largest moon, Io, is a mass of erupting volcanoes. Lava on its surface makes it look like a huge, mouldy orange!

JUPITER: VITAL STATISTICS
Diameter: 142,984 km (88,846 miles)
Average cloud-top temperature: −110°C (−166°F)
Length of a day (sunrise to sunrise): 10 Earth hours
Length of a year: 11.9 Earth years
Distance from the Sun: 779 million km (484 million miles)

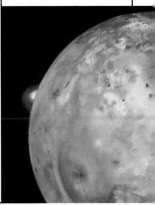

25

Spectacular Saturn

All four gas giants, Saturn, Uranus, Neptune and Jupiter, are braceleted by rings made up of millions of chunks of icy rock, ranging from pebble-sized to boulders as big as houses. The widest and most spectacular of these rings belong to Saturn. They glitter and gleam in the Sun's light and are bright enough to be seen from Earth through good binoculars.

Saturn is the second largest planet in the Solar System, but it's also the least dense. In fact, it's light enough to float in water if you could find a big enough bucket!

All aboard
Apart from Superman, only a few JLA members can fly, let alone travel through space. When it comes to interplanetary travel, these nonflying super heroes usually hop on board a supersleek jump shuttle.

Many of the JLA's high-tech gadgets are dreamed up by the scientists who work in the US government's S.T.A.R. Labs.

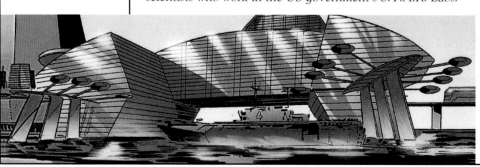

The gas giant Saturn and its incredible rings.

Saturn's rings are 100,000 km (62,000 miles) wide but are less than 1 km (0.6 miles) thick.

The *Cassini-Huygens* spacecraft is due to reach Saturn and its moons in 2004, after a seven-year journey. Scientists are eager to study Saturn's largest moon, Titan, because it is the only moon in the Solar System with its own thick atmosphere.

The JLA uses a teleporter to bring equipment and supplies to its base on the Moon.

SATURN: VITAL STATISTICS

Diameter: 120,536 km (74,897 miles)

Average cloud-top temperature: –140°C (–220°F)

Length of a day (sunrise to sunrise): 11 Earth hours

Length of a year: 29.5 Earth years

Distance from the Sun: 1,434 million km (891 million miles)

Unusual Uranus

There's something very strange about Uranus. Unlike all the other planets, it rotates on its side, at right angles to its orbit around the Sun. This makes the warmest place on Uranus its poles!

All of Uranus's 21 moons are also lying on their sides. At just 480 km (300 miles) across, its largest moon, Miranda, is about one-seventh the size of Earth's moon.

Like the three other giant planets, Uranus has rings and is mainly made of gas. Its beautiful green colour comes from the gas methane in its atmosphere.

The planets Mercury, Venus, Mars, Jupiter and

Scientists think that a collision with a gigantic space rock billions of years ago may have pushed Uranus on its side.

Emerald warrior
One of the younger members of the JLA is Green Lantern Kyle Rayner, owner of the willpower-controlled Power Ring.

Herschel constructed this large telescope in 1787–89.

William Herschel was born in Germany in 1738 and settled in England in 1757.

Saturn can all be seen from Earth with the naked eye and have been known since ancient times. Uranus, Neptune and Pluto can only be seen through a telescope and weren't known until long after its invention. Uranus was the first planet to be discovered through a telescope, in 1781 by the astronomer William Herschel. He built his own telescopes and later discovered two of Uranus's moons.

URANUS: VITAL STATISTICS
Diameter: 51,118 km (31,763 miles)
Average cloud-top temperature: –195°C (–319°F)
Length of a day (sunrise to sunrise): 17 Earth hours
Length of a year: 83.8 Earth years
Distance from the Sun: 2,873 million km (1,785 million miles)

Green menace
The colour green has a special link with Superman. It is the colour of kryptonite. The deadly radiation given off by these fragments from Superman's home planet can poison the Man of Steel.

Stormy Neptune

Neptune is similar in size and colour to its neighbour Uranus, although bluer.

Super-speedster
What's speedier than the winds on Neptune? Superman, of course! No one knows exactly how fast he can fly, but his top speed is near the speed of light – nearly 300,000 km (186,000 miles) per second!

Howling windstorms rage through the atmospheres of all four giant planets, but the roughest weather of all belongs to Neptune. Winds tear across its surface at speeds of up to 2,000 km/h (1,250 mph) – more than four times faster than in the worst tornado ever recorded on Earth.

Astronomers discovered the planet Neptune before 1846, when they first saw it through a telescope. They had predicted its position using maths, after they realised that neighbouring Uranus's orbit was being affected by an unknown object's gravity.

The spacecraft
Voyager 2 produced
this image of Triton
during its close flyby
on 25 August 1989.

Eleven moons have so far been discovered around Neptune, and its largest, Triton, has a very odd habit – it orbits the planet backwards. That's not the only strange thing about Triton. It's one of the coldest places in the Solar System and has active volcanoes that spit out ice!

Greased lightning
Another of the JLA's super-powered speedsters is the Flash (Wally West). Powered by the Speed Force, he's also able to run at near light-speed.

NEPTUNE: VITAL STATISTICS
Diameter: 49,528 km (30,775 miles)
Average cloud-top temperature: –200°C (–328°F)
Length of a day (sunrise to sunrise): 16 Earth hours
Length of a year: 164.8 Earth years
Distance from the Sun: 4,496 million km (2,794 million miles)

Puzzling Pluto

At one-fifth Earth's size, the farthest planet from the Sun, Pluto, is also the smallest. With an average surface temperature of −225°C (−373°F), it's also the coldest planet. Unlike Neptune and the other three giant planets, Pluto is a solid ball of rock and ice.

In fact, some scientists think that Pluto isn't a planet at all, but one of the space bodies they call ice dwarfs. Ice dwarfs are similar to asteroids, but instead of being solid rock, they are a mixture of rock, water ice and other frozen chemicals. Thousands of ice dwarfs are thought to orbit the Sun beyond Neptune, in a region known as the Edgeworth-Kuiper Belt.

Pluto was the last planet in the Solar System to be discovered, by American astronomer

Pluto is just two-thirds the size of Earth's Moon.

Ice bound
When Superman wants to cool villains down, he doesn't need to exile them to chilly Pluto. A single gust of his flash-freezing breath is enough!

Pluto's moon Charon (right) is much larger in comparison to its planet than any other moon. This photograph was taken by the Hubble Space Telescope.

Clyde Tombaugh in 1930. No spacecraft has ever visited it, but scientists hope to launch a mission to investigate it in 2006. The spacecraft should reach Pluto by 2015 and the Edgeworth-Kuiper Belt about 10 years later.

Space snowballs

Comets are lumps of snow and dust that usually orbit the Sun in and beyond the Edgeworth-Kuiper Belt. Some comets, however, break free and speed through space towards the Sun. As a comet nears the Sun, the heat makes the snow turn to gas, which streams out behind it in two tails.

PLUTO: VITAL STATISTICS

Diameter: 2,390 km (1,485 miles)

Average surface temperature: –225°C (–373°F)

Length of a day (sunrise to sunrise): 6.4 Earth days

Length of a year: 248 Earth days

Distance from the Sun : 5,870 million km (3,647 million miles)

The Milky Way

Just as Earth is one of a family of planets, so the Sun belongs to a star family called a galaxy. The Sun is in the galaxy we call the Milky Way – it was named by the ancient Greeks, who thought it looked like milk streaming from the breast of their goddess Hera.

The Milky Way is made up of around 500 billion stars.

The Key
The goal of chemically enhanced supervillain the Key is to rule reality. The JLA has so far managed to stop him.

Galaxies are like islands of stars in the vast ocean of the Universe. There are billions of galaxies, each containing millions upon millions of stars.

Distances in space are so huge that scientists measure them in light-years, the distance light travels in one year – 5.9 million million miles (9.5 million million km). The Milky Way Galaxy measures 100,000 light-years across and is 4,000 light-years thick. It is shaped like an enormous bulging disc with

An irregular galaxy.

An elliptical galaxy.

Galaxies galore
Not all galaxies are the same shape. Some are spiral-shaped like the Milky Way. Other galaxies are irregular (with no particular shape) or elliptical (ball- and egg-shaped).

Alien star
Starro was a starfish-shaped alien from another galaxy who tried to enslave the population of Earth until stopped by the JLA.

long spiralling arms, and it contains an astonishing 500 billion stars – far too many to think about, let alone count!

The young stars that scientists call protostars.

Tiny titan
An experiment with the fallen fragment of a white dwarf star helped physics professor Ray Palmer shrink his body and begin battling crime as the Atom!

A Universe of stars

The stars may all look alike when you gaze into the night sky. But if you could get closer to those twinkling lights, you'd see that they come in all sizes and colours.

The biggest stars are the giants and supergiants – a red giant can be 10 times the size of the Sun, while a supergiant can be 10 times the size of a red giant. There are smaller stars than the Sun, too. White dwarfs can be Earth-sized, while the smallest stars, neutron stars, are the size of a big city.

All stars are born, shine for a time and then die. The Sun is a medium-sized, middle-aged star. It was born about five billion years ago and has enough gas fuel left to last another five billion or so. It will then start to die.

Stars are born inside vast clouds of gas and dust called nebulae. Inside each nebula, gravity pulls gas into ever denser, ever hotter balls, which eventually start to spin and glow. These young stars are called protostars. They get hotter and hotter until they shine steadily, as true stars.

Shaping up
Patterns of stars in the sky are known as constellations. They are often named after a mythological creature or person, such as Orion.

The Sun is a type of star known as a yellow dwarf. Here, other types of star are shown in relation to a yellow dwarf.

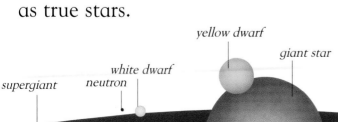

supergiant   neutron   white dwarf   yellow dwarf   giant star

Star death

Most stars start to die when the hydrogen gas fuel in their core runs low. Stars like the Sun then slowly swell into a red giant. Eventually, the red giant's outer layers are puffed off into space, while its core collapses in on itself to become a white dwarf star – thousands of times smaller than the red giant but still very hot. It takes

Superman Red

All change
When the Sun was consumed by "Sun-Eater," Superman lost his powers. Attempts to restore them caused him to split into Superman Red and Blue.

3. It balloons into a supergiant star 100s of times bigger than the Sun before going supernova.

1. A massive blue-white giant star begins to die.

2. It swells and changes colour, turning yellow then red.

38

A supernova explosion.

Heavy weight
The matter, or material, in a white dwarf star is incredibly dense and heavy – so much so that on Earth, a matchboxful of white dwarf would weigh as much as an elephant!

Split personality
Superman Red was hot-headed, but Superman Blue was cool and rational.

billions of years for the star to cool and fade to a cinder.

Some more massive stars than the Sun have a far more dramatic ending. This kind of star swells into a supergiant before blasting itself apart in a vast flash of light called a supernova. A supernova is one of the brightest objects in the whole Universe – giving off as much light as all the stars in an entire galaxy combined.

Superman Blue

A Hubble Space Telescope image of a whirlpool of hot gas fuelling a suspected black hole.

Spaghetti junction

If an astronaut fell into a black hole, its gravity would pull so hard that his or her body would be stretched out like spaghetti!

Black holes

When a star goes supernova, its core collapses in on itself and is pulled tighter and tighter and smaller and smaller by gravity. The dying star's core may end as a tiny neutron star. Sometimes, though, a neutron star carries on shrinking and becomes a black hole.

Black holes are among space's biggest mysteries. Their gravity is so powerful that it sucks in anything that comes near. Even light cannot escape – that's why the "holes" are described as black. Because our eyes cannot see without light, finding a black hole in the blackness of space is very difficult. Scientists do it not by looking directly at them but by detecting their effect on a nearby

Stars that come in pairs are called binary stars. If one of the pair has collapsed into a black hole, it may be sucking in gas from its companion star.

star. The telltale signs are the invisible X-rays that are given off as a black hole's super-strong gravity hoovers up the star's gas. The gas spins around the black hole like a whirlpool, becoming extremely hot – up to 100 million °C (180 million °F) – and making it give off X-rays.

Rising pulse
A pulsar is a neutron star that spins rapidly, giving off pulses of radiation.

A pulsar.

Supersight
One of Superman's powers is his X-ray vision. It allows him to see through all solid materials, apart from lead.

Otherworldly
Superman's enemies are not limited to Earth creatures. General Zod is a formidable alien foe, who is intent on world domination.

Superman and the alien Massacre trade blows.

Is anyone out there?

Are we alone in the Universe or are there aliens somewhere out there? An alien life-form might be anything from a tiny bacteria to an intelligent being, but one thing is certain – there's no scientific proof that any kind of alien exists, let alone creatures capable of inventing spacecraft that can travel across the vastness of space to visit Earth.

Scientists have proved, however, that there are other stars apart from the Sun with planets. Since the first was detected in the early 1990s, more than 100 planets have been found outside the Solar System.

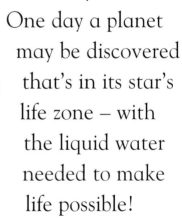

One day a planet may be discovered that's in its star's life zone – with the liquid water needed to make life possible!

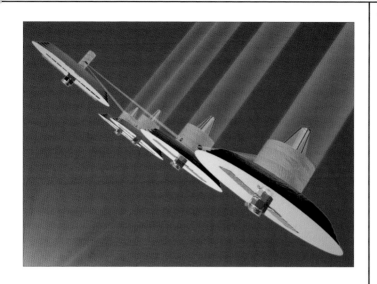

Scientists are coming up with ideas for new spacecraft all the time. This illustration shows one idea – a spacecraft that will carry telescopes powerful enough to detect faraway planets.

The SETI@home website is at http://setiathome. berkeley.edu

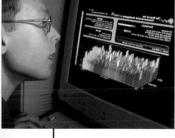

SETI

Scientists are using radio telescopes to listen out for radio signals broadcast by aliens. This program is known as SETI (the Search for ExtraTerrestrial Intelligence).

Some people say they have been abducted by aliens. The extraterrestrials are often described as little green or gray men.

43

Time lord
The Lord of Time is an enemy of the JLA. He is able to travel through time, and his goal is to conquer time and space.

Some scientists are trying to develop solar-sail powered spacecraft like this, which will capture the Sun's energy and use it to fuel journeys out of the Solar System.

Interstellar travel

Even if humans were to make contact with an alien civilisation, they don't have the technology to visit another solar system. The stars are just too far away.

The closest star to the Sun, Proxima Centauri, is 4.3 light-years away. Travelling in the space shuttle at 28,000 km/h (17,000 mph), it would take 166,000 years to reach it.

Time isn't the only problem. The journey wouldn't be possible because

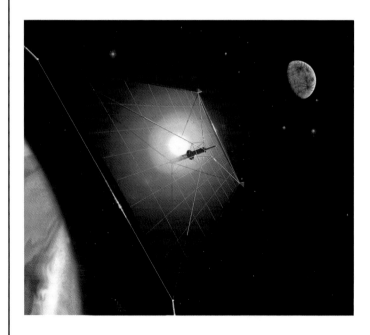

Strange things might happen if humans could travel close to light-speed. Five years might pass for one twin who journeys into space in a spacecraft, while 50 years pass for the twin who stays behind on Earth. When the journey ends, the Earth twin would be much older than the space traveller!

the shuttle couldn't carry the vast amount of food and rocket fuel needed to travel so far.

If human beings are to make it to the stars one day, scientists will have to invent a way of travelling at near light-speed, using little or no fuel. One idea is a spacecraft that won't need to carry its own fuel. Instead, it would have a huge solar sail and be pushed through space by the Sun's energy, in much the same way that wind blows a sailing ship.

Prankster
Qwsp is a silver-haired sprite from Zrfff, a place in the fifth dimension.

The Big Bang

The Universe isn't just huge, it's getting bigger all the time. Most scientists believe that it began about 13 billion years ago, when an infinitesimally hot and tiny speck of something suddenly exploded. This explosion is called the Big Bang, and it was the beginning of time, space and everything!

The Big Bang was so powerful that in less than a second the Universe grew from smaller than an atom to bigger than a galaxy. It is still expanding today, with the galaxies speeding farther and farther away from each other. Humans may have figured out how and when the Universe began, but no one knows

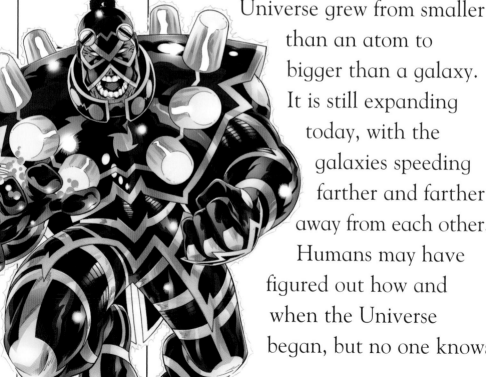

whether it will ever end. Most
scientists think it will continue to
expand forever. Others believe that
one day the Universe may start
shrinking and that eventually
everything will crash together in
a Big Crunch!

Early Universe
This image was
taken by a
satellite
launched by
NASA in 1990,
and it shows
what the
Universe looked
like about
300,000 years
after the Big
Bang. The blue
areas are cooler
clouds of gas.

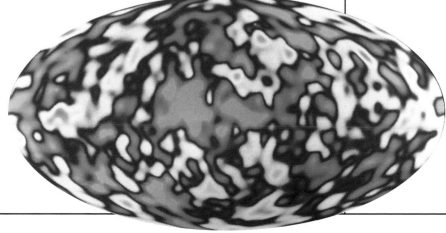

Glossary

Algae
Life forms that range in size from a tiny single cell to seaweeds 50 metres (160 feet) long. Most algae live in water.

Asteroid
A rocky space body that orbits a star but is much smaller than a planet.

Astronomer
An expert in astronomy, the scientific study of space and space bodies such as stars, planets and moons.

Atmosphere
A layer of gases that surrounds a planet or moon.

Atom
The smallest part of a chemical element such as hydrogen or oxygen.

Bacteria
Most bacteria are single-celled life forms that are so tiny that they can only be seen under a microscope.

Core
The innermost part of a star or planet.

Crater
A bowl-shaped hole in the ground left after a large space rock lands or a bomb explodes. The mouth of a volcano is also called a crater.

Diameter
The length of a straight line drawn from one side of a circle or ball shape through its centre to the other side.

Infinitesimal
Extremely small.

Invisible
Something that cannot be seen.

Laser
A device that produces a very powerful, narrow beam of light, capable of cutting through metal and concrete.

Missile
A flying weapon such as a bomb.

Moon
A space body that orbits a planet. Unlike stars, moons cannot produce their own light. They appear to shine only when sunlight bounces off them.

NASA
Short for National Aeronautics and Space Administration, the US government agency that researches into and carries out space exploration.

Orbit
The path of one space body around another, more massive object.

Planet
A large, ball-shaped space body that orbits a star. Unlike stars, planets cannot produce their own light.

Radiation
A form of energy, such as light or radio waves.

Satellite
An object held in orbit around another, larger object by its gravity, such as a moon or spacecraft orbiting a planet.

Solar system
A star and all the space bodies trapped in orbit around the star by its gravity.

Star
A hot, shining, vast ball of gas, which produces heat and light energy in its core.

Telescope
An optical telescope is a device that, when you look through it, makes faraway objects appear larger. Radio telescopes collect invisible radio waves from space.

X-ray
A form of radiation that can pass through many substances that light cannot. Doctors use X-ray machines to take photographs of bones and teeth.

The Loss Adjustor

Aifric Campbell

A complete catalogue record for this book can be obtained from the British Library on request

The right of Aifric Campbell to be identified as the author of this work has been asserted by her in accordance with the Copyright, Designs and Patents Act 1988

First published in this edition in 2011 by Serpent's Tail
First published in 2010 by Serpent's Tail,
an imprint of Profile Books Ltd
3A Exmouth House
Pine Street
London EC1R 0JH
website: www.serpentstail.com

ISBN 978 1 84668 731 0
eISBN 978 1 84765 232 4

Designed and typeset by sue@lambledesign.demon.co.uk
Printed and bound in Great Britain by CPI Bookmarque Ltd, Croydon, Surrey

10 9 8 7 6 5 4 3 2 1

Mixed Sources
Product group from well-managed forests and other controlled sources
www.fsc.org Cert no. TT-COC-002139
© 1996 Forest Stewardship Council
FSC

The memory throws up high and dry
A crowd of twisted things;
A twisted branch upon the beach
Eaten smooth, and polished
As if the world gave up
The secret of its skeleton
Stiff and white.

TS Eliot, *Rhapsody on a Windy Night*

Part **one**

1

I WAS BORN IN A PLACE that presumed departure. A strip of kerbless road that claimed village status but was really only known for its proximity to other larger, more substantial places. When I was six years old our lives were transformed by the opening of a bypass that took all the traffic away and turned us overnight into a dead end. From then on we were access only and would stand astride our bikes in the new cul-de-sac where we practised our wheelies watching lost drivers make sloppy U-turns, gears screaming in reverse before they sped off to their true destination two miles further south: a thriving town, a retail park and all the other places where people actually wanted to go. This was how we became both a wrong turn and an unsustainable community that, according to the planners, was not earmarked for growth but destined to shrivel up and die.

From the gate at the bottom of our front garden I could survey the entire limits of my childhood universe with a sweep of the head: twenty-eight post-war semis thrown up on surplus farming land when a chicken factory was built nearby and then shut down fifteen years later after the owner fled a contamination scandal, leaving a trail of job loss in his wake. Our house was attached on the right-hand side to Estelle's and if I leaned out of my bedroom window I could look down on the tiled slope of her porch. Just a few feet away on my left was the perspex roof of Cormac's leaky conservatory where a nest of blackbirds once settled in the gutter late in the season, as if they'd run out of time to find a better home. The houses were set back from the road behind long, narrow gardens separated by privet hedging that took my father a full day to cut. There were child-sized gaps on both sides that led into Cormac's and Estelle's, little crawl spaces that we began tunnelling as toddlers, but these have long since disappeared. New neighbours have run fencing along one side and the holes in the privet have filled in as if the three of us never existed.

I do not recall a time when I did not feel my friends' presence on either side of me. I do not remember a single moment when I experienced the solitariness that could have come with being an only child. From the earliest days I was part of both their families and wandered in and out at will. Mealtimes at their houses were large, messy occasions with high chairs and spillages and interrupted chatter that contrasted with the silent triangle at home. I often slept over, in the bunk below Cormac's that had been abandoned by a succession of older siblings or in the room that Estelle shared with her two sisters, curled up on a jumble of beanbags, surrounded by teddy bears and dolls and dust balls.

My own family organised itself around sudden exits. When I was twelve years old my father suffered a fatal coronary at the kitchen table one Wednesday morning in May. Strangely enough, it is not his choking slide from the chair that I remember most clearly but how my mother rose from the table and made the emergency call, calmly spelling out the address as if she had been rehearsing this moment for years. She stood in the hallway while we waited for the ambulance, cradling the

Bakelite phone that my Dad cherished as a relic of times past
– a sweeter, better time when objects were heavy and durable
and anchored to the wall.

Two weeks after my father's death, Spike hurled himself
under the wheels of a passing car as I left for school. I dis-
tinctly saw him turn his head to check that I was watching
before he ran at full speed into the path of a car that had just
completed a U-turn and was accelerating back to the bypass.
Although no one but Estelle believed me, as the only witness
I knew it was a deliberate act. Even as a puppy Spike had
never shown the slightest interest in traffic and would lie
in the front garden, head resting on his front paws, behind
a fence that he could have cleared in an instant. His eyes
might appear to be closed but border collies are always on
high alert, constant vigilance is a hallmark of the breed; they
are like aspirational scouts always at the ready for some unex-
pected twist of fate. After the killer-driver was absolved and
dismissed by my mother, I stood looking down at Spike with
Cormac and Estelle beside me, her hand slipping into my
palm. I thought how it looked like he was sleeping except for
the blood puddling beneath his head and the strange angle of
his neck. But I should have known then that Spike's suicide
was an omen, a warning that life as we knew it was poised to
unravel and that we were on the brink of a future he could
not bear to witness.

'Poor Spike, poor Spike,' Estelle kept repeating in a flat low
voice, tugging at my hand. Cormac said nothing, just stroked
my head as I bent low over the black and white fur. Already
at eleven and three-quarters he understood the power that
resides in silence, a talent he has since honed to perfection
under the blaze of light that follows him wherever he goes.

There didn't seem to be much point in going to the vet
just to arrange for incineration and there was the problem of
transporting the body, so we buried Spike in the back garden

beneath the laurel hedge that looked out over the open fields where he liked to chase rabbits in the early mornings. Digging a hole that was big enough was surprisingly difficult with one small spade so we took turns, Cormac, Estelle and I, but Estelle just made doll-sized indentations in the earth and quickly tired. My mother stood by the back door tapping a cigarette by her side. She'd taken up smoking in the days after my father's death and had not yet perfected her technique. Her mouth was slightly agape and for a while I thought she might be about to speak but she was somehow preoccupied – with what I do not know – except that for the rest of my childhood she exuded an untroubled vagueness that may possibly have bordered on neglect.

On the night of Spike's funeral, Estelle, Cormac and I lay pinwheeled under the stars, legs and arms spread like spokes, staring up at a midsummer constellation until the grass chill crept along our spines and Estelle's mother called out in the darkness and we went inside. The next day Cormac showed up in my front garden with a chisel and slab of sandstone in a wheelbarrow. We spent all morning hacking Spike's name and date into the stone and then hauled this secret memorial the half-mile up to the church and placed it by the western wall, hidden behind a spreading gaultheria. Every time I visit the graveyard it is that moment of solemn reflection that comes to mind: the three of us holding hands, Estelle in the middle at her insistence. I can still feel the dry heat of her clasp, Cormac's pulsing palm on my right, both held in a grip that seemed eternal. And although I should be used to it by now, I am still periodically astounded that only one of us remains, that I have been left alone to brood on the complications of the past.

Sometimes I try to force a little perspective and remind myself with a spare summary of events: Estelle died two weeks after her fifteenth birthday. It was sudden, violent, explicit. Shortly afterwards, Cormac decided to leave. After that was new time, the very texture of experience was forever altered and I was left with the sense of empty seats all around me, as if my life had become a theatre for one.

Immediately after Estelle's funeral, Cormac locked himself in his bedroom for three days. His mother left brittle boards of buttered toast on a tray outside the door and I sat on the landing listening to the silence of his headphones. I could picture exactly how he would look from the bottom bunk where I used to lie staring up at Springsteen's matted poster hair while Cormac sat on the floor inches from the speaker, playing 'Jungleland' over and over and over again.

Hwuuuuuuuuuuaaaaaaaaaaaaaaaaaaaa

Every couple of hours his mum appeared in the landing gloom and bent down to lift the tray, a big fat tear rolling to a halt in the furrows by her mouth. 'Grief-stricken,' I heard her whisper on the phone downstairs, but I knew different. Cormac was in New Jersey on a boardwalk he had never seen, washing his own sorrow in someone else's story. And Estelle was bathed in a halo of memory, already elevated to so much more than she had ever been: stupid, silly, unpredictable, unreliable – all the things that infuriated but none of it her fault, of course, and none of it ever enough of a reason to make it possible to walk away.

'Take this, dear,' his mum handed me a mug of tea. 'I'll leave his here just in case,' she said, placing another on the floor beside me. I wanted to fling it at Cormac's door, this ownership of grief that was nowhere near the true story.

On the third day he emerged backlit at noon by a sun that shone right through his T-shirt. He stood on the threshold without speaking. I leaned my head back against the wall, I wouldn't look at him until in one movement he crouched down in front of me and took my hands in his.

'I'm leaving soon,' he whispered.

'Are you asking me to come with you?'

He shook his head, let my hands flop down on my lap.

'Good. That's good,' I said. 'Because I would say no.'

That was the last time we spoke. A few weeks later I watched him pack up his dad's car from my bedroom window. Cormac gave no sign that he knew I was there until the engine was running and then he stood in the passenger doorway wearing his *Born to Run* T-shirt, staring straight up at me and waving, a long slow side-to-side motion like semaphore, as if he was wiping all traces of us clear. I did not return his gesture, could not entirely decode the signal, but I could tell that this baggage would not weigh him down and I knew he could see clearly where he was going now and that the journey wouldn't take long.

'Is this a retrospective?' said Cormac last night. 'Because I'm not dead yet.'

The interviewer laughed. The studio audience laughed too and although I have lost count of how many times I've replayed this scene, I still smile at each repeat. For unlike Estelle, Cormac is very much alive although we have lost touch through my own meticulous doing. But everyone knows where he is. I could lift the phone right now and track him down in less than an hour and he would take my call. Instead, in the twenty years that have passed since Estelle's death, I have watched him closely from a distance, studied his work for any signs that the past might be infecting his present. I press my hand over his screen heart, it has a strong and steady beat and I am convinced he remains untroubled by history. He has successfully absorbed or perhaps deflected the past while I am stalked by guilt.

The interview was first broadcast a week ago to launch the

publicity extravaganza that is building up to Cormac's forth-coming appearance. His billboarded smile trails me around the city, I touch his laminated face in bus shelters, I even stood amongst the shifting crowds in Piccadilly Circus on Tuesday and watched him stride across the giant video screen in endless thirteen-second loops. And last night I lay on the couch freezing the frames, cataloguing all the ways in which he is both recognisable and different. Cormac leans back in the leather armchair, one arm slung over the side, his right ankle balanced on the opposite knee. He used to sit this way at school, tilting back on his chair, tapping a pencil against his thigh, sometimes even humming in class. His jeans are stone-washed and there are intricate patterns etched in the side of his oxblood ankle-boots. He wears a white T-shirt with a burst of swirling colour on the front, green, red, blue and yellow and some Japanese calligraphy running a vertical black line from shoulder to waist. A tall lean frame that can fold effortlessly into yogic poses. His arms and hands are strong and he does not carry any excess weight. He still has his mother's colouring, pale skin lightly freckled in an off-beat symmetry about the nose and cheeks, the same summer-blue eyes. And his hair has remained long with dark blond curls that fall to his shoulders in lustrous tangles. He has acquired a mid-Atlantic twang that suits him. Even in this pixellated rendering, he glows.

A counsellor once told me that a successful bereavement consists of a period of intense mourning followed by the vig-orous rebuilding of a new life that will make you realise you can dispense completely with the dead person. The initial stage should last no more than three months. After that, excessive grief is an indicator of pathological tendencies and intervention is recommended before the problem gets out of hand. Survival depends on being able to cut loose, to believe that the dead are not as central to your happiness as you

might think. *I cannot live without you. Without you I am nothing.*
But how do you grieve when the one you have lost is *not* dead,
when the object of your passion is still out there? How do
you plug a human-size hole? There is no strategy other than
a simmering acceptance when your heart is pierced by a sharp
object, but such palliative remedies are no more than puncture repair, patching you up so you can battle on, hurtling
towards the next disaster on the horizon.

'I am getting tired of all these sad stories,' said Nicola at
Friday's monthly meeting. My boss is not usually given to
emotional reflections and prefers to focus on the practical
resolution of difficult cases, but pregnancy has triggered a
style change as if new life demands that old certainties be
re-examined.

'It never used to bother me before. But now…' she leaned
back in the swivel chair, her voice trailing away, her hand
comforting the growing bump.

'Foreseeability,' shrugged the forensic engineer, closing
the file in front of him. 'Her husband was warned that the
brakes were faulty. He should have made sure the car was
taken off the road.'

'Yes, I *know* that,' snapped Nicola with a fierce jerk of the
head, 'but he *didn't* know that his wife was going to use the car
to do the bloody school run when her own one wouldn't start.'

The engineer glanced at me as if looking for guidance
about how to proceed. This new unpredictability in Nicola's
mood was taking some adjustment and he was still learning
how to tiptoe through these meetings without setting off the
alarm. And of course, the human cost was not his problem,
he had done his duty and had no intention of being drawn
into a lingering exploration of lives that have been blighted
by loss.

'They'll suspend the sentence. He won't do time,' he offered in an attempt at consolation.

'He'll be doing time for the rest of his life,' she muttered but he did not respond, just tucked the folder under his arm and stood up, waiting for the right moment to depart. Nicola frowned and hunched forwards, inclining her head. I have noticed these moments of still attention before, it is as if her unborn baby can communicate on some frequency that only she can hear. I held my breath, the engineer did not move, both of us suspended in anticipation of some pre-natal announcement and then Nicola sighed, levered herself out of the chair and returned to the public space. 'Sorry,' she smiled wanly. 'Blame it on the hormones,' and he nodded and left us both wrapped in a rare silence staring out the window at a sunstreaked skyline, Nicola with her back to me and one palm pressed flat against the glass.

'How *do* you come to terms with killing the one you love? How do you manage the guilt, Caro?' and I flinched at this sudden accusation but when I raised my head I saw that this was not a charge flung at me but out the window where Nicola stood shaking her head at the beak of a receding crane as it swung blindly away over the City.

2

I PASS BENEATH THE TWO stone eagles that guard the grand entrance to the hotel's estate. A single-track road leads past the cricket ground which is empty now but will soon busy up with members of the local archery club who congregate here on winter Sundays. Middle-aged men and the occasional woman, many of them dressed in green, form a silent line and take aim at coloured targets arranged like giant dartboards on the edge of the boundary. They fire on a single cue but many of the arrows miss their targets and come to rest at strange angles in the grass. One morning just after dawn I watched a longbow archer in a Robin Hood costume practise alone, his arrow slicing the air with an audible quiver before thudding hard and clean and deadly straight into the bull's-eye.

As I pull up to park by the churchyard wall an old woman emerges from the gates on a motorised chair, a little England flag taped to the handlebars. I have seen her walk quite sturdily and without the aid of a cane but when I stopped to open the gate for her some months ago, she told me that she no longer drives and cannot manage the quarter mile walk from the house to visit her dead husband. She waves to a smiling woman in a grey anorak who stands by the church entrance holding a rake – one of the volunteers who tend to the grounds, burning leaves, cutting grass and sweeping up the confetti that is supposed to be thrown only in the area immediately outside the wooden gates, but the wedding guests are mostly out-of-towners who make their own rules.

Two years ago this place was included in *Bride* magazine's list of the top ten most picturesque venues within a fifty-mile radius of the city. The sandstone church dates back to the thirteenth century and is in an elevated position overlooking a deep wooded valley and a lake. In late spring the distant woods are carpeted with bluebells and the sloping lawns are visited by nesting ducks and Canada geese who waddle across the grass in an afternoon foraging ritual.

Just a few hundred yards away and discreetly obscured by enormous rhododendrons is a grand country-house hotel that was once the family seat of Lord Liverpool who presided over this 800-acre estate and who, in 1830, had the entire village moved a mile to the north so that he could enjoy an uninterrupted vista from the stone terrace at the rear. Summer wedding parties can walk the short distance between church and hotel and it makes a fine sight – bridesmaids skipping along in dresses with big bows and mini bouquets and the bride following slowly behind. The vicar, however, will only agree to two weddings a month. He is unhappy about SUVs churning up the grassy verge, cigarette butts in the church grounds and the hotel's recent ad for helicopter weddings which will involve the bride and groom hovering above the church and sweeping over the countryside for a panoramic glass of champagne before landing fifteen minutes later on the lawn. The owner – a city financier with a portfolio of country hotels – is trying to tempt the vicar with donations for a restoration of the rose garden on the eastern side of the church, but the vicar refuses to budge.

Or maybe he is holding out for more money, for just as the secular population is expanding, the congregation is

dwindling. I have learnt all this from Hannah, one of the volunteers who seizes any opportunity to engage mourners in
conversation. Most of the others keep a respectful silence as
they go about their work. They are lean and diligent retirees
who cling to a sense of community that is under siege from
frantic commuters as house prices force city workers even as
far out as here – a fifteen-mile drive to the nearest station and
a fast train to their desks. Men line the platforms like skittles
at dawn and return under cover of night. Mothers ferry their
children between nurseries and schools and part-time local
workplaces.

My life now seems to revolve around tending to the departed
and the absent. Of course there are other distractions: there
is work to be done, a world to negotiate, but I often think
– stalled at traffic lights or running on tarmac in the early
evening – it is reality that feels illusory. As if there has been
some sort of reversal in the physical laws so that the tangible
eludes my grasp, as if the here-and-now is two-dimensional.
I fulfil my commitments. I go to work, clean the car, pay my
taxes, recycle my glass and plastics, but it is history that
appears in three dimensions, loaded with colour and scent.
I try to convince myself that it is an irrelevancy, that all that
matters should be the now and the next second, but present
moments dissolve, slipping by like fast-moving rapids, and I
am washed up again in the lagoons of the past. So it is that I
find myself back in the place where it all began, lured here by
memory and a certain guilt and all the accumulating losses to
which I cannot be reconciled.

There was a time when I came here every week, but these
days I ration myself to a fortnightly visit – I have a fast car
and get up on Sunday morning when the city is still asleep,
straight into jeans and sweatshirt so that in seventy minutes'

time I can be cosying up to the dead. This was the landscape of our childhood. Cormac, Estelle and I came here in autumn for the shiny conkers that fell in their hundreds from the horse chestnuts that line the southern perimeter wall, we picked blackberries by the churchyard gate, inspected the famous poet's brother's grave on a nature walk from school and took half-hearted bark rubbings. We played in the shade of the giant yew that is said to be two thousand years old and whose heavy branches veil ancient gravestones that are sinking into the needle-covered earth and will eventually be completely submerged. The branches conceal a shadowy inner chamber where the huge trunk has cleaved to form three hiding places, deep lacquered grooves that shine as if glossed by a recent rain. From this secret spot we used to spy on weddings and funerals, crushing the cerise berries between our fingers. We would lie back in the folds of the trunks during choir practice on Thursday evenings, the voices spiralling upwards and out across the graveyard. Sometimes Cormac led us down the valley, through the woods to the other side and an out-of-bounds housing estate where we crouched behind the bushes and watched teenagers burn tyres and drink cider.

In the weeks after my father's death we used to come here to contemplate the site of my future interment: a small granite cross and a rectangular strip of chipped gravel beneath which I would one day be laid to rest on top of my grandparents and parents. I would live out a lifetime – which a female could expect to be 77.3 years – and then be consigned to silence in the place where I was born. But I do not come here now to visit my father's grave and neither does my mother, judging by its forlorn condition which is in stark contrast to the neatly tidied plots that surround him. Clumps of weeds have worked their way to the surface in one corner, an old wreath has fallen apart to reveal its skeletal core and a stubborn moss clings to the edges of the stone. No doubt the volunteers disapprove, for they expect the living to honour their dead. They have their hands full tending to those who have no one left on earth to rake the gravel, scrub the lopsided tombs and scrape away the lichen.

I take up my usual position on a wooden bench by the wall that backs on to the car park and is partly shaded by the branches of an alder. There is another seat much closer to Estelle but I prefer this vantage point at a clear diagonal to her notional resting place. The Garden of Remembrance is tucked away in the south-western corner and separated from the cricket grounds by a wire fence erected as temporary cover when that section of the wall was destroyed by the storm of 1987. The estate lost over two hundred trees and some of the lightning-scorched stumps still stick out from the hillside like animal carcasses in a desert. But the smashed wall remains unrepaired as local sandstone is expensive and there are more important priorities – Hannah tells me that the church bells are being restored, some copper from the lightning conductors on the tower has mysteriously disappeared and the congregation is struggling with the burden of maintenance. The volunteers have planted ivy in the hope that it will train along the fenceposts and hide the wire but the soil seems curiously hostile and the leaves are speckled with a queasy pigment. A rusted sheet of corrugated metal hides a compost heap in the furthest corner. Thus the Garden of Remembrance feels like a paupers' resting place in a graveyard that is otherwise filled with customised tombstones and grand family vaults.

'Estelle,' I say aloud, for I am still captivated by her name, there is a phonetic perfection about the sibilant and the closing labial that lingers like a whisper in an enchanted forest. 'Estelle,' I repeat for the familiar effect – ephemeral, insubstantial, a name that conjures up a moss-covered gravestone askew in an old churchyard and a tattered wedding dress. Estelle's mother believed she had named her daughter after the heroine in *Great Expectations* but when her eldest son brought Dickens home from the library and showed her the error, she didn't seem to think that substituting the 'a' for an 'e' obscured the reference. She used to remind Estelle of her literary connection as she brushed her flaxen hair each morning before school – twenty steady strokes while I stood fidgeting in the kitchen. 'You girls,' she'd murmur, shaking her head, with a smile that sometimes seemed close to tears. When we turned to wave goodbye as we rounded the corner, she would be standing on the porch with little Harry on her hip. She seemed to be frowning at some complexity on the horizon and I wonder now if she could somehow foresee a cloud scuttling across our futures. There are people who have a sixth sense, there are dogs that bark long before the door-bell rings. Perhaps, like Spike, Estelle's mother could already sense disaster looming up ahead.

When I re-read Dickens after Estelle was dead, her fictional namesake struck me as an inspired choice although at first glance they seemed to have nothing in common. Estella had brown hair, she was beautiful and haughty and liked to make young boys cry. Estelle's manipulative powers were chaotic and spontaneous, never premeditated, her anger was like a sudden squall precipitated by frustrated impulses. But Estella's froideur could have been interpreted as that missing part that singled Estelle out. Cormac, of course, saw meaning in her differentness, endowed it with a sort of mysticism. For a while he even toyed with the idea that she might be in possession of superior truths and watched her more carefully than usual, listened to her chatter as if he might detect an undiscovered profundity.

The real Estelle has no corporeal remains and, as far as I am aware, no memorial other than this communal garden, an uninspired square of grass enclosed by a straggly box hedge that refuses to flourish. The occasional bunch of roses in fogged-up cellophane is left here as a further reminder of decay but there are few visitors. It is as though those who were happy to consign their relatives' bodies to the furnace do not feel the need to keep returning to pay their respects. A slate slab in the centre of the miniature garden urges visitors to 'Remember those whose ashes are buried here'. But technically speaking the ashes are buried in the rectangle of cheap gravel off to the side that is overlooked by another yew and constantly in shade. Small squares of granite record the details of the dead and Estelle is in the middle of the third row, a simple note of her name and dates etched in thick blunt capitals, a bleak and spare announcement of all that could not be said.

This memorial gives no clue to the grim circumstances of her death and perhaps that was the family's intention, as they did not want the site to become a ghoulish shrine. Estelle, however, would not have approved of her send-off: she would have chosen something far more glamorous than cremation at a non-religious service to which only immediate family were invited. Her parents – although her mother did not attend the proceedings, she was too distressed, too drugged – wanted the whole business excised from their lives; there was, after all, her brothers and sisters to consider and little Harry was only eight years old at the time. It is possible that they kept some of the ashes for a private memorial elsewhere but I do not know if they did because her family moved away just a few weeks after the funeral. A red and black truck pitched up outside their house early one morning and three men in overalls cleared the contents in a couple of hours while I watched from my bedroom window. They stood around smoking and drinking from a thermos until Estelle's father came out and spoke briefly to them. I did not see the rest of the family leave – Estelle's mother and the kids, the cat and the hamster – they must have slipped away while we were sleeping and I never found out where they went. The postmistress knew, of course, but for once Mrs Harris kept her mouth shut. 'If they had wanted anyone to know their business they would have said so,' she replied to a stream of enquirers that afternoon. 'Doesn't the whole country already know enough about that family's grief?'

After the truck had rumbled away, Estelle's dad locked the front door behind him and hurried down the drive, trench coat flapping loosely around his shoulders. He seemed to have shrunk to half his size in a month. I pushed through the hedge and ran after him but he spun round and raised a hand, his palm outstretched to deflect, finally and for ever, any further communication. Then he got in the car and drove off, never checking the rear view mirror.

No one comes to visit Estelle any more although there used to be a family delegation on her anniversary and I would park down by the hotel and watch them arrive in varying groups – first her mother, in the morning and usually alone. Her father came in the afternoon, speaking of a rift that has never healed. It always had the look of a long-distance drive and for a few years he arrived with a large capable-looking woman who held his elbow as she clicked along the tarmac path beside him. Once he stumbled into her as if his legs had buckled and she pulled him close, put both hands to his face and kissed his forehead, but he broke away from her the way men do on screen. She let him go and knelt down to stroke the memorial stone as you would smooth a child's head. I thought it a kind act from someone who only knew Estelle's story and not the person.

Estelle's older brothers and sisters grew up tall and heavy and arrived in a convoy of people carriers with sweet wrappers blowing out of the windows. Little Harry had become a man but he still had the loping stride of the boy I remember, fists thrust deep in his trouser pockets. The children were never taken into the graveyard. Jenny stayed behind to chaperone, distracting the little ones with bubbles while the teenagers slumped in the back seat plugged into earphones, occasionally craning their heads out through the window to watch the proceedings. After the others returned, Jenny would nip in quickly as if she was taking a cold bath. She blessed herself unfamiliarly, rearranged a flower and hurried back along the path with her arms wrapped round her front against a cold that wasn't there. The oldest sister never came, not even once.

Six years ago Estelle's dad stopped coming, but of course, he may be dead, he has reached the age where men disappear overnight without warning. For the last five years I have waited till nightfall but no one has come. It is as if the family has reached some agreement that observing the anniversary is no longer appropriate or necessary. Perhaps they have decided that they can more usefully spend their time amongst the living.

I bumped into Estelle's mother three years ago at Victoria station. She was queuing at the excess ticket office on platform 19, her outline blurred by a crumpled raincoat. When she turned to look at me I saw her reflex-check over my shoulder as if Estelle might be trailing along behind like she always did, but the expectation vanished in a small collapse of her face. There was a worn peace about the way she hugged me and she smelled of ginger, which I said and she laughed. 'Still baking, always baking, you remember, dear,' her voice teetering on the brittle high notes. The queue shuffled forwards and she was at the window, time was slipping away, she clutched at my sleeve but I had a sense she would prefer that I refused her invitation to keep in touch. I was a creature walking out of the sea, a reminder of what she had struggled so hard to forget.

And there is no gain in the further expenditure of regret. I see this often in my line of work – on Wednesday this week, for example, when Nicola asked me to step in on a case with a couple who had lost their little girl in a fire three months ago. These cases are rare enough and responsibility always rests with the forensic engineers when there is loss of life. But my colleagues are sometimes squeamish about the face-to-face, many of them have children themselves now and their empathy is unmanageable. 'I'm worried they might find my condition upsetting,' Nicola said, patting her swelling tummy as if reassuring the unborn child. 'And you are so good at this kind of thing, Caro,' she added, meaning that I have all the style of a seasoned undertaker. I have learnt to compartmentalise and I do not over-identify. I am unflappable in the face of misery, my emotion concealed behind a mask of professionalism like a walled-in corpse.

Under normal circumstances, meetings are always conducted at the clients' home and I was apprehensive about this deviation from the usual routine since the office environment is somewhat clinical. But Nicola's secretary told me the husband held firm, quietly resisting the idea of a visit at their temporary rental. We sat in a room on the fifteenth floor which is suitably muted for sensitive discussion, with an oblique view of the city that is not too distracting, a Persian rug with priestly purple swirls, a subdued landscape painting whose earthy oils suggest endurance, a circular teak table with six comfortable carvers and a selection of refreshments that the couple refused. The wife gave very little sign that she was even aware of her surroundings, pinched her lips every now and again and occasionally lapsed into a compulsive nodding. She was flushed – a side effect of medication perhaps – her forehead beaded with sweat although the room was fiercely air-conditioned. Her husband wore a thick jumper and said he would be returning to work within the week.

'What, what?' she shouted suddenly as I was explaining

the procedure for assessing the quantum. I paused, he squeezed her hand and she stared down as if appalled by his touch. He turned to me with a quick tip of the chin to indicate I should continue and I read aloud from the list of contents on file, ticked the boxes as the husband gave curt yes and no replies. When we reached the discussion of valuables the wife's nodding reached a frenzied pace. I began winding up with a summary of the terms of reparation. We would bankroll their shiny new childless life, we could replace everything that was lost except the only thing that mattered. The walls around us screamed with the omission, the human cost not itemised in the inventory of loss.

The husband prised his wife from the chair, led her shuffling to the lift, and the receptionist bowed her head as if a funeral procession was passing. We emerged into a lobby flooded with brilliant autumnal sunshine and the wife shielded her eyes, almost doubled over at this point, swinging from her husband's arm. He shook my hand and stepped away with the grim determination of one who has resigned himself to the worst possible outcome. He may have to cast her aside if he is to survive this. Her heart will break, is already broken. Statistically I think she will never entirely mend.

always the same cheap bouquet in the same sickly lemon, mean pinched petals that look as if they expired before they flowered, the very antithesis of blossom. His choice of flower makes me think he did not much like the dead person he is visiting or – if the carnation was their favourite flower – that they themselves were unlikeable. There is a distinct air of the reluctant visitor about him, the service station price sticker clearly visible on the plastic wrapping and his insistence on keeping a distance from his dead charge, for I have never seen him tend to whatever grave brings him here. The flowers suggest a woman and wife is the likely suspect, but of course it could also be a mother or sister. My theory is that it is someone about whom he was ambivalent, someone to whom he was connected through the accident of birth or the permanence of marriage. Although I sometimes leave before him, I have never seen him actually place the flowers on a grave, instead he leaves them to wither on the bench. But still he visits, a slave to duty, or perhaps he too is stalked by guilt.

His regular seat is a bench diagonally opposite me that backs on to the northern perimeter wall and marks the highest point in the churchyard. Laurels and rhododendrons partly obscure his view to the east, but it is otherwise an excellent and private spot that allows him to observe while remaining screened from most angles. The graves in that area are all more than a hundred years old with inscriptions so weathered they are barely legible. Three lopsided stone crosses flank each side of the path approach so that in a certain light his bench has all the appearance of a throne. Shortly after he sits down, a wiry little Jack Russell comes trotting up along the central pathway, pausing to make a thorough snout inspection of the grassy verge. He springs up on the seat with surprising vigour and assumes his usual position beside the old man, leaving a sizeable gap between the two of them. The Jack sits erect and stares straight ahead like a sentry on watch duty. From time to time he shivers violently, as if he has seen an apparition, some ghost dog perhaps, come to remind him of the bleak future that beckons. Otherwise man and dog ignore each other with a relaxed familiarity. It is always the same routine.

The Jack has his own business to conduct. Each time the gate opens, he hops down and scoots over to a low stone vault which affords him a good view of the arrival. He does not usually bother with dogs the same size or smaller but makes immediately for any larger breed, barrelling down the path to ambush owner and dog. Sometimes a barking scuffle ensues but the old man never intervenes, just watches from behind his hedge screen while the frustrated owners look around in desperation before escaping through the back gate to the open fields of the estate. 'Is this your bloody dog?' a woman screamed at me last month while her Golden Retriever cowered in front of the Jack, who stood snarling in the middle of the path. I looked across at the old man, whose face was turned upwards as if he was searching for something in the blank blue. 'Oh, for God's sake, Archie, don't be such a baby,' she yanked at the lead and the Jack suddenly lost interest and sauntered off to the tap by the gates for a long and noisy drink from the plastic dog bowl before returning to the bench to wait for the next encounter.

I do not know how long the old man has been coming here but it is probably a year since he first walked past my bench. There are certain similarities in our routines. Neither of us tends the grave we are visiting as if we are both wary of being publicly associated with our dead. Both of us come in all weathers – in February, for example, we sat through torrential rain, shuffling to the edge of our respective benches to take partial shelter under foliage. Like me, he has the capacity to remain very still for extended periods, occasionally stretching his arms out in front as you might on a long-haul flight.

Sometimes he folds them in wings behind his neck and tips his head back into his hands. He might even close his eyes but I am not near enough to be sure of this. On other occasions he drapes his arms over the back of the wooden bench and stares unabashed at other mourners. Occasionally he appears to crack his knuckles and the Jack swings his head around in disapproval.

The first and only time we spoke was six months ago in the spring. I had noticed that he did not show for a few weeks and when he reappeared he was startlingly slow, the stick marking exact time with his progress. Instead of passing by my bench he took the direct route to his own, the Jack keeping pace by his heel as if making sure that his owner made it all the way. He sat down heavily and let both arms dangle by his side like a marionette. It was clear that he'd lost weight, his face was gaunt with a distinct sharpness about his profile and the maroon scarf was muffled tight on a windless day. He has been ill, I thought, and he is clearly not better. After a time he rested both hands on his lap and coughed, a dry light sound. When a dog walker arrived and the gate creaked open, the Jack stood square-shouldered on the bench glaring at the tethered spaniel but he did not leave the old man's side.

The next week he did not come. And then he did and the scarf was gone, the Jack was no longer tracking his heels and the stick was swinging again. 'Hello,' I blurted out impromptu as he passed and he stopped, casting me in the shadow of a weak sun. Close up he seemed even taller, his eyes were a soft brown, his face unevenly shaved with patchy white stubble above the jawline. There were veiny splotches about his cheekbones and nostrils and deep lines by the mouth. 'Morning,' I said and he arched a brow as if I'd managed to amuse him but he did not speak. The dog looked from me to his owner as if wondering how long this diversion would take and then the old man dipped his head in an exaggerated bow and continued towards his bench. When he left, after a much shorter visit than normal, the bouquet remained on the seat. I watched him all the way to the gate before getting up to follow.

'You left your flowers on the bench.'

'As usual.'

'I just thought… maybe you'd like me to put them down for you. If you have to go.'

He considered his stick, lifting and weighing it in his hand as if testing for some deficiency, and said, 'She won't notice.'

But of course I knew he did not believe this. My hunch is that – like me – the old man suspects that we are being watched by the dead, that they monitor our mourning, curious to see how we perform in this theatre of loss.

The volunteer has disappeared inside and the churchyard is deserted now that summer is gone and a sharp September chill bites into the mornings. The clouds hang low and heavy, today is a whiteout with a vaporous aspect to the trees, which are completely immobile. Occasionally a branch quivers as a squirrel makes a dash but it is otherwise a still life, the sky a dirty blur. And the birch leaves are turning – the brilliant ochres and golds and reds of last week are starting to fade. This is the lightless advance of winter that bleeds the colours and renders the world in an unremitting grey. And it is easy in this non-light to imagine the souls of the departed sneaking out of their lairs, pushing aside the stones and peeking out into the world to survey all that they once knew. I imagine them winged, angelic, a curve of silvery feathers transparent as gossamer folded behind their backs, which lends them the hunched appearance of playful vultures. They perch on the churchyard wall, inspecting the passing cars, the dog walkers and the bridal parties, nudging each other at the best man jabbering into his mobile about some hitch in the proceedings. They are hungry for evidence of exciting change, something worth missing – new generation cars, outrageous fashion – but apart from births and marriages and the occasional funeral there is not much entertainment and they bemoan the lack of events. There will be even fewer weddings in the months ahead, the odd winter bride taking advantage of lower rates at the hotel will arrive in a horse-drawn carriage with a little fur stole on her bare shoulders and stand shivering in the church, wishing away the ceremony. The funeral business is also slow, over the years it seems there is less death or else the locals are being interred elsewhere. Or perhaps every-one is cremated now, perhaps the whole death business has become more discreet. I imagine that the ghosts stay close to the site of their eternal rest rather than taking flight to the nearest town. I suspect them of teasing, this disparate lot thrown together by the injustice of death, and eventually they grow bored and resort to playground games, grave snatching and trivial desecration. Familiarity dulls the lustre of memory and dissolves into contempt for what they once had and have now lost: the ecstasy of longing. They tire quickly and slink back to their graves.

Although my father lies a few feet from here, I have never felt his presence amongst the ghosts, he refuses to be con-jured up. This could be because of the absence of a defining memory, the very word 'father' is flat, deflated of personal resonance, and dangles weightless, nothing attached other than a bald statement of fact. Closing my eyes, I struggle to remember what he looked like. I see a figure bent over the front tyre of my bike pinching the grooved rubber between his fingers and then pumping hard while I hold on to the handle-bars. He unscrews the nozzle and we both listen for the hiss of escaping air. He always executed these tasks with a word-less gravitas but it was clear that it was not me he was seeing as I wobbled away down the road, for his wave was mechani-cal, like a toy soldier. Tall, almost emaciated, his shirt ballooning around his concave chest, a green and brown checked weekender buttoned to the neck. A fierce concentration etched on his brow as if the detail of living perplexed him.

But I can easily imagine Estelle in the centre of the ghostly departed, she has no doubt found someone to take my place in the afterlife, someone to watch over her since my betrayal. A motherly type who knows the full story and would wreak havoc with my life if voodoo was in her power. Someone to protect her from the bullying that must be a regular feature of ghostlife, brought on by the monotony of their condition. Estelle excelled as both victim and perpetrator, it was always easy to wind her up, provoke a petulant foot-stamping that quickly bloomed into a pink-eyed rage. I remember once in Reception class when a little girl in plaits and pinafore called her 'Estie Pestie' after an argument over a ball of plasticine and Estelle slammed the wooden desk lid on the girl's fingers leaving her with a thumbnail that turned black and eventually fell off.

I have never once brought flowers for Estelle but I do not come here empty-handed. Instead I bring little trinkets: a tiny feather, a little crystal, coloured beads, shells, shiny pebbles, crumpled silver wrapping from a Kit Kat so she can smooth the wrinkles with her nail. I bring food, as the Egyptians do, those chocolate fingers she used to suck right down to the ginger bone. I bring treasure, anything glittery – penny rings, bubble gum, crinkly sweet wrappers folded into little shapes, those plastic balls from dispensers outside the post office with little prizes inside. These are the kind of baubles that Estelle adored and would not hesitate to steal without making any attempt at disguise.

One day after collecting us from school her mother stopped in town to buy a birthday card and Estelle picked up a bracelet made from seed pearls, crabshell pink with a silver clasp. She tried it on and held out her arm to admire. When her mother was finished Estelle turned to walk away and the shop assistant said, 'Excuse me, miss, but I think you forgot to pay for that,' pointing to Estelle's arm. Her mother went to remove it but Estelle refused, held her arm behind her back, ignored her mother's pleas and my offer of letting her wear my own bead bracelet all the way home. 'NO!' she screamed and made a break for the exit. Her mother grabbed her arm but Estelle spun round and caught her on the side of the cheek with a loud slap. The assistant stepped back horrified, looking behind her for support that did not materialise. Estelle's mother touched her chin and, blinking against the sting, managed a smile. 'It's OK, it's OK, she didn't mean it, did you, love?' but Estelle held firm and we both knew she would lash out again. 'Please, love, be a good girl now,' her mother pleaded. The shop girl looked down at the floor, twisting her finger around a fold in her skirt. It ended with Estelle's mother paying for the bracelet, which she slipped off when Estelle was asleep and returned the following morning. When her mother said she must have lost it, Estelle flew into a rage and smashed a mug against the wall.

We often had to resort to using trinkets to shift Estelle's sudden moments of intransigence. She could refuse to be budged, would cling to the swing with her eyes darkening, and the beginnings of a wail. She would bite, kick out with all her strength. The best strategy was distraction and I learnt to carry little objects that would grip her attention – a clam shell, a keyring, best of all was my silver chain with a crystal that sparkled in the sunlight – and she would abandon her protest and come running. Cormac could create a diversion with music, sing a funny song that he made up on the spot. Once at dusk Estelle sat swinging her legs on the branch of a massive oak and refused to come down. We were already an hour overdue home and my patience was unravelling. I flipped a silver coin, slapped it on the back of my hand. 'You can't stay here, Estelle. You know we'll get in trouble and then they won't let us out in the fields again in the evening.' She looked away with airy contempt, Estelle didn't respond to punishments or sanctions or loss of privilege, she did not extrapolate or dwell on contingencies and you could not appeal to a better nature that did not exist. Inside her world the laws of government were different, impulse-driven, random, unpredictable. We were the unstable system constantly thwarting her plans with our impenetrable logic.

Cormac climbed up on the branch and swung upsidedown. 'Estelle, you're going to land us in hot water. *Splash,*' he said, dipping again and then he dropped to his feet and rolled in mock agony on the grass, 'Oow oow I think I've broken my ankle. I might even have broken my hand,' he clutched at his arm, 'I might never play the guitar again.' Estelle peered down with interest. 'Never again, never again, never again,' he sobbed on his knees now, his curls burning red-gold in the low light.

'You can still sing,' said Estelle, leaning forwards on the branch. 'You haven't broken your voice.'

'That's true,' he sprang up. 'You're absolutely right. I can still sing, *I can sing, I can sing.*' And then he stood with his hands apart and sang 'Stella is so bella, She is not a fella, Stella is not yella, Stella Stella Stella.' She giggled. 'Again,' she clapped her hands. 'Stella is so bella, She is very mella, Stella is not yella' and Estelle called out 'bella, bella' and edged backwards along the branch, Cormac serenading her from below until she jumped without warning, knocked him over and rolled along the ground until she came to a halt.

'Stella, what d'you think –' but she was laughing, her feet sticking up in the air and Cormac going, 'You're crazy, you could have broken –' '– my voice!' she shrieked and he took up singing again, 'Stella is not crazy, Stella is not lazy.'

I stood over them. 'Come on, we have to go.'

'Caro is right, you know,' he said. 'Get up before we tickle you,' and Estelle scrambled to her feet, half-ran all the way down the hill, stopping every now and again to taunt him. Cormac lunged, making a great show of catching up with her, letting her edge forwards through the gap in the hedge, chasing her all the way up the front garden.

Since Estelle always enjoyed hide-and-seek I do not leave my offerings in the Garden of Remembrance but place them somewhere close to the bench, either on the ground, or tucked into a crevice in the sandstone wall, and imagine the fun she will have finding them. When I return after a couple of weeks her presents have always vanished. It may be that the volunteers mistake them for rubbish but I prefer to think of Estelle losing them in some spectral squabble. Today I have brought a piece of coloured glass and I can picture her turning it over in her ghostly fingers, marvelling at its soft edges, holding it up to the light. I see her still in the blue dress that she was wearing on her very last day – her favourite colour, but not the most flattering for it seemed to highlight the web of veins that lived so close to the surface of her white skin, as if her entire life-support system was on display. Estelle used to call them rivers of blood and giggle in that maddening way she had. There is a trainee in the office with the very same complexion and I can barely speak to her when she comes to me with a question.

'You've left your lights on,' the old man stops a few feet short of my bench.

'My lights?'

'On your car,' he adds sternly, pointing over the wall behind me where my headlights shine weakly in the daylight.

'Oh hell,' I turn back to face him. 'Thanks for telling me.'

'I should think a good car like that would have a beeper alert for the lights when you open the door,' he says, tapping the stick on the ground, and there is a clear assumption in this remark that I am the type of person who pays no attention to warning signals.

'I didn't hear it.'

'The battery might not be completely flat. You haven't been here that long and you've driven a good distance to get here.'

The Jack sniffs at the foot of my bench, gives the wood a cursory lick and then lifts his leg to piss right beside my foot.

'How do you know how far I've driven?' We are both taken aback by the edge in my tone. The old man inclines his head. He must be at least six foot two or three and I feel like a cheeky schoolgirl. There is nothing frail about him now, he is in much better shape than he was six months ago and has even gained a little weight. Whatever illness gripped him has vanished and left him rejuvenated.

'No great mystery. The city garage sticker on your car is the give-away. And you have the look and manners of an out-of-towner.'

The Jack trots towards the gate and stops to look back at us. 'Come along then,' the old man swings his stick. But I do not like sudden departures and my pocket hand remembers the little piece of glass. I do not want to reach down and leave it in full view.

'I wasn't leaving yet.'

'I think an hour and a half amongst the dead is sufficient for a Sunday morning, don't you? And we need to make sure you can start that car before I go.'

We walk forwards in silence and he holds the gate open for me. 'There is just something I forgot,' I mutter and run back to the bench, stopping to glance over the wall to check if he is watching, but he walks on feigning incuriosity. I crouch down and place the little piece of glass between the wall and the back leg where visiting children will not easily find it. The ground stinks of the Jack's piss.

The old man stands frowning at the bonnet of my car. 'You have a dent here,' he points his stick at the driver's door and takes a few steps back to check the bodywork, 'and a scratch about the wheel arch.' Of course he assumes that my reckless driving is to blame, that I spend my time speeding round in expensive German cars that I cannot be bothered to maintain. 'Shame not to get those fixed on a car like this.'

I turn the key and the radio blasts out at high volume.

'Not surprised you didn't hear the lights alarm. Your ears would be buzzing with that,' he says, leaning on the open door.

'Thanks again.' I tug hard on the seatbelt and rev the engine.

'You were lucky.'

'Well, goodbye now.' He straightens up to let me close the door. The Jack sits a few feet away on the ground by his Jeep, a muddy old Defender and the only other parked car.

Through the windscreen I see clouds massing above the treeline. A swirl of dry leaves shuffle and scatter on the ground by the graveyard wall. There is a sudden furious rustling in the trees and I fancy Estelle has begun her treasure hunt. I imagine the blue dress hovering about her ghostly form, she is fleshless beneath it like a line drawing, a complex cross-section of hollow joints and bone. Her hair is so long it brushes the ground, it is no longer white-gold but a dirty yellow like trampled straw. Her fingernails are long talons with soft jagged edges where she bites them still and her teeth are fully exposed in a skeletal grin, the gums long since shrunk and disappeared. There is a sound of clinking bone as she closes her fingers around the glass and cocks her head to one side. I wonder what she has to say. My guess is that Estelle would begin with an accusation about something trivial, like how, on her very last day on earth, I refused to lend her my necklace to wear with the blue dress on the grounds that she was careless.

We were standing on the path in her front garden, I could hear Cormac's guitar through his bedroom window that was open against the sticky heat. Estelle's mother came out on to the porch and bent down to pick up the milk bottles, sniffed and shook her head – it was 10 a.m. but the August sun had already been beating down for hours.

'You'll only break it,' I said, clutching the necklace to my neck, imagining how she would tug too hard and the string would snap and the beads fly up in a shower of glitter and scatter all over the gravel.

'You are so mean. I *hate* you,' said Estelle, her face so close I could smell her breath stained with cereal.

'You haven't brushed your teeth,' I wrinkled my nose and turned away.

'Give me the beads,' she said an hour later in Cormac's bedroom and made to grab them from my neck. 'I hate you *both*. I hope you die,' she shouted as she fled down the stairs.

This was the last time I saw her alive.

With the benefit of hindsight she would be able to point out that this was also her last chance to wear the necklace and I wouldn't let her, but perhaps I am wrong – perhaps Estelle has grown up in the afterlife, matured into an adult sensitivity that she never attained on this earth. Perhaps she would look on me sadly now and accuse me of a betrayal, of having led her towards such pain. Estelle might have figured out what I know and what Cormac would never accept: our complicity in the horror of her final moments.

. . . . .

There is a sharp rap on the glass and I jerk sideways banging my knuckle on the steering wheel. The old man's face looms in my window.

'Sorry to startle you,' he says, bending down as I open the window. His long fingers rest on the car door, flecks of brown scattered on the back of his hand.

'I wanted to ask what it was that you left on the bench?' His nose is oddly beakish at this sideways angle. 'Just idle curiosity I know. But it will be on my mind all day.' His smile intends charm but instead simply emphasises a slight over-bite.

I rub the curve of the wheel feeling faintly ludicrous as if some eccentricity is about to be exposed. 'Why should I tell you?'

'You know about my flowers. And of course I could always go back and look for it.'

I swing my head to face him and a vision of me chasing him through the gate with the Jack snarling at my heels.

'Forgive me,' he straightens up. 'I'm sorry to intrude.'

'It was just a piece of coloured glass. For someone to find.'

He nods gravely and steps back. I put the gearstick into reverse and pull out on to the road, watch him raise his hand in a quasi-formal salute in the rear-view mirror.

lingered at the little counter tucked into the corner while the postmistress distributed stamps and news in hushed tones from behind the glass screen. When she retired her unmarried daughter took over with a vision of a grand renaissance. She started stocking milk and bread and vegetables and even opened for Sunday newspapers, but after a couple of enthusiastic weeks the papers lay unsold – a new service station had opened up along the bypass and the village discovered a need for fresh doughnuts and Danish pastries and aisles of choice, so the daughter finally took her frustrated ambition elsewhere. For the last few years the business has been run by Mrs Harris's widowed younger sister who has moved into the daughter's old room upstairs. Mrs Harris herself limps about rearranging the shelves and chatting to the customers. On sunny days she takes out a kitchen chair and sits on the pavement, her swollen feet planted wide in slippers, watching the unchanging road. She is one of the few neighbours left who still knows me as the girl I was and never misses an opportunity to tell me how she often thinks of my little playmate and those terrible times. And remind me, of course, how well it has turned out for Cormac. 'Imagine such a celebrity in our midst,' she sighs with a searching glance over her bifocals.

In the early years I made a conscious effort to ignore his growing success, flicked past the radio stations and avoided the gossip mags at the hairdressers. But then I fell upon them like a lapsed smoker so that now I can barely restrain myself from tracking his every move. And even if I chose to ignore him it would be difficult not to know anything about Cormac's life. His shift from the private to the public domain has been so comprehensive that his true biography appears like an artistic conceit. He was the cliché afterthought, the beautiful mistake, with a host of older siblings who adored him, it was a constant hair-ruffling indulgence. An older brother's guitar was the beginning – all of this is now public knowledge –

Cormac's arms were too short to reach around the body so he balanced it flat on his knees. At school he was constantly drumming a beat or scribbling lyrics on a page during lessons, but his effortless charm defeated even the teachers, who reprimanded him without enthusiasm. From the age of ten he carried plectrums in his back pocket, little coloured plastic triangles scuffed at the edges. His fingers often bled. This is already the stuff of rock legend.

Twelve years ago, on 12 October 1995 on stage at Wembley Stadium at the end of the first set, Cormac leaned into the mike and said: 'This one's for Caro. You never called me back.' The moment is recorded on DVD and I may be the only person in the world who knows what it means. Four years after he had waved goodbye at my bedroom window, he rang my mother's house. It was the summer of 1991, I was away at university and she posted his number on a slip of paper that I carried around in the pocket of my jeans to lectures, to the library and the canteen till it became soft with wear and I had to transcribe it into my diary. It was coming up to the launch of Cormac's first album and he'd told my mother he wanted to see me. But I was stubborn and refused to hurl myself on the phone just because he had deigned to call for the first time. The album was launched some weeks later to huge acclaim and Cormac was billed as the most exciting rock debut either side of the Atlantic in years. I waited some more and then I dialled the number. The person who answered said I should call the lettings agent, who told me it was a short-term let and refused to divulge any more details. If I wanted to write a letter they would undertake to forward it although they couldn't guarantee that it would be received.

I didn't write. I didn't try to contact his agent. And he never called again.

· · · · ·

'It's only me,' I call out from the utility room.

'I'm here,' my mother replies and even before I open the kitchen door I know that I will find her exactly as I have always done ever since I was twelve years old: tucked in the armchair smoking a cigarette, her feet keeping warm in Spike's old bed. The sole additions to the scene are the plastic reading glasses that she buys from the pharmacy and never removes, as if there is no need to be able to focus on anything further away than the printed page. She does not get up but peers over the edges to inspect the middle distance where I stand facing her in that awkward moment of greeting. We do not have a pro-tocol of touching, but whenever we meet, which is only here and only every six weeks or so, she stares at me like none other. It is as if she has some special power in those blue eyes, as if she is reading signs or checking a gauge. But she never comments on whatever it is that she sees.

Like all visits to my mother, this one is unannounced. After my father and Spike died we lapsed into a cohabita-tion that was mostly silent and without event. From time to time things would break – the TV, the toaster, the lock on the bathroom door – and they wouldn't get fixed. One day the car refused to start and then my mother lost the keys. For months it languished undriven until Cormac's father explained that an engine needed to be turned over and arranged to sell it for her. The grass grew long, smothering the little rockery at the front and every so often one of the scouts would call and my mother would let them loose with a mower. But what we soon discovered was that these things didn't really make a dif-ference – there were buses, you can always eat bread instead of toast and you can let a garden grow wild. It didn't feel like a decline, more like an elimination of the non-essentials. For all that it might sound callous, the truth is that nothing important really changed after my father's death. There was less money but there was a pension. His departure simply revealed his irrelevance, just as I believe mine probably did to my mother when I left home six years later. 'How sad,' Nicola once remarked but it never seemed strange to me. In fact I think such solitude prepared me well for the life that has followed.

'Coffee?' I say, moving away to the kettle, and she nods, rummaging in her pocket for a pack of cigarettes. She has stopped reading but she never entirely disconnects from her book, just smooths the open page, sometimes tucking it under her arm as she moves about or frowning at the cover as if she has just discovered some new detail. She wears her usual long navy woollen cardigan, jeans and thick outdoor socks. A rumpled purple shawl hangs over the back of the armchair to keep her warm in the long still reading hours. Sometimes, when she drapes it at a certain angle across the front and swept high up on the shoulder with her hair folded at the nape of her neck, there is a discernible elegance about her side profile. When she raises her head to savour some sentence or thought that hovers silently in the space in front of her, there is a fleeting air of the grande dame in the uptilt of her chin, the strong curved jaw. Her hair is uniformly white and still long, possibly to her shoulders but I do not know because it is always in a chignon with fine wispy strands that fall forwards as the day wears on. When I was a child she used to sit at the table while I cut it with the kitchen scissors. My mother is not otherwise interested in her appearance. Age spots have appeared like paint spatter along her hands but the skin on her face is still surprisingly taut and smooth although it is splotched pink in places. I have never seen her apply anything except Vaseline on her lips in winter and the tube of hand cream she keeps on the window sill behind the taps. She is light, almost lithe from all the walking and the fact that she eats very little, snacking on bananas or porridge, a boiled egg, a tin of tuna. After my father died, mealtimes quickly

rearranged themselves around hunger rather than conven-
tion. Cooking was time-consuming, smelly and complicated
and even I still have a preference for fruits, vegetables and
cereal, anything easily prepared.

I turn my back on her and stand at the sink looking out at
the garden framed in the window. Occasionally I almost convince myself that I drive down from the city to visit my mother
and this is a pretence that she appears to find amusing. Thus
she sometimes greets me with a sardonic arch of her eye-
brows as if these sporadic visits are a lame and predictable
joke. She knows of course that it is not her I come to visit but
the churchyard up the road and Estelle's grave. It is possible
she has guessed that I drive down more often than I visit, that
she has even spotted me taking a detour through town. But as
far as I am aware my mother does her shopping on Thursdays,
returning with a carton of cigarettes and a supermarket bag of
food that she eats for sustenance rather than pleasure. For it
is reading that sustains her, the piles of books that she buys
in bulk and lugs home in plastic bags from second-hand bookshops in nearby towns. She reads with a fierce concentration,
sitting by the Rayburn in the same high-backed armchair that
she hauled into the kitchen the week after my father died. It
was warmer there and she could dispense with setting the
fire in the living room which was an evening ritual he always
insisted on. At first the reading seemed like a grief response
and indeed neighbours who came to us with stews and pies
noticed that although the food was barely touched, the books
they brought were devoured, big fat historical novels that
kept her company during the long nights of bereavement.

In the months after his death my mother began reading
late into the night, falling asleep in the kitchen armchair, and
eventually she dispensed completely with her bedroom. I was
left with the full run of the upstairs and shuttled between
my own and my parents' abandoned room, using the electric

blanket, spending hours in front of the dressing table and taking as long as I wanted in the bath. I would find her early in the mornings with the overhead light still on, her feet resting on the empty dog bed, her hand slack against the open pages of a book, little heaps of misfired ash around the heavy glass ashtray that still lies on the floor.

After she had worked her way through the neighbours' shelves she discovered the library in town, a grey stone building whose columned entrance lent it a grandeur that was not matched by its contents. Ignoring the fiction section – which was mostly crime and romance bestsellers with a smattering of the classics – she began to work her way through the history shelves along the back wall. She seemed possessed by a hunger for events, as if she had suddenly realised how much had just passed her by. One day calling in from school to get a book for some project I saw her sitting on a stool lost in a book about Elizabeth I. She did not notice me standing in front of her, and when I said 'Hello, Mum,' her eyes wandered slowly over me as if she couldn't quite place who I was. She waded through the monarchs and started on wars – the Boer, the First, the Second – and then leapt back to the Roman Empire, big heavy hardbacks with thick plastic covers that I used to scratch with my thumbnail leaving a ripple of tears.

She drifted into biography, I remember a book on Stalin, a black-and-white photo in full uniform and his name in huge scarlet letters across the front. It was after this that my mother branched out into science and natural history – books on bird migration, archaeological expeditions in Egypt, out-of-print volumes with pencil drawings of churches, grainy photographs of the surface of the moon, the lost tribes of the Amazon, the history of inoculation. She spent months on the Polar explorers and I have noticed that is one of the themes to which she continually returns. The story of men and the difficult things they have done in harsh conditions seems to hold a particular fascination but I have never asked her why.

It took about a year before she exhausted the resources of the library and began to move further afield, buying from charity shops and then the second-hand bookshops that she still travels to by bus. I have offered to drive her but she politely declines. 'I'm very slow at making up my mind. You'd have to wait for too long,' she says. I have told her I can source second-hand books online but she says she prefers to see the physical book and make her own choice. I notice that her reading seems to have become more focused in recent years and there is even a vague cataloguing system with volumes arranged by subject matter in piles on the floor or in the dresser that now serves as a bookshelf.

My mother has always been a very companionable reader who slips quietly away into another world when she opens a book. We might be sitting at the table after I came home from school when her hand would stray towards the open page and I'd get up and scramble an egg or heat some beans. The book is always held open between her palms, which seems to emphasise her reverence for all that is contained within, and she studies diagrams and pictures with great concentration. She is meticulous about looking after library books and turns the pages with care, never folds a corner, always uses a book-mark and never endangers the spine by leaving it face down on the table or out in the garden where a sudden shower could destroy it.

I do not know what my mother is doing with all this knowledge that she has accumulated over the years for she rarely speaks about a book and then only when pressed. There is no evidence that all this reading is having any effect, no indication whatsoever that it is impacting on her life in any way. She is a loving reader who does not skim, who will dignify a poorly written page with full attention, so I some-times wonder how discerning she might be and how much exactly she retains. Perhaps she is not reading at all, perhaps it is a form of therapy. Maybe the act of visual concentration is transporting or induces a catatonic state. Whenever I pick up a book from the table and ask 'Any good?' or 'Are you enjoying this?' she simply says 'Yes' and won't offer any further comment. It seems to be a private business, like bathing or sex. If I insist on knowing more she will say, 'Why don't you read it yourself and see what you think?' My mother has no instinct to divulge or share her opinions and manages to make me feel as if an answer requires too much effort or there was something inappropriately intrusive about my question. Sometimes I interrupt and say, 'What's it about then?' but she just shrugs and offers a terse description: 'the hibernation habits of polar bears' or 'a collection of Napoleon's letters'. It is never anything related to me or her or the fragile thread of family that connects us.

I take my place at the table in the chair where I have sat since I was a child. I can remember being so small that I could swing both feet clear underneath and sometimes Spike would come and lie below and I would bury my toes in his fur. My mother's hand drifts over a large hardback photo book of the Grand Canyon and comes to rest on a history of the gold rush with a torn cover. Her head bends low over a small paperback whose cover I cannot see. This is how we pass the time together reading when I call, for I too will pick up a book or a newspaper that I have brought with me and keep her company at the table. I have learnt not to wonder why I bother to come here at all, rather to say it is what you do when you are the only surviving relative. We do not communicate at any other time. She never calls, although she has a phone. She does not write. And at Christmas, if I visit as I usually do, the routine is unchanged, although I may bring a bottle of wine and a miniature Christmas pudding, the way you might tempt an invalid into appetite with a little delicacy.

Once I brought her a present of a lavishly illustrated history of the Ottoman Empire and she eyed the cover suspiciously.

'Maybe you would read it first?' she said, sliding the heavy volume towards me.

'Why?'

'I prefer to read a book already read.'

'Why?'

She ran a finger along the table edge. 'I prefer the feel of used books.'

There is a sense of my own redundancy in her resolute self-sufficiency. But I do not believe that there is any message behind her imperviousness other than the confirmation that we are both linked by biological fact rather than anything more meaningful. The truth is that I am not needed for anything. I used to imagine that one day if she became infirm she might need me to take care of her or at least find a place in a good nursing home and visit her at weekends.

'You only ever use one room,' I said. 'Why don't you move to an apartment? There'd be less to look after.'

'I only look after what's important. As you can see very well,' she said, spreading her arms to indicate the kitchen, the books piled up on the floor.

'But when you can't manage any more...'

'I have made arrangements,' she said, smiling not unkindly.

'What?'

'A swift exit when the time comes,' she patted the arm of her chair. 'But none of that need concern you.'

'But I am your daughter.'

'You are your own person, Caroline. You do not exist to take care of me.'

'Thank you,' she says as I place the mug on the table by her armchair, her face folding easily into the kind of smile you would offer to a passing child or a friendly dog. A gesture that perhaps depends on transience for its apparent warmth. Hers is an insistent self-containment although I suspect she would be a good listener if I had something to say. Her great skill is never to ask questions, to trust that if something needed to be said it will rise to the surface. Whether this is out of respect for my privacy or simply a statement of disinterest remains unclear. I do not think it is the latter but I have sometimes thought so in the past. My mother's disinclination to enter into conversation is nothing new. This was always how she was – silent, peaceful, untroubled. I do not recall ever thinking her distant and aloof but rather like a creature who has found its perfect habitat. The truth is I am jealous of her books, her life seems serene and rich and ageless and there is nothing at all wistful in her isolation. In order to limit well-meaning calls from concerned neighbours she maintains visibility by visiting the post office once a week to buy eggs and also to show her support for Mrs Harris's sister. The odd neighbour calls round from time to time and she is quiet and polite and no doubt considered somewhat eccentric, but there is a gentleness to her inattention which can be interpreted as forgetfulness. I assume her mind is on other things. This is the default position. She finds her worlds in books and that is where she chooses to dwell. She has never asked me anything other than the most practical of questions and in general always answered yes to my requests. I was not a handful. I was independent. And I was mostly next door.

There are other daughters who would be sitting here unburdening themselves of intimacies, like Nicola for example, who often opens some story about her weekend with 'When I was round Mum's on Saturday'. I am always struck by these mother–daughter relationships that appear to be based on a genuine friendship. I see them out shopping, ducking in and out of changing rooms, fingering each other's choice of outfits, one smoothing the other's hair. Nicola has told me how her mother was an absolute rock during the divorce eight years ago, popping round to cook impromptu dinners to make sure she was eating properly, encouraging her to get out and see people, book a holiday, get her hair cut, all the small practical nudges that keep a life afloat in rough waters. But what could I say to my mother now, how would I divert her attention from the page? Chat about work, feed her slices of office gossip, entertain her with some juicy stories of loss? Or tell her how I lay sleepless on the couch last night, the remote control sweaty in my palm, flicking backwards and forwards, staring at the frazzled stills?

The Madison Square Gardens gig three years ago was part of the eighteen-month world tour that accompanied Cormac's fifth album and the biggest grossing rock event ever at the time. I bought tickets for one of the London dates even though I knew I would not go. I do not know exactly what I thought might happen, but isn't that the point about anxiety? The effort to try and rationalise the fear can fail and leave you hyperventilating. Once during a commercial break at the movies Cormac appeared unexpectedly in front of me with other musicians in an advert raising money for Africa. His face filled the big screen, his voice boomed in the darkness around me and I couldn't breathe, had to scramble and kick my way from the middle of the row, ran down the aisle and collided with an usher. In the end I gave the tickets to Nicola on the morning of the gig. She was overjoyed and insisted on paying for them but I told her they'd been a present from someone who thought I was a fan and it seemed a waste.

The opening sequence of the concert is predictable: stadium searchlights scan the crowds who are stamping their feet and chanting *Mac Mac Mac Mac*, the fans' pet name that follows him all over the world. There are drum rolls, a mournful solo from an invisible lead guitarist and then the rising roar as Cormac strides out of the shadows into the spotlight and grabs the microphone with both hands. At this point I often switch off the sound. It has taken long enough just to be able to watch to here and I am still training myself to listen. There is a theory that says if you have a phobia you should expose yourself to the stimulus, that aversion therapy is the most effective cure, so you should surround yourself with close-ups of spiders and snakes. Whenever I watch this silent concert late at night it takes me back to the bottom bunk in Cormac's bedroom where the pillow smelled of his skin and he lay on the floor beneath me, the rich steel thrum of his twelve-string reverberating around the room, wrapping me in its layered sound. I was his audience of one but we could both sense the larger effect, could already hear the roar of applause. Cormac was oblivious, feeling his way with the instincts of a blind mole, and I was the screen. Sometimes I would open my eyes and see his mother or one of his older brothers standing on the threshold, lured upstairs by the performance. They shook their heads in amazement. He was so good you forgot to clap.

Once I sat cross-legged on the floor while he played a new song, the words flew past in snatches – a running girl and a dark street, it seemed to be about nothing and everything. Even before the last chord I was floundering at how to respond, what to say. Was the girl me, something about a shadowlight on her face? Perhaps I was concealed, a secret presence looking out through her eyes. 'It's great,' I said, 'it sounds great' – but how to comment, how to *receive* when you are deaf to the medium. Perhaps my indifference to music should have been a clue that our relationship would never survive. Can you love someone who cannot share your passion?

'I don't know what else to say,' I pressed my hands against the floorboards.

He spun round on one foot holding the guitar aloft and

said, 'It doesn't matter, Caro. You are an audience,' a remark which reassured me at the time but has since returned to me with a different interpretation.

Last night I spoke to his screen image. I said, do you remember one afternoon how the sun streamed through the fingerprinted panes of your bedroom window as we lay without clothes on the rug? The rare quiet of your house and Estelle away on some assessment. 'My favourite place ever,' he used to say, face lying on my breast. But this is not a place that he has ever revisited in a song.

I was in my second year at college when his first album was released. I bolted up the stairs in hall, ripped off the plastic and lay back on the bed expecting a message encoded in the lyrics: an explanation, a confession, something that would fill in the gap between that last wave from his father's car and the four years that had followed. There were images of sky and water, doors slamming, a foghorn and a cityscape at night but there was nothing, NOTHING where I appeared, no identifiable reference to me or to our time. I could not find us anywhere and I did not recognise the specifics. I studied the folded lyric sheet, read it all aloud but the words emptied senseless and small into my little white room. It all came from a place I did not know. Since then I buy each album and read the words without listening to the music. I have been waiting for some common ground that I would recognise but even the playground Cormac sings about in the last hit is unfamiliar – the creaking metal swing, the rusted roundabout – it is not the real world one that still stands on the edge of town. There are still no messages for me, I am not in the script.

In the small print at the bottom of the page of that first album was a long list of names he thanked. It ended with 'And Katarina'. Without knowing anything, I knew.

. . . . .

My old room is sterile now with a non-specific damp. A single bed, a naked mattress with a green blanket folded on top, a white chipboard wardrobe with one handle missing, a blue tasselled lampshade and, in the corner underneath the window, a dark stain on the carpet where I once spilled a Quink bottle. There are little pockmarks of exposed plaster on the wall where there used to be posters of dogs and rock stars, most of them put up by Estelle when she had run out of space on her own bedroom wall. I tore them down not long after she died, stripped the walls methodically, gathered up the traces of our conjoined lives – the photos, the dolls and drawings, the beads, the sea shells and lucky stones – hauled them all out to the back of the garden and stuffed them in the bin. I knew I had to make some gesture at dismantling the past and no one told me what else I could do.

The heat rained down on us in the aftermath, nights hung wakeful and airless. Cormac played his guitar behind a locked door into the early hours and even when he stopped the strings still hummed in my ear. I leant out the window and called his name but he would not reply. Everything had been transformed by Estelle's death. Even when I experimented with moving back into my parents' old room at the rear of the house I could still hear him play, an incessant strumming, as if the music could heal. And it was here, kneeling on this narrow bed looking out this window, that I watched Cormac wave goodbye and in the slow arc of his hand erase the future that I had fashioned. For the first time in my life I was truly alone. For fifteen years it had always been the three of us but three is a number fated to become unworkable. The impact of the extra one is way beyond its magnitude. Three-ness is an unstable configuration, a circuit that threatens to blow when it is overloaded with emotional charge, when the alternating current of affection that sparks and fizzles between the nodes finally short-circuits and self-destructs.

After Cormac left I was rendered invisible. I suffered a compression, was made small by the shrinking space I occupied in other hearts. It was not always this way of course, for I had been muse and protector – the wise one, if not the inspirational one. I was the oldest of the three by almost six months and so it fell to me to be responsible for road crossing and time monitoring, the division of sweets, the administering of encouragements and iodine. I had a natural aptitude for the health and safety role, born perhaps out of a relative caution, a preference for not falling out of trees, for watching and observing from the sidelines. I had no obvious leadership talent and no creative inspirations – it was always Cormac who had the ideas and Estelle who was the enthusiastic follower. According to the Myers Briggs profiling which was recently conducted at work, I am an ISFJ. The de-briefing psychologist in Human Resources described how this kind of personality is characterised by a desire to be needed. It seems that I exist to serve and am therefore likely to be often taken for granted – an unappreciated doormat with a high work ethic, a reliable backroom drone who is utterly dependable. He gave me an explanatory printout of my identity during our five-minute slot in the conference room. I am unlikely to perform very well in group situations, he began with a faint smile. I will struggle at parties, refuse the mic at karaoke and shrink from the dance floor. I have a deep appreciation for conventional behaviour and so I am not likely to strip off at the Christmas party or lie by omission on my tax return. My friends are few and close and I am fiercely loyal, sometimes dangerously so. I am prone to silent sulking and unable to articulate my feelings, which is apparently something I should watch out for. The psychologist pointed to the bottom of the page and a list of famous ISFJs that included Robert E. Lee, Jerry Seinfeld and St Teresa of Avila. 'She used to fantasise about angels piercing her side with a golden spear,' I said as he rose to indicate that our time was up. 'They're only examples,' he said, opening the door and beckoning to the next in line.

'Let's talk about your musical influences,' said the interviewer last night and Cormac settled back in the chair and began to describe how he spent an entire month listening to Leonard Cohen when he was twelve. This is the story he always tells, but he never says that the records were Estelle's, he does not describe how she inherited a stack of albums from an older cousin who was killed in a head-on collision on holiday in the Costa Brava. Estelle did not know her well and I did not know her at all, but this cousin had apparently taught Estelle how to ball socks and blow bubble gum and her grieving mother could not bear to have the records in the house. Thus Estelle showed up one afternoon in Cormac's bedroom with a collection that bestowed a sophistication in musical taste that was ten years older than us: Joni Mitchell, James Taylor, Neil Young and early Van Morrison. Cormac has often described how this treasure opened up another world and a new kind of lyricism that sent him off on a transatlantic drift and proved a counterweight to the music of our times – big sound, big hair Eighties with swooping synths, and reverb – and laid the groundwork for his extraordinary appeal.

Cormac tells the interviewer he spent hours copying Joni Mitchell's guitar technique, trying to imitate the twelve-string abundance with open tuning on his six-string acoustic. But he does not say that this was because 'Big Yellow Taxi' became Estelle's favourite song ever, that she made him play it over and over again while she sang along *DOOOOOOOOO BOP BOP BOP BOP*, her off-key little girl's voice capturing the mischievous innocence of the song. Cormac taught her the triangle but her timing was wildly irregular, she preferred the castanets she'd got in a Christmas stocking with the outline of matadors painted red on black and she would click them as she twirled barefoot around the room. She was surprisingly agile, her dancing far more accurate than her beat, her long white-blonde hair streaming behind her like a silk flag.

Cormac talks on, punctuating the story of his musical development with anecdotes about meeting his heroes face to face, but he does not describe how we built a little shrine to Estelle's dead cousin in his bedroom, on the desk beside the tape recorder. The only photo she had was a blurry representation that we glued on to an old Christmas card and placed beside a white candle sealed to a saucer. The cousin was aged about twelve, wearing a short white skirt and top and she is holding Estelle on her lap. There is a rag doll by her feet on the grass. The cousin smiles into the camera and Estelle – who is probably two at the time – reaches out for her hair with a chubby little hand. Sometimes Estelle arranged daisy chains in a necklace round the base of the candle and insisted that Cormac light it whenever we listened to the records. She would dance around or conduct while he lay beside me on the floor stroking my hand. 'Those whom the gods love die young,' he murmured once, turning his head to the photo, and it seemed like a sort of consecration, a pronouncement that might seduce another teenager into suicide pacts, but not him, not Cormac whose blue eyes glittered with a glacial and clear-headed ambition. This first exposure to tragedy infected our perspective on premature death with a romance that was based on an insufficient grasp of its immutability: that the state of being dead is eternal, that loss is a permanent condition, that its pain is chronic and enduring and leaves you like a gutted apple, the core hollowed out by a sharp paring knife.

My mother stands by the Rayburn with her hand on the kettle.

'I'm going now.'

'Coffee before?'

'No thanks. I need to make a move.'

She follows me out to the utility room. The day is fading fast and a breeze blasts through the back door ruffling the hanging coats. A school gabardine of mine, my father's padded black anorak that he got from a fireman friend and that is the warmest and most unstylish outdoor coat imaginable. Spike's old lead dangles from a hook, the leather dried and crusty.

'You don't have to come by, you know,' she clutches the cardigan collar about her neck.

'What do you mean?'

'You can just go straight to the graveyard.'

'I know. I come because –' I look down at my car keys.

'I never really understood why you were always so close to her,' she says, repeating the first and only comment she ever made twenty years ago about the actual event. And I still do not know the answer, except that it was not always benign. Perhaps blood relatives are the only ones who can detect it when your scent is no longer pure and true.

Out on the road the house lights twinkle in the dusk. The scooter has been tidied away and the curtains are drawn in the window above the post office where Mrs Harris and her sister will be settling down to a night's TV. The shuttered 'For Sale' house broods in the gloom. Somewhere I hear a door slam and the yapping of a small dog. On the back of Cormac's third album there is a shot of this road, a black-and-white still taken in winter with a dented rustbucket car, the glint of smashed glass by its rear tyre. The windows of his parents' old house are curtainless black rectangles and the door is menacingly ajar. The photo hints at the miracle of how genius flourished in such unlikely surroundings. An art-directed triumph over adversity. There is another picture of

Cormac sitting on the green Dralon couch holding the neck of a guitar that is far too big for him, trying to position his little fingers along the fretboard. His head bends in a pose of fierce concentration, curls falling forward over his face. He is five years old and wearing a green jumper with a brown felt guitar sewn on to the front which his mum knitted for his birthday. I remember that jumper clearly, I remember Estelle insisted on having it, how she flew into a rage when we sat down at his party tea. 'Give it to ME, me, me, me, ME,' and then she lashed out, caught Cormac on the mouth while the rest of us stared, sucking on our straws. He took off the jumper and stood there in his little white vest. Estelle snatched it from his hand, her mother had tears in her eyes and Cormac's mother had them rolling down her face and all of us kids sat with our Rice Krispie cakes staring at this little boy with the bleeding lip who gave away his special birthday jumper to Estelle.

she continually returns, spurred on by a conviction that time is running out and a curiosity about the reason why. 'I don't believe there has never been *anyone*,' she said one night after an offsite dinner. She had insisted on limoncellos after the others drifted away from the table and we stood swaying in the hotel lobby before clattering into the residents' bar. 'I think you had your heart broken, Caro.' She was stabbing at an intimacy, hoping for a story that would extend the evening and I was refusing to oblige. 'You never give anything away, do you?' she sighed, twisting her empty glass.

It was a year after her divorce, the sparkle of singledom had faded and she was ready to start afresh. Nicola is a fixer, which makes her an excellent manager. Practical, activist and not afraid to bulldoze over sentiment when required. Crucially she is unafraid. 'I lost my fear of heartbreak after Joe,' she explained. It was an early mistake marriage, they were childhood sweethearts and one beer was never enough even when he was thirteen. Even as she ran through a hail of confetti in her fairytale dress Nicola knew that Joe was already married to the bottle and she would have to content herself with second place. A story like a bad movie she said, showing me the little white scar on her temple where he'd slammed her head against the doorjamb. An accident, or at the very least, not deliberately done. 'You know, the funny thing is, it was the smell that bothered me most. He smelt of – squalor. And even when he was all scrubbed up and sober that was all I could smell when he was near. Like it was lodged in my nose for ever. And I thought, I can't live with that. So I decided not to fight it, to just let him become a bad smell. And that way I could just learn to stop loving him. There's nothing left now. Really. I saw him last year, I was driving past the station and there he was staggering along the road looking like the drunk he is, looking really terrible. I stopped the car and stared out at him and all I thought was: there goes that bad smell. And d'you know that was the same guy that made my heart race for ten years.'

'So what is it?'

'Sorry to dump this on you, Caro. But Michele, my fifteen-year-old niece, is coming in for work experience this morning and I had it all arranged for Jim to keep her busy while I'm at a committee meeting. But he's just left a message to say he won't be in. Some gastric flu thing.'

'No problem, I'll look after her. When's she coming?'

'She's here.' Nicola steps back into the corridor and beckons with a wave. 'You're a star, Caro, I know it's a drag but all the juniors are out travelling. Michele is actually very sweet.'

Nicola spreads her arms wide and then wraps them in welcome around a tall fair-haired girl wearing a short blue coat, a striped scarf and a turquoise shoulder bag so tiny that it reminds me of the doll accessories that Estelle loved to play with, how she'd wind the plastic strap tight around Barbie's shoulder to stop it slipping down her arm.

'Michele, this is Caro,' says Nicola and I shake her finger-less gloves.

'You're in great hands, love. Caro is the best. I'll see you lunchtime.' Nicola reaches up to pat her on the cheek and Michele moves into my office with an apologetic stoop as if she has not yet adjusted to her height.

'Wow,' she says making straight for the window. My corner room always attracts comment from first-time visitors since the jagged edge of the neighbouring building completely obscures over half the view, as if some architect miscalculated the distance between us. The protrusion is a geometric play of interlocking glass and steel and as the sun drifts west, darkness steals across the room like a giant blackout blind that has been cut with pinking shears. I have grown fond of this shifting play of light and dark but others find it disconcerting.

'That is so weird,' she turns round. 'Feels like you could reach out and cut your hand.'

'You get used to it,' I say. 'Come, let's get a coffee and I'll show you around.'

Michele is refreshingly unrehearsed, unlike the graduates that we have on rotation in the summer whose desire to impress means they are often afraid to ask the obvious questions. As we wait by the lift doors she tells me this is her first corporate outing, that her father – Nicola's brother – is a GP, with a practice in the converted garage at home so she can't play loud music on Thursday nights when he has late surgery. By the time we've travelled down fifteen floors I have learnt that she is pretty good at maths and science, that she once threw up in a high-speed lift on a family holiday in Dubai, that she would like a really good job that involves working with people but is quite technical too ('but not in a totally boring way') and that as well as being the absolute best aunt ever, Nicola is also her role model. She stops short at the alcove that opens on to the basement cafeteria and takes in the spotlights, the enormous canvases on the white walls, the slate grey floor, the constant stream of people hurrying about the shiny steel islands of plenty. 'It's like a cross between an art gallery and a food hall,' she says. Women in coats and trainers with shoebags slung over their shoulders whip past clutching coffees, pink-faced men fresh from their early morning workouts balance trays of fruit and cereal and the sports physio is deep in conversation at the juice bar queue, a towel snaked around her neck. In the ten years since I joined, the company has ballooned in size and profitability, gobbling up the floorspace all the way to the top of the building. Back then this was a giant storage area and we used to grab our coffees outside the Tube from one of the little Italian delis that have been swallowed by the chains. 'No tables,' Michele looks around. 'You eat at the desk,' I say. 'Better for productivity, maybe worse for the digestion.'

'I have to admit I don't know anything about insurance.' She sits in a narrow carver in front of my desk clutching a smoothie, one long slender leg wrapped around the other. 'Or anything about your job. But everyone's always telling me I'm a quick learner.'

It is rare enough that I get asked about my work. I am more often greeted with the suspicion afforded tax inspectors and policemen, someone who threatens to expose a secret or a lie. I am at best a reminder of an irritating or upsetting event, at worst a reminder of devastating loss. I arrive on the scene when the smoke has cleared and the drama of event is over and begin my search for the truth. I ask the probing questions, consider unsullied fact: how did it happen? What do we know? My business card conjures up images of a Dickensian bookkeeper who counts the cost of the disasters that threaten to drown us in catastrophe. I am the person you hope to go through life never having to meet. Like an undertaker, I will always be a consequence of bad news. Except that death, of course, often brings mercy or relief.

But I have always been entranced by the romance of my job title and I was quick to order an extra supply of my existing business cards after Tuesday's announcement when Nicola gathered us together in the conference room to run through some departmental changes. Last year the company hired a top line management consultancy to steer us through an expensive rebranding exercise which is designed to sharpen our competitive claws in the global arena and will involve, amongst other things, a change of logo and a review of our job descriptions. The transition from 'Loss Adjustor' to 'Loss Assessor' seems to me to ignore a crucial element of a job that is, in my view, part counsellor, part prosecutor and part judge. An active management of the client will not only ensure that our financial liability is equitably administered but also that the client is restored, in as much as this is possible. As well as looking after the company's interests I consider it my personal responsibility to help our claimants adjust to their loss. Empathy and careful handling can, I believe, contribute to a better outcome. Thus my job title is a vote of confidence in the survivability of misfortune.

Naturally the company's concerns are entirely financial. There is no correlation between profitability and successful adjustment to loss so the company is interested in the welfare of its policyholders only to the extent that they keep their lives as safe as possible and continue to pay the premium. The tendency these days for insurance companies has been to outsource loss adjustment and I occasionally get calls from headhunters who want to take me to lunch and discuss how I could cash in on my excellent reputation with a career move.

Nicola is amused that I keep turning them down. 'You could get much more money, Caro,' she said at the end of my 360 review last year. 'It's the way of the future.' The impending birth has exaggerated her directness, as if she is making sure that there is nothing left unsaid before she goes on maternity leave. But I have never considered moving. This is a cradle-to-grave business and I believe in the relationship between underwriting and risk. Outsourcing creates unseemly gaps in what should be a connected process and I prefer to stick with an organisation that still provides a comprehensive service.

Sometimes I walk down to the thirteenth floor to watch the army of underwriters quote for new risks to brokers and occasionally direct to clients. They sit in front of the screen and tap in the permutations, check the postcode and answer the questions: How much will it cost to insure my new car?

What will it cost for my wife's life? Do I need locks on the upstairs windows? What if someone else's kid falls off the trampoline in my garden? We offer protection for the stolen handbag, the mysterious illness that renders you incapable of work, the malicious scrape of a key down the side of your new car – only last week the evening papers led with a story about £250,000 of malicious damage caused by a gang of schoolchildren who vandalised sixty-two parked cars in one of the more elegant suburbs. The whole business took less than fifteen minutes and was watched from a bedroom window by a Filipino nanny who, unable to decide if this constituted a genuine emergency, did not call 999 but rather enterprisingly used her mobile to take a high-resolution photo which was reprinted in all the papers and clearly showed the faces of a girl and two boys either side of a BMW.

The company depends upon a certain paranoia to make money and an ideal operating environment is a world where the scales are tipped towards dangers that never become reality. A world where nothing ever happens. Thus the climate of fear has had a very positive effect on negative sentiment: 9/11, the spectre of the terrorist prowling our cities, stranger danger, the daily warnings of imminent threat flashed across our screens confirm that the whole business of existence is fraught with risk. This is the way we live now. Panic and distrust fuel our revenue growth and in general this has been excellent for business, if it were not for the apparent increase in natural disasters on a national and global scale. This may be a blip of course, but the debate about climate change preoccupies the boardroom. Like all the other big players we are a global operator and the scale of our exposure is impressive. The shockwave from an earthquake ten thousand miles away will be felt in the increase to your household premium.

· · · · ·

I place a stack of glossy brochures on the table and Michele opens the one with a child's crayon drawing of a blue house with a brown roof and a large daisy by the front door, all of it enclosed within a wobbly red heart and drawn by Jessica, aged nine, who won last year's art competition that was part of our Investment in the Community Programme. She flicks through the pages – Buildings cover, Contents cover, Personal possessions, Claims conditions, Policy exclusions – while I walk her through the fundamentals. The company promises peace of mind in return for a fee. We collect protection money from men and women who are worried and the list of worries is endless: the water tank that could spring a leak; the old wiring that could short circuit; a thief that could jemmy open the conservatory window, download your computer data, steal your passport, appropriate your identity and drain your bank account; the carnage that greets you after the holidays when you turn the key in the door to find laundry all over the hall, the crockery smashed to pieces, the carpet sodden and stinking with the water that has overflowed from a sink deliberately blocked, the kids' mattresses slashed, the spongy entrails of their disembowelled teddies strewn across the bedroom floor.

But with life comes event risk. With flesh comes disease and decay. With ownership comes loss and malfunction. And our business thrives on anxiety and dread. Who knows what nasties are brewing in the sewage pipes underneath your lawn? What is that shadow on the X-ray, there by your left lung, like a rain cloud massing in a grey sky? Who knows if someone is sitting in a parked car on the corner of your street, watching you pull out of the drive at 8.15 a.m. with the last frazzled child strapped into the back, or following you along the platform as the midnight train approaches, threading their way through the drunken crowds, trailing you from a distance across the footbridge, edging closer in the low-lit cut-through, reaching out for the briefcase in your hand? The flash of a knife, the tsunami that rips into your holidays, the consultant's grave face. We cannot stop the screaming alarm at 3 a.m. – the best deterrent would be not to own anything. Or not to care, not to love. If you do not love, you cannot lose.

Michele has more practical concerns and wants to know if I spend most of my time in the office. I describe my visits to policyholders all over the country, inspecting burnt warehouses and flooded homes, long hours watching CCTV footage, talking to building surveyors, meetings with the police.

'Oh, will you be seeing anyone today?'

'No, I haven't got anything scheduled. I work the larger cases and I'm afraid this is a quiet week. Otherwise you could have tagged along with Jim to some of the small cases but we're a bit thin on the ground today between sickness and travelling.'

'I'm here next Monday too.'

'Well, maybe there'll be something then.'

'Sure,' she nods without conviction, for Michele is still young enough to be wary of adult assurances about the future that so often disappoint.

'So is this the job you always wanted?' she says, looking doubtfully at Jessica's painting.

'It has its attractions.'

'Sorry. I didn't mean –'

'It's OK,' I smile. 'Come on, let's take a tour round the building and I'll tell you on the way.'

Mine was an accidental career choice, not a vocation or a gift. I went to university because I was offered a place and it was an option at a time when the horizon was bleak and unpromising.

While my fellow students graduated to house shares I spent three years in halls, in a grubby 14 x 10 room with a mini-fridge that hummed at night. I spent my time reading and wandering around the campus, a grey homage to concrete and glass surrounded by green fields that I tramped in all seasons. In summer I sat on an auditorium of steps outside the cafeteria watching skinny boys play football on the paving below. I was a diligent student because it was a way of passing the time. I spent long nights in the library, sometimes dozing off amongst the crammers in the countdown to exams. I sat in large noisy groups in the Union bar on a Friday night and flipped beer mats, drank cider and perfected the art of slinking off without anyone noticing. There were boys who stroked my arm and mouthed things I could not hear above the music but I felt as if my skin belonged to a stranger. Once a boy with a tattoo on his shoulder and a black bandana rode me home on his handlebars but when we kissed I found I could not breathe and fell back gasping. Desire snuffed out. I could not taste anything outside myself and I could not imagine ever being lost in the wonder of another person again, that soaring feeling, the conviction that all the industry of daily life has got some point.

There was a girl who briefly befriended me, who wore her brown hair in thick plaits at night to frizz it for daytime. She took to sitting beside me at lectures or in the canteen, talked endlessly about her parents who had announced they were divorcing on the very day she started college. 'They actually thought I should be fucking grateful because they waited until I had left home,' she said and then she cried and I looked away for words of comfort that I did not seem to know. She too was an only child and thought this commonality grounds for friendship but all I could do was shuffle cutlery around my tray and ask if she wanted another coffee. Eventually she drifted off to other tables and other girls who could offer what she needed.

On days without lectures I worked early and sometimes double shifts in a newsagent near the train station where even the regular customers never lingered longer than it took to exchange pleasantries. I went home in the holidays and lay on the bed dreaming of Cormac and Estelle and avoided the post office and neighbours who were curious to monitor my progress and asked for news of him that I did not have. I worked in a succession of jobs in the town during the summer; my favourite was the supermarket checkout at peak times and the conveyor belts that spoke of transience. I saw my mother infrequently but I was not lonely, I was simply alone. In my final year I got a job in the library administering fines and civic leaflets, stamping and shelving books, idling over breaks in the staff room where women in outsize skirts rested their stockinged feet on stools at lunchtime, dipping digestives in their tea.

I graduated with a 2:1. I could probably have made a first but such overachievement seemed wasted on someone without drive or ambition. It just didn't seem to matter. And then I was hoovered up as graduate intake by a commercial bank that trained me to become a business development manager. My days were spent cutting a swathe through someone else's ideas, asking the difficult questions, feeling for the pulse of a viable business, doing the numbers on creative endeavour, stripping away fantasy from reality to expose the beating heart of a project. I learnt to be a bloodhound sensitised to variables that would indicate risk or failure, pored over spreadsheets that told stories of desire, grand visions woven into the fabric of the numbers, swelling the bottom line with a feverish optimism. I became a dream breaker. It was my job to prick the balloon, deflate to verifiable facts and reasonable assumptions and present the neutered odds to a management committee of two, for start-up projects less than half a million. But I knew it was the wrong place for me. I had flown too close to the sun before and needed to step back from the thrust. Something more restorative and ordered would be better and this was what I found with a sideways move to a large insurance company ten years ago.

Once I dreamt that I was standing by the water cooler in the dead centre of our Underwriting department and the phones were completely silent, the office workers were flicking through newspapers at their desks. Two girls sat in front of their screen watching a movie. Others played online poker. One man lolled snoring in his chair. I looked out the window at the people walking about down on the concourse, buses inching along the street, traffic lights shifting from red to green, life carrying on as normal and I wondered how we had managed to miss this. Behind me a woman sat at her desk arranging photos in an album.

'What's happened out there?' I said.

'I guess someone told them there's nothing to worry about,' she smiled and rose to stand beside me, pressing her fingertips against the windowpane. 'Maybe they've just decided to take their chances. See what life brings and take it on the chin.'

This may or may not be the perfect job for me, but who can tell? It is certainly the perfect marriage of my personal and professional interests. Unlike Cormac, I have punched below weight for most of my life. Upward career progression at this point requires a commitment to managing people and Nicola knows that I am not interested in being responsible for the welfare of others. She tells me I am a manager's dream because I do not use her as nursemaid or therapist. I do not wish to become involved in other peoples' dreams again. There is plenty of work and plenty of time to brood and reminisce in my black swivel chair with its obstructed view and this large wooden desk with a surface so glossy that I cannot be sure it is veneer without destroying it.

6

FROM HIS VANTAGE POINT on the other side of the graveyard the old man has me under surveillance. I gave him short shrift when he arrived today but he remains undeterred. A new routine has been established since his auto rescue some weeks ago and he now insists on conversation each time he arrives.

'You're not a doggy person, are you?' he began on the first occasion. The Jack stood staring up at me with dark goiterous eyes. 'I could tell the very first time we walked past.'

'I don't remember.'

'Jack just sniffed your leg and moved on. He's never bothered with you since which is most unusual because it's always women he prefers.'

'I used to have a dog actually,' I said looking over to the corner where Spike's memorial is hidden. I would have liked to tell this man that mine was a nice dog, unlike his scabby little terrier who terrorises other dogs and pisses on bench legs. I would have liked to say that old age is not a licence for blunt presumptuousness and intrusion.

'He was my wife's dog. Beth made me promise to care for him after she'd gone. I suppose she knew I'd try to palm him off at the first opportunity. As if I didn't know it would be impossible to find a home for a cranky old terrier who doesn't like men and can't be trusted with children.'

Jack sat with his ears pricked, eavesdropping on these home truths. No doubt such a betrayal is exactly what he had expected and he was unsurprised by such disloyalty. The old man wiggled his stick and the dog looked away in disgust, but he is not going anywhere, the damnation of the dead keeps him safe. The two of them bound together in reluctant comradeship by a promise to a dead woman, Jack gritting his teeth against life's dwindling pleasures: no more extra scraps or tummy tickling or napping in Beth's armchair, the smell of her still steeped in the cushion, all over the house.

'Your car still OK then?' The old man appears suddenly in front of me and stands, eyes flickering over my bench. He is curious to see this week's trinket and I squeeze the little silver charm in my palm, staring straight ahead like a stubborn interviewee.

'Yes.' My rudeness is out of character but I am wary of his expectations and the commitment to enliven his solitary visits with a friendly chat. There is a bossy inquisitiveness about him that could quickly become repellent and it is easy to imagine him harassing his Beth with questions. He strikes me as the over-monitoring type, a paternal busybody who sticks his nose into domestic minutiae and never misses an opportunity to draw attention to shortfall. I used to see a man like this – dark-haired and immaculate in Italian suits and handmade shoes. He liked to know what I was doing even when he wasn't there. In the beginning I mistook it for jealousy, but in fact there was something almost effeminate about his interest in my movements, like a girlfriend who might chitchat about the weekend. On the nights when he slept over he spent long hours in the bathroom, taps running on and off, the sounds of a complex bathing routine. He had a foldout washbag with special sections for each grooming implement that reminded me of a little boy's toolkit. And there were peculiarities about touching that went unarticulated but which he managed to convey by an insistent manipulation of my body parts. He didn't like his clothes being removed by anyone other than himself. Ties could not be slung over a wardrobe door. Suit jackets had to be hung. He managed to multi-task his way through shirt-folding while maintaining an erection. He always came inside me with a precision that convinced me he was worried about spillage for he would get up quickly afterwards and shove a hand towel under my ass. He inquired about my cleaner and always plumped up the pillows when he got out of my bed. He had ideas about storage improvements I could make to the bathroom.

At first he was enthusiastic about shower sex, which started out as an adventure but his interest in water as a cleansing agent had a sobering effect. I didn't appreciate being excessively lathered into a squeaky-skinned tightness as if he was preparing a vegetable. I do not recall being bathed as a little girl but it reminded me that I might have been and seemed to form an unfortunate link between the splashing horseplay of childhood and the shivering sponge baths that awaited me in old age. As he turned me round to soap my bottom for the second time, it seemed I was being diligently washed rather than experienced in water. I pressed my ass back into his hard-on in an attempt to revive some present tense and a desire that was draining steadily down the plug-hole. But he steadied me upright and continued with a slow methodical soaping which quickly became unbearable, like a ticklish massage, and I stepped out, slamming the shower door. We stood staring at each other through the rain-soaked glass. There was no diminishment in the extraordinary angle of his erection. My jump-start would be sufficient for him to power on his own momentum and if I left the bathroom he

he cocks his leg on the grass, throws me a quick glance and moves off to the side.

'Never stare down a dog,' I used to warn Estelle but that only made her do it more. She would corner Spike in the bedroom when he was a puppy and stare at him until he barked. Once he scratched her bare leg jumping for a stick and she hit him hard on the nose. He yelped and cringed and I flew at her. 'You stupid idiot, what d'you think you're doing.' She pushed me away howling and pointed at the graze on her thigh while I cradled Spike, buried my head in his fur and told him it would be all right. The stick had left a small scratch on his nose. But he got used to her eventually, like we all did, learnt to make allowances for the swinging pendulum of her moods. When Estelle showered him with unsolicited affection, Spike would lie with his ears back and would not move a muscle but wait until she was distracted before slinking noiselessly out of the room. He never made the mistake of trusting her, his instinct was true, he could sense how she could turn in an instant. But Estelle always believed he loved her and whenever we visited his memorial she would kiss it and say, 'I bet Spike really misses me.'

Now of course they are united again. The Garden of Remembrance is less than a hundred feet from Spike's stone which is completely hidden now beneath a thicket of foliage. Estelle would be pleased with this company as Spike was easier to negotiate than people and far less confusing than the human condition, which was fraught with complications. And he will be a good and loyal companion to her. I imagine his fur a distinguished grey like a grand old silvery wolf, his blue eyes yellow, his paws a snowy white. Estelle will have made him a crystal collar and I picture him loping along by her side as she air-runs, a graceful flowing slipstream that only ghosts can do. Her straw hair flaps out behind her, the blue dress is just a blur at this speed and for a moment they are both transformed to hot breathing flesh. And although I know that bad things cannot happen to Estelle ever again, it is still comforting to think that Spike will protect her from harm, stretched out Sphinx-like in front of the stern slab.

'Why does he do that?' I point to Jack who is over by the church porch licking the stone wall like cows who slather great hunks of stone with their fat grey tongues.

'An instinct for something he's missing,' says the old man. 'A mineral, some deficiency. Like the way he eats grass to make himself throw up. Dogs are intuitive about health, they listen to their bodies when we do not. They don't need to be rushed off to the vet like we go down to the doctor's every five minutes.'

Jack starts off along the path with a stiff little three-legged gait as if he is rehearsing for a future as an amputee, one of those dogs you see with a furred stump, looking like battle-scarred veterans from another age.

'He's lame.'

'We both have a touch of arthritis. He's rickety in these damp mornings so I give him Metacam to ease the pain.' The old man stretches his right knee slowly outwards. 'In fact I take it myself.'

'What?'

'Metacam. Jack's arthritis drug. Comes in a liquid, a little syringe that I squirt over porridge in the morning. Can't taste it, but it works a treat, I can tell you.'

'Why don't you use a human drug?'

'Can't be bothered with the waiting,' he sniffs. 'Sitting for hours in surgeries full of old people with all their miserable ailments and doctors that look like schoolgirls. I can get the dog's stuff on repeat. Just walk into the vet and renew it. He's registered at two surgeries so I get a double dose.'

'Don't you worry about side effects?'

'We've all got to die of something.'

A little flurry of cool air snakes round my neck and I fancy that Estelle is creeping closer. We have an audience, the ghosts can smell the breeze of a story in the air and nudge forwards.

'So what happened to your dog then?' he says.

'What?'

'You said you had a dog?'

'A border collie. When I was a kid.'

'Name?'

'Spike.'

'Excellent name, perfect choice for the breed. Lots of character. People round here choose such ridiculous names. Tinsel and Jewel and such rubbish. You know what the test of a dog's name is?' he leans towards me. 'Try shouting it out in a public place and see if you sound like a fool.' He nods enthusiastically. 'SPIKE. SPIKE,' he roars in demonstration and Jack comes belting out from under the yew. 'Yes indeed. One strong syllable.'

He rests both hands on the stick. 'So what happened to Spike?'

'He was run over by a car when I was twelve.'

'Hard to teach dogs about traffic in the countryside.'

'Spike knew all about cars. We lived in a cul-de-sac, he was always wandering around.'

'Drunk driver?'

'Actually it was suicide.'

He swings his head round and I instantly regret my frankness. 'Suicide,' he repeats as if he is testing the theory.

'I saw him do it. He turned to look at me and then he ran right out in front of the car.'

And the old man does not smile but instead takes this information under consideration, looking up at the sky, thinking it over, and then he turns to face me. 'Well, I'm sure we're not the only species who must feel it's all rather pointless from time to time.'

Jack shuffles his rear against the ground, scratching his bottom.

'He barely tolerates me but I'm used to him now. Beth gave me all the instructions, she was very firm towards the end – no more cajoling, just that bossiness that we all always took comfort in. Of course it's women make the structures, the rules that dogs and children live and die by and with Beth there was always a routine. Jack would sit waiting by her heels while she stood in front of the hall mirror. Knew all her habits – she only had to take the lipstick from her bag and he knew it was walkies. At first he refused to adjust, like he was keeping vigil for his real owner. I still find him sitting at the bottom of the stairs in the morning like he's waiting for her to come down. When I appear on the landing he turns away with a flick of his snout. I fill his bowl at seven o'clock when I make my tea but he won't touch it till eight. Sits there waiting, drooling by the bowl.'

The wind ruffles the white fur around Jack's neck as he sits on the ground with his back to us, nose twitching at some scent on the air. He is not about to waste his time learning new tricks, he will stick with the original plan, a cussed loyalty to a dead owner whose rules he refuses to change.

'I even have to take a biscuit on his walk, something Beth never had to do, he always came when *she* called him. I can shout till I'm blue in the face but he pays me no mind. And he sits in the front seat of the Jeep. Ruins the driving experience with his filthy looks.'

I remember once leaving as the old man was arriving, Jack peering determinedly through the windscreen and shooting worried sidelong glances at his chauffeur.

'You lost the wrong one, didn't you, Jack?' He throws his head back and cackles, an astonishingly loud bark. Jack shuffles off, embarrassed by this raucous truth. 'I even said this to Beth in her last week in the hospital. And do you know what she said to me? She said, "Tom, you'll have to make a bigger effort now. Remember you're the adult."'

He tightens the muffler. A chill creeps around the back of my neck; it is ghostbreath, Estelle playing games. She has shuffled closer with her companions, like herons inspecting a still pond, looking for the flash of scales before they swoop. Something lies beneath, there is a story here and it is not good. An old man's misery, some saga of familial ruin that lies now like a stinking heap atop his dead wife's grave.

'Oh yes. People die and pets and children mourn the passing of the one they really loved. Jack lost the wrong one. And Charlie too.'

I rewind the scarf around my neck but the cold presses ever closer as the light fades and I must ask the question that goes begging: 'Charlie?'

'My son. He's lived in Australia these past seven years. Lectures at the University of Melbourne. Mi-cro-bi-ol-ogy,' he says, slowing down each syllable in faint mockery. 'He's made his home there now. Married a local girl.'

'Nice place to visit.'

'I don't.'

He is poised on the brink of a story that I hope will be choked off by his habit of reticence, but I have the feeling that this good habit is being unlearnt in my company. It's something about being a good listener and I know from my work how a quiet attentive manner can be the most effective prompt.

'You talk to your friend, don't you?' he turns to me. 'Oh, don't look so shocked. People often do around here. Even I find myself talking to Beth sometimes and that's something I did very little of when she was alive.'

A drop splashes on my forehead and then another and I look up at a sky sullen with cloud.

'There are those who say they can see the dead. I wondered if you did? Sometimes you look as if you are watching something.'

'Rain.'

'I don't feel it,' he tips his face upwards and crinkles his nose.

But my cheek is wet and I cannot stifle the conviction that Estelle is up to some mischief. When we were eight she went through a water pistol obsession that dragged on for months. She would creep up at any moment and get you right in the ear, even in the eyeball if she could manage it. Once she sprayed my homework, then my mattress, and howled with laughter 'Caro wets the bed, Caro wets the bed.'

'Would you like to tell me about your friend?'

'No.'

'Well then, tell me about your job. I presume you must have a good one to afford that car of yours.'

'Why are you trying to coax me into conversation?'

'Why not? We've got nothing else to do but sit here and talk to the dead. Why not talk to someone who can answer you back? Don't men ever try to talk to you?' he grins. He has clearly amused himself with this little witticism.

'Maybe I come here to be silent.'

'Think of it as an act of charity. Today I brightened an old man's day by talking to him.'

I cannot resist smiling but I do not look at him.

'Now you see I have amused you. So you owe me a chat in return. Tom Warren,' he says extending a hand. 'Nice to meet you.'

'Caroline.'

'Caroline?'

'Yes.'

'Never mind. A young person's thing to introduce with a first name.'

The dog trots over, peers up at me with his head cocked.

'Ah yes. And Jack of course.'

'Hello, Jack,' I say and bend forward but he growls and backs away.

'He's a miserable sod. Makes up his own mind about who touches him. So shall we proceed in the traditional manner?'

'How d'you mean?'

'Public servant. Retired,' he crosses his long skinny legs. 'And you?'

'I am a loss adjustor.'

'Hardly a pair to set the blood racing,' he chuckles. 'But never mind, Caroline, let's keep it moving along, shall we? Nothing more tedious than a boring conversation. Why don't you tell me something eventful that happened at work this week. A run-in with the boss, a bit of gossip? Better still, tell me how you adjust a loss.'

Tom Warren balances the stick by the edge of the bench and settles back, arms folded and expectant. The Jack returns to sit directly in front of us, ears cocked as if he too is waiting for the entertainment to begin.

'This week I met with a woman who left her five-year-old daughter in charge of her handbag while she looked at earrings in a department store. The little girl was just a few feet away playing with a doll on the floor while the mother chatted to the sales assistant, during which time "a nice lady" asked the child for the handbag.'

'And she gave it?'

'Of course. The mother was distracted, had a fretful baby

in the buggy. She was going to her sister's thirtieth birthday party, she hadn't been out in months and her husband had said, go on, treat yourself, buy something nice.'

'What an inventive thief!'

'We found it on CCTV. An impeccably dressed woman with huge sunglasses. Probably a wig.'

'What was in the handbag?'

'Credit cards, a small amount of cash. But the real problem was her husband's watch which she'd just collected from the jeweller's after a service. An antique Rolex Oyster inherited from his father on his deathbed. And of course, not insured – the husband thought the quote for an all-risks policy was too expensive.'

'Ouch. I bet that was worth a few bob.'

'Six grand.'

'Poor woman,' he clicked his tongue.

'She was so cross with her daughter that she smacked her and the girl cried. All recorded on camera. When I met her she was desperate, she hadn't told her husband about the Rolex, he thought it was still at the jeweller's. He would never forgive her she said. He was always saying she couldn't cope.'

The little girl stood in the kitchen scrunching her bare toes on the linoleum. She followed me to the front door with tears in her eyes, asked if I was going to bring back Mummy's bag. But I have limited powers, I could not save her or her mother from the truth that would have to come out.

I interview, take the testimony, collate the facts, gather and weigh the evidence, collect the receipts, seek expert advice when necessary, assess the damage and estimate a reserve. If there is anything suspicious I will call in the authorities. Of course restitution is not always possible: the replacement ring is beautiful but it is not the original, that exists only in sensory memory and indeed many women report that exact replicas feel different on the finger. The photos of the honeymoon vanish with the stolen camera and the whole experience must be entrusted to storage in a personal memory vault that no longer feels secure, for memory seems like a poor second, as if we were unreliable witnesses to the lives we have lived. The recorded event is more substantial because we were not paying attention to the unfolding moment, we were too busy fiddling with the video and fretting about how reality will appear in replay. 'Oh look, Jim *was* there and I don't remember him at all.' So now the camera tells us what happened, our lives are captured on a running ticker tape.

'The whole honeymoon is ruined for me,' said a woman whose laptop was stolen. 'I can't bear the idea of somebody looking at the photos.'

I told her that the most likely scenario is that the thief wiped the hard disk before selling it, but she wasn't listening, she was dabbing angrily at her eyes. 'It's like some stranger was there in the hotel room, in the restaurant, everywhere.'

'The thief will want to get rid of your laptop as soon as possible. No one wants other peoples' snaps.' This is not in fact the case, but I offered her this reassurance instead of the inside truth which is what the police tell me – that they are amazed how often everything is deleted *except* the photos. It seems that even petty criminals have a fascination with the lives of others and love to peruse pictures of family outings, the Christmases and christenings of strangers. Or perhaps it is the idea of the dream life that is seductive, for we don't photograph the lows – the bitter fights, the funerals.

I asked her if the photos were compromising. 'No, no,' she snapped. 'It's just everything was on there – my niece's birthday party, the hen night. They can do anything with graphics these days, you know. Makes me feel physically sick just thinking about it.' She crushed her empty plastic cup, thinking about body doubles, her niece's face advertised on some trafficking site.

'Extremely unlikely,' I said, although I could see she would look good as an emaciated dominatrix. A spiky haughtiness about the chin.

'That's what my husband says, but you don't know. Who knows what those perverts do?'

Who knows indeed? Her lip trembled at the vision of her wedding face atop a naked torso in some carelessly orchestrated porn video where the bride and her maids cavort with their bouquets before being deflowered orgy-style by the priest. It must exist. Everything exists, more or less.

'So Caroline, you have become an expert on loss,' Tom smiles resting both hands on his stick.

'The irony is not lost on me,' I sit forward on the bench. 'And now I'm afraid I have to go.'

He chews his lip, a little disappointed, he had settled down for a good old chat that might fill a chunk of his empty day.

'You need to leave first,' I remind him.

'What?' he looks up confused. 'Oh yes, yes. I was forgetting.' He rises stiffly, hand comforting his lower back. 'Thank you for the conversation,' he says. 'I look forward to a continuance,' and he raises his hand in a gesture that is midway between a salute and a doffing of his hat and walks away with Jack trotting behind him.

The silver charm has made small pink indentations in my palm. The perfectly formed 'E' reminds me of the one Estelle lost from her bracelet when, despite her mother's warning, she insisted on wearing it out in the fields. We searched everywhere but to no avail and Estelle ran home screaming, kicked open the kitchen door and threw the charmless bracelet in the downstairs toilet. It lay unflushed for two days, her mother told everyone to use the upstairs. Estelle inspected the bowl after every use, it was a perverse sort of punishment for the bracelet that had carelessly lost its prize charm. On the third day, she herself took it out with a stick and threw it on the garden bonfire. Never spoke of it again.

I start the engine and turn up the heater full blast. A long line of conifers shivers in the wind as I reverse, the whip of rain on the windscreen will double the journey time back to the city. Tom's tail lights disappear under the stone arch, he will be home in minutes. I asked why he never comes on foot, for he could easily walk here from his house using the path that cuts past the old gate lodge, but he said the engine needs turning over and there is a road to cross and Jack detests the lead. I imagine the two of them moving about in the kitchen, Jack waiting for an evening snack, the old man opening the fridge door contemplating the tedium of cooking for one. Drinking his tea at the table, thinking over his inventory of loss.

7

THE BRIDGE IS JAMMED with a queue for the slip road up ahead and down below a sea of red lights pricks the motorway gloom. I settle back in the seat and fiddle with the tuner, the news channel murmuring on low. I have learnt to be careful with the radio when driving, the sudden assault of music when I am hurtling along in the inside lane and all concentration can leak out of the car. Once I was stopped at dusk, blue lights rearing up behind me, the shadowy outline of a dark figure behind the windscreen. It was spitting rain when I pulled over and cut the engine thinking how the reflector yellow of the bulky jackets is less threatening than the fitted black uniform, speaking as it does of the outdoors, of sandwiches and thermoses. The policeman bent down at the window and warned that deer can ambush at any turn. 'I should give you a ticket,' he said, 'but you look like you've had a hard day. Don't let me catch you again.'

Cormac's CD lies on the passenger seat. The cover shows the band in a moody playground with Cormac standing side-ways by an empty swing, hands in the pockets of his jeans, head turned towards the lens as if the cameraman has just called his name. The drummer is draped uncomfortably over the central pivot of a seesaw while the bass player and lead guitarist pose on the graffitied roundabout that appears in the title track, 'Playground Chains'. A crushed can lies on the ground by their feet. It is a winter scene with bare trees in the background and the whole composition is aggressively forlorn. The outer edges of the photo are blurred, an effect achieved by smearing Vaseline over the lens, at least still engineered this way by the purists who eschew Photoshop. This was the album released nearly two years ago that chronicled the hard times endured by some of the band members in the fulfilment of rock star cliché. A recent actuarial report at work described how new research indicates a high mortality rate amongst musicians. It is apparently a lifestyle that kills, which would put Cormac in the danger zone although he has so far managed to escape disaster through clean living and emotional stability. This is exactly what I would have predicted. Cormac has not fulfilled the bad-boy persona. He never had the constitution for a drug habit, I can remember him retching in the bracken after a cocktail of cider and Carlsberg and he never even progressed beyond the trial stage with smoking. Such single-mindedness does not allow any time for recreational drug use and any moments of misbehaviour have been kept out of the public glare.

The other members of the band have however embraced the cliché with genuine zeal. According to the gossip mags the heartbreak of the album is not Cormac's own. This post-party collection was released just as various crises exploded on the scene: the bass player's bitter custody battle, the sudden death by heart attack of the drummer's parents (rumoured to have been precipitated by the malfeasance of the offspring), the suicide of a sibling (the lead guitarist's younger sister, from an overdose ruled accidental by the coroner) and of course the drummer's very public break-up when his wife took four-year-old Pollyanna and Binky the spaniel to Palm Springs and filed for divorce. Road rage, mayhem and general hotel room trashing ensued. Their home in the foothills sat empty because the drummer could not tolerate the reminders of family life that taunted him. He grew dangerously thin, was unusually foul-mouthed to the paparazzi who snapped him clinging to the necks of various groupies or falling into limos at 3 a.m. And then he disappeared. Frantic speculation was quashed by the band's publicist, Penelope Fisher, who confirmed that he had checked out of his hideout suite at the Chateau Marmont and into the Dale P. Vermont Clinic and asked the press to respect his privacy. His rehab has been heavily photographed – aerial shots of the Arizona site, dry and punitively sharp as if the very air could burst into flames. The drummer was followed shortly after by a pap shot of the lead guitarist being chauffeured through the gates of the same clinic in a car driven apparently by Cormac, although all you could clearly see were two hands on the steering wheel.

The drummer emerged from rehab a few months ago clean-shaven and contrite, his trademark ponytail still intact. He had paid his dues, he said, and found that the answer to life's great mysteries does not lie in cocaine or champagne. Excess was simply that. He is as good as new and happy to fall on his sword on any chat show in town. There is even talk of marital reconciliation. The lead guitarist is reportedly doing fine although he has so far avoided the limelight and headed off to a secret location to spend some quality time with himself. Throughout it all, Cormac stood firm, a true friend to these true friends who have been together since the early days. They are a happy family who really do holiday together.

On the inside flap of the new album is a close-up of Cormac's winning smile and there is something almost Christ-like about him, a radiance that makes me think of the boy child in the 'Selfish Giant' story. An absence of malice, a ruthless positivism, an evangelistic belief in possibility. He has become the adult of the boy he was and all the world adores him. When I think of Cormac it is of a system whose working parts are all in perfect order. A model human if you like. The blueprint that God must have had in mind and that I so badly wanted to be.

A sublimated ego is a rare commodity in his business but producers report that Cormac is a joy to work with, gracious and receptive to artistic input. 'Inspirational', the critics write of his lyrics and also of his live performances, the 'boy-next-door' who gives his all on stage. Fans comment on his sincerity. 'The thing about Cormac,' said a tearful brunette interviewed after one of his concerts (Seattle 1998), 'is that you look up at the stage and you just know that he really means it.'

While the band members' stories played out, Cormac spent six months alone in a studio in New Mexico, an experience that kick-started what promises to be – according to the previews – a sea change in his song-writing which is moving from anthemic to ballad. From the public to the personal. Out there in the desert in the subzero nights, he had an apocalypse and is ready to square up to his biggest challenge: *Unplugged*.

My hunch is that ever since Cormac saw Springsteen do his acoustic tour he thought, what bravery, what courage. And so he has opted for small venues only, just Cormac and his guitar, and everyone wants a piece of this intimacy, the tour is a sell-out before the tickets are even printed. Apparently it takes enormous courage to stand in front of 8,000 fans armed with only an instrument. The legend of reputation does not shield you from disaster. Although of course the simplicity of *Unplugged* is illusory – to put Cormac on the stage in a pair of jeans and guitar looking as if he has just rolled out of bed requires a road crew, sound technicians, sparks, lorry drivers, stylist, the whole entourage that has characterised his appearances to date.

'How does the band feel to be left behind?' asked a journalist at the press conference.

Cormac smiled. 'The boys are happy. They're solid guys. A hundred per cent. It's a chance for them to take a break.' Talk of a split is unfounded. 'We'll be back in the studio next year. The dates are already booked.'

The music world is in a frenzy of anticipation for his forthcoming show and I too am impatient for this creative *pièce de résistance*. I expect it to have the tag of a great story, perhaps dredged from his youth with all the frisson of real life behind it. For Cormac is approaching that age now where rock stars are expected to be reflective as the energy for new work is on the wane and the challenging business of being the megastar consumes so much time outside the studio. He has written some great songs, he says in interview. In his own view, his best work. Has tunnelled deep inside to explore places he has never been.

'Was he wrestling with any demons?'

He fingered his Perrier, waved a dismissive hand, tugged on the legendary curls. 'If I could talk about it I wouldn't have to write the songs.' This chastening remark was delivered with a disarming smile.

Unlike his band members, Cormac has managed not to have a long lens record his every move. Neither he nor his wife has ever dignified the media with a single comment about their private life. We do not know what Katarina makes of *Unplugged* or indeed of anything. There are occasional red-carpet smiles and in rare shots she appears mute in goggle-size sunglasses, shepherding their two little girls in and out of cavernous SUVs, the youngest one often clinging to her, nuzzling her hair. The eldest has Cormac's strawberry curls. She always wears a white smock dress and carries a fox glove-puppet on her hand. Katarina endures paparazzi attention with the forbearance of a pioneer woman. She refuses to engage, in the politest way possible. She is also effortlessly stylish in a no-frills manner. I imagine myself in her flip-flops. Cormac appears to have married the kind of woman I would have wished to be – I could have managed the self-effacement with flair but I'm not so sure about the mothering. I know Katarina's skin to be smooth and flawless, have myself traced its imaginary outline many times, followed Cormac's hand down the curve of her neck, the delicate crevice of her clavicle, the slight swell of her breast, my lips following his lead close round her nipple, my hand trailing his as it slides up her thigh. I lift my head with his and our mouths press down on her surrender. I am with them.

For Katarina is where I always was and where I would still be if it weren't for Estelle. Even now after all these years I can be suddenly overtaken by fury at the cost of her loss since it was her death that precipitated Cormac's departure. I would still have him if she had not been so stupid as to get herself killed. How I struggle with forgiveness, for it is so often a way of just letting people off the hook and the youthful dead have the unfair advantage of being finished with all the pettiness, the tragedy of their circumstances apparently absolving them of any blame. Sometimes I think Estelle took the easy way out, she was always in or close to trouble, everyone knew it and there was a sort of safety in that, her fatal trusting in the kindness of strangers.

People say that seeing the body facilitates closure but I think it simply sparks a new beginning. Death invites revision of history and deflates the urgent business of living. Estelle's corpse was unmarked and quite beautiful, a bluish tinge lent her an elegance that eluded her in life. Her skin had a waxy sheen to it as if it might come off on your hands – although I didn't touch, that wasn't protocol. I wasn't even supposed to be there, had lied my way past the funeral directors. But I did surreptitiously finger a strand of her hair and found it disconcertingly cold and dry, winter hair that would carry on growing in the coffin. Did they wash it, I wondered? I can see her reflection now in the dressing-table mirror of her mum's bedroom, her finger tracing the silver-backed brush set that was just for show. When we sneaked in after school I would warn, 'Don't brush hard, your mum will see the hairs, she'll know,' but Estelle carried on brushing, not listening, behind those pale blue eyes there was always a flat perspective between somewhere and nowhere.

Once I took inspiration from an agony aunt on a radio phone-in for people who cannot stop picking at old sores. 'Write a letter,' she urged a tearful caller whose daughter hadn't spoken to her for twenty years. 'Tell her what you feel. You cannot take this to the grave, it will destroy you. We must address the deceased, talk to the dead.' I set my dining table for three and lit a pair of ivory candles – Estelle always liked the drama of low light, sparkling glass. I could see exactly how she would sit on my left, tilting the flat blade of a knife to catch her own reflection, twisting her head from side to side to monitor the effect. To my right, Cormac would flit about, somehow never entirely seated. He would be up changing the music, reading a CD cover, telling a story, showering us with his overabundance, like static in a room. I sat like a nodding dog at my own table. What could I say?

'You are both gone.' I flipped my eyes open. 'One dead, one basking in the public gaze.' The candle flame flickered in the downdraft of my accusation. 'And look. Look what I am left with.' I could see Estelle's frown, a lock of white hair slipping forward over her shoulder. She put the knife down. It was always tone not content that reached her. 'And YOU,' I shouted as her hand pawed at the napkin, the beginnings of an anxiety that would quickly erupt.

Cormac squeezed my hand, his fingers curled around mine as if to take possession of the charge. I stared at this grip I had known since childhood when he used to tug me along through the grass on the way home from school. 'I used to wiggle your knuckles against each other and you'd scream,' he said. 'D'you remember, Caro? Do you remember?'

I wrenched my hand away and Estelle cried out, one palm flailing in front of her.

'Shush now, Caro,' he said, 'you are making too much of things.' He leaned forward with his chest abutting the table's edge and took both of our hands. 'Girls,' he said, 'my girls,' and for a moment we were back in his sun-striped bedroom, Cormac on his back playing guitar on the floor, Estelle kneeling in the corner carefully stacking draughts in monochrome piles, me lounging on the bed, head propped on an elbow, watching his fingers fly up and down the fretboard and thinking that life would always be a variation on this theme.

8

'OH, I LOVE THOSE,' says Michele, pointing at the glass pods sliding up and down the corners of the huge atrium filled with plants.

'Shame our meeting is on the ground floor then,' I say but she has stopped to watch a lift's ascent. With her chin tilted upwards and a child's gaze of longing, all pretence at sophistication is forgotten and I almost expect her to swing round and tug at my sleeve like Estelle once did at the fairground, begging me to go on the waltzer with her just one more time.

'Sorry,' she skips to catch up as I step into the lobby of a small retail bank. Reception is unmanned so I press the desk buzzer and wait while Michele crouches down in front of a large aquarium and taps at the glass.

I found her this morning standing by the photocopier watching Nicola's PA wrestle with a paper jam and she clapped her hands with delight when I told her she could come along to an interview. 'It's a small claim that Jim is handling, but he's still out sick. It was going to be rescheduled but seeing as it's only a few minutes away and you were so keen I thought I'd do it for him.'

· · · · ·

'So do people ever lie?' she'd asked, buttoning up her coat as a blast of wind hurried us across the open sweep of the concourse and down a side alley on to Bishopsgate.

'There was a survey done last year that showed six per cent of policyholders made false claims. Mostly personal technology items – laptops, iPods, that kind of thing. And mostly younger policyholders.'

'So how can you tell if someone's not telling the truth?' she turned towards me, hair blowing across her face.

'We are very thorough. And we make it difficult. Policyholders have to provide evidence – proof of ownership, receipts, police reports if there's been a theft.'

I have my own personal theory about story-telling techniques in interview and how a claimant's narrative style can hint at falsehood. For example, the confusion of pronouns – the 'I' and 'we' – and the specificity of adverbs – the 'definitely', 'absolutely' – or a stubborn insistence on temporal and geographical vagueness. Unlike some of my colleagues, I believe the emotional consequence of material loss is often underrated so I keep these theories to myself even though it could reduce the company's payout. But in any case, it is often difficult to establish intent. Fraud, to be fraudulent, is an amphibious and flabby word, the tight echo of the vowel conjures up tawdry circumstances involving mean-spirited corner-cutters. A cheap and cowardly deceit perpetrated by narrow-shouldered men who were bullied at school and jeered at by girls they longed to know. In fact the lie is often prompted by embarrassment – the claimant is desperate to mask negligence or foolishness and a fraudulent claim might seem justified as a reward for the years of premiums paid. Like tax evasion, it is rationalised as a victimless crime. But my job is not to wonder why, rather to establish the facts, assess the damage and pass the file to Claims who will issue the cheque.

. . . . .

Anna Murray emerges from a door behind us and mumbles a greeting. Her black hair hangs limp on her shoulders and there is a sleepless look about her face, a bruised shadowing about the eyes and a chubby nervousness in her fingers. After a moment's hesitation where she scans the corridor left and right as if checking for traffic, she leads the way wordlessly down a corridor and into a cramped room with partition walls so thin that I can hear each passing footfall. I sit down opposite her at the outsize table and watch her unfold a crumpled copy of the claim form and smooth it down beside her mobile and a pen. There is a faint trace of a number biroed across the back of her right hand. In accordance with her observer role, Michele sits as instructed a few feet away from the claimant and not at the table but in a chair pushed back against the wall. While I run through the assessing process Anna Murray nods miserably at the table without looking up. She confirms that the incident occurred while she was on a week's holiday but her unnecessary embellishments speak of some discomfort. Her boyfriend is English, they haven't been together very long, it was his first time in Dublin and he didn't really enjoy it. 'Spent most of his time taking the mick out of everybody's accent.'

'Tell me about the video camera.'

She straightens up in the chair and swallows hard. 'A Panasonic. HDC SD7.'

'And you bought it when?'

'Uhm. About a year ago.'

'You didn't include any proof of purchase with your claim.'

'I haven't been able to find the receipt.'

'Credit card statement?'

'It was cash.'

'Where did you buy it?'

'One of those places on Tottenham Court Road. I can't remember the name exactly.'

'"I believe the camera was on the seat beside me,"' I read aloud, '"but when I turned my head I saw it was gone."'

'The pub was really crowded, you know, there were coats everywhere. It must have been nicked. Or something.'

'So you reported it to the police in Dublin?'

She shook her head, chewing on the inside of her cheek.

'We, um, didn't have time, you know? I mean we would've had to wait for ages in the station and we were in a bit of a rush, we had to get the bus for the ferry.'

'Had you taken a lot of footage?'

'Um no, well, a bit, I suppose.' She fiddles with the plastic lid of her pen.

'Hard to get the hang of, aren't they? I always find they wobble when you're trying to zoom in.'

'My boyfriend was better.'

'More of his thing then?'

She looks to the side, blinking rapidly.

'I'm so sorry, Miss Murray. Sometimes people find losing objects more upsetting than they expect.'

She looks up at the ceiling, a tear trickling down her cheek.

'Is it the footage that you lost – something very special?'

'No. No, it's not that.'

'I've obviously come at a bad time for you.'

'My boyfriend kept going on about how stupid I am. Like the bloody camera was the most important thing ever.' I pass her a pack of tissues and she pulls one out, blows her nose. 'He went mad, started shouting out on the street. And then it was a terrible crossing to Holyhead and I was sliding all over the place. I went up on deck, I was sick as a dog up there in the pouring rain while he got plastered in the bar.'

'So you got the blame for losing your own camera.'

'Oh, he called me every name under the sun. I'd never seen him like that before. Himself and another fella had biked across the Pyrenees in the summer and he had hours of footage on there. They were going to make a documentary or something. I thought he'd kill me and all I could do was puke my guts up.'

The crushed tissue sits in a wet ball on the table.

'So he borrowed your video camera for his biking trip?'

She shook her head, staring at the tabletop.

'He took it without your permission?'

'No,' she says, her voice watery. 'No. I mean yes, yes, he borrowed it.'

'He borrowed it.'

'We're not even going out any more,' she mumbles. I let the silence settle. A snatch of conversation floats past the door.

'A Panasonic HDC SD7, right?' She nods, biting her trembling lip.

'And you say you have no receipt?' She shakes her head.

'I do need you to tell me where you bought it.'

'God, I can't do this,' she throws her head up to the ceiling. 'I – I never wanted to do this. But he just kept going on and on about it. He's such a bastard.'

Michele is straining forward in the seat, I can tell she is holding her startled breath, looking from me to the girl whose head is bent now, tears dripping on her clasped hands. 'I'm so stupid,' she mumbles as I stare at her side parting, at the bone-white scalp of a child.

'Michele, why don't you pop outside and get Miss Murray a glass of water? Just ask at Reception.' She hesitates and then springs into action, manoeuvring herself carefully around the table, and closes the door gently behind her.

Anna Murray takes a deep breath, closing her eyes, gritting her teeth. 'The camera's not mine. It was never mine. It was his. He lost it one night out with the lads. I wasn't even there.'

'And I take it he doesn't have insurance to cover the loss.'

'Doesn't believe in it.'

'It's a serious business, a fraudulent claim.' I point to the form in front of me. 'See here the declaration that you signed? … "the information I have given is true and accurate".'

'Can't I just cancel it? Please? Tear up the form. Oh Jesus, I can't believe I did this. He filled it out, made me sign it. My flatmate said I was mad to do it. Isn't there anything I can do?'

'Your claim is on record. You exist as a live case.'

'I'm so stupid,' she shakes her head slowly from side to side.

The room fills with the sounds of her distress, her gulps and swallows, the splash of a teardrop on the claim form. I look down at my own original, at her signature on the dotted line – blue and small and perfectly legible, the careful hand-writing of a diligent schoolgirl. I picture the boyfriend standing over her tight-lipped and insistent and I too am suddenly tired of all these sad stories, the smallness of it all, trapped in this airless room with this wretched little screenplay and the wrong one getting away. An image of the boyfriend in a smug leather jacket draining a triumphant pint as he celebrates his little scam.

'Miss Murray,' I lean forwards, folding my arms on the table. 'Anna,' I say loudly. She sniffs and raises her head. 'Sometimes claims are made for an item that is subsequently found. Sometimes an item has not been lost, but simply mislaid.'

She blinks, frowning and opens her mouth, but I raise a silencing hand.

'I once arrived for an interview where the claimant told me that she had found the reported item that very morning.

On her way to work.'

She nods repeatedly, dabbing at her nose. 'A watch that had gone missing months before turned up at the bottom of her briefcase. She guessed that she must have taken it off at the gym and forgotten all about it.'

'I see.'

'In *that* case the policyholder immediately called the Claims department and withdrew the claim.' I gather my papers together. 'Of course, I had a wasted visit, but there was no loss to adjust. And the policyholder learned to be more careful in her routines.'

'Thank you,' she whispers, picking up her mobile and smoothing the claim form.

The door opens as she is dialling the number and Michele appears with a plastic cup of water and places it on the table in front of her. 'Thank you,' mouths Anna over the receiver and Michele beams, happy to be able to contribute at last. She settles down again in the chair ready for the next instalment.

'Is that the Claims department?' says Anna, tucking her hair behind her ear. 'I need to cancel a claim I made.'

'We're leaving, now,' I say to Michele who is staring at Anna with her mouth open.

'*Now*,' I say sharply and she quickly picks up her coat from the chair and steps out into the corridor.

'Yes, I need to cancel a claim because the missing item has been found.'

'Thank you for your time, Miss Murray,' I say with my hand on the door handle and she blinks her first smile at me.

Michele waits expectantly in Reception while I fiddle with my BlackBerry, feigning distraction with some urgent message.

She is gagging for a debrief, can barely contain her curiosity and I am stunned, winded by the full impact of my transgression.

'So what happened?' she says as I set a fast pace through the atrium.

'She's calling the Claims department to say the camera has been found.'

'But how? What happened? Who found it? Did the boyfriend call her? Did it just turn up? Oh, I'm so happy for her. Poor Anna, she was so upset. Imagine that timing though, right in the middle of the meeting!'

'These things happen.' A taxi horn blares and I grab her elbow, steer her with a jump over an oily puddle on to the pavement.

'So it's all sorted?' she says.

'All sorted.'

'My God, what a complete so-and-so, though, her boyfriend. What a loser.'

'*Ex*-boyfriend.'

'At least she dumped him. You know, when I was sitting there listening she reminded me of a friend of mine – Katie – she had a bloke just like him last year, a real bully, we all thought so but of course she wouldn't listen until –' and Michele spins her teenage story for me as we hurry through the lunchtime crowds and I try to figure out what it is that I have just discovered about myself. And why after all the years of listening to these tales of loss I would choose this moment to seize directorship of the plot and write a different ending. Some instinct to spare from pain, some latent contempt for procedure? It is the smallest tweak of the rules, a technical breach, but a breach nonetheless, for it is my duty simply to inform the Claims department and let them handle Anna Murray from there.

We round the corner on to Liverpool Street and a light

drizzle glitters on the sleeves of my coat. Michele has switched tracks now and I nod along to her story about some scandalous advice given by a careers advisor at school. I hitch my brolly over our heads, hold it high and conduct an internal risk assessment of the situation, calculate the cost. It is a zero sum game: no claim means no payout and a favourable outcome for the company. And Anna Murray's claim will be cancelled by the time I get back to the office. A cross-referencing email from me on file, the records updated, the case closed.

9

'I BROUGHT YOU THIS.' Tom wiggles the flimsy stem trapped in his glove. 'I thought you wouldn't be wearing one.' In this wintry light the paper petals have the brownish hue of dried blood. 'You haven't got a clue, have you? Remembrance Sunday?' he gestures behind me over the wall to where a warden is directing traffic on to the grassy verges. Another man in an outsize anorak waves impatiently at a stalled car. People are streaming along the path to the entrance of the church, a volume that far exceeds the usual congregation.

'For God's sake, take it,' he says, thrusting the poppy into my hand. 'Put it in your buttonhole.'

'This is a ski jacket. It only has zips.'

He sighs, shakes his head.

'But you look very smart,' I say, taking in the shirt and tie underneath his raincoat, brown shoes polished to gleaming.

'I can't believe you sat here and didn't notice all that fuss behind you?'

'I was thinking.'

'Your generation spend too much time contemplating their navels.'

'You mean we don't care.'

'Yes. I suppose that is what I believe.'

I have grown used to these caustic observations in the last

few weeks since Tom decided to foist his company on me. He has an insatiable appetite for stories about my job – 'You are the one out there in the world. I was pensioned off, remember' – and I have a huge inventory to keep him amused. I have entertained him with the engagement ring lost in a tiramisu at the Cipriani, the serial loss of pedigree Labradors, the million-pound canvas accidentally slashed. He listens with great attention to my tales of loss and pesters me with questions about the legal issues, the calculation of reserve, the regulatory environment, the adjudications. Last week he argued the case on behalf of a couple whose newly planted rose garden had been ravaged by deer.

'Look, here they come,' says Tom. Two young Beavers in full uniform lead the procession slowly out through the church doors. Between them they carry a large red wreath down the slope to the cenotaph that records the names of the thirty-seven men from this parish who 'fell in the Great War for freedom, truth and righteousness'. There is a nod to the Second one inscribed at the base, for the memorial was erected in 1920 when no one dreamed it would be necessary to leave space for another catastrophe. The congregation fans out behind the boys, stepping carefully around the graves, but a bottleneck jams the exodus from the church. The two Beavers lay the wreath on the white marble and stand upright. One fiddles with his toggle, uncertain of the script now that the primary task has been executed. The Beaver leader signals impatiently and they scurry off to take their positions in the pack.

Four veterans move to the front, one of them scanning the sky above as if expecting an aerial signal. Another is wheelchaired in full military dress and clutches a wreath that is slipping down on his lap. He catches it just in time and leans forwards but the grass verge prevents him from reaching the spot he wants and one of his comrades bends to assist. The bell announces the minute's silence and Tom is on his feet beside me. Jack stands a little way away watching the crowd, on the ready for any sudden canine appearance. I get to my feet although I am not sure that we remember any better standing up and I have already spent many hours of silence held hostage by the dead, although not these war dead. Tom is right about introspection. I think back to the black-and-white of history lessons, the droning voice of a teacher, the endless repetition of human error. How little that stuck.

A wind ruffles the Beaver banner. A baby cries. The minute strains, stretches out like elastic suspending all of us in this state of heightened consciousness and I feel a sudden emphasis on the physical, a prickling in my nose, an urgent need to sneeze or cough. I imagine the ghosts of the dead jostling for position on the churchyard wall as they monitor this choreographed homage. They chatter and point and crane their heads, they can do this without disrespect, for death has long since lost its mystery, it is the drama of the living that enthrals. And they are out in force today, even the younger ones are perched on the elders' shoulders, their gossamer wings glistening like pixie dust. These child spectres are rarely visible except on special occasions, I think the elders are protective of them and keep them out of sight.

A couple of the little ones run about and play, they are at their most mischievous, excited by the spectacle and they sidle up to the crowd, press their vaporous faces close to the living flesh to see if they can make them laugh. Estelle leans forward and I know that she is staring at the medals on the veterans' chests. And being the most daring, she fly-hops down from the wall and approaches the wheelchair veteran, stretches out a finger bone to tap the shiny medal. Flicks his poppy. Leans into his beret and blows in his old man's ear.

A visible shudder runs through his body that is registered by the living around him who put it down to the flashback horror of the battlefield. The veteran steels his jaw, he too believes it is the power of remembrance that accounts for the icy whistle in his ear. Estelle slips to the side and presses a chilled palm over the hand of a standing veteran. He stiffens and she pulls back smirking and turns to her ghostly audience on the wall, checking for effect. An elder beckons her back, he is indulgent until she oversteps the mark. They see the humour in solemnity and there are veterans amongst them inured now to the ceremony. Death has improved their humour and taught them to lighten up.

Estelle skips coquettishly, threads a roundabout route through the crowd by the gate. A prancing colt, a Tinkerbelle wreaking havoc. She peers underneath a woman's hat to examine an earring and then hops back on the wall, squeezing in amongst the others. But the elders are hovering overhead now and beckoning to the hordes who drift over the still living towards their resting places, guiding the little ones to the right gravestone, chivvying along a boy ghost who tries to sneak under a grand vault. Estelle floats above the Garden of Remembrance, turns her head to check that I am watching just like she always did in the flesh world. I have learnt to meet that stare and not to look away, not to flinch from the skeletal permagrin of the dead and her party trick – a slow 360-degree revolution of the head. Folding her wings, she slides her ethereal form beneath her little stone square.

The bell tolls, the crowd is released and falls into a loose semblance of a parade led by the wheelchair. But it is an unsatisfactory ending that needs music to lend it some dignity. People break away already in the car park – a younger man drifts off to the side and takes a Marlboro pack out of his pocket, another man turns on his car radio through the open window. Others linger to plant their own remembrances in the soil at the base of the cenotaph, little wooden crosses with a poppy at the centre, many of them with personalised inscriptions – Malaya 1941–1943, Northern Ireland 1984, Kosovo 1990. Most of these new additions will not survive the winter but collapse under the beating rain or be picked up by passing puppies.

'So what age were you in the War?'

'The worst age,' Tom sits down. 'Born 1933. Too young to be of any use but old enough to remember too much.'

'Your father fought?'

'He was also the wrong age. Wounded in the First and then too old for the Second so he volunteered in the Home Guard. He used to do lookout duty in the spire here.'

'You don't join in the parade?'

'This is not usually where I come. There is a better place in the Forest.'

'A better place for what?'

He stands up again, suddenly enlivened. 'I'll show you. Come for a drive.'

I hesitate and he grins, amused at the shock effect of his suggestion. 'For God's sake, girl, I'm not asking you out on a date. What's to think about?'

'How far is it?'

'A ten-minute drive.'

Tom takes the S bends at fifty, ignoring the hazard signs as the road carves through a heathland of subdued colour into the treeless forest. Scrubby bushes and young oak line the roadside and the grass is shorn by roving herds. He stops for idling sheep at Duddleswell when a thick-set ram pauses in front of the Jeep and stares into the distance as if considering its options. Tom leans out the window shouting 'Hoosh Hoosh', slapping his hand on the door. We pass a field where years before Estelle stopped a bike ride to taunt a dejected Charolais. The bull stood with its head aloft in the centre of the field, grounded by a bulk so massive that his hooves had sunk in the soft ground. Estelle waved her arms and shouted, 'Come on you big bully-bull, come and get us.' We climbed over the padlocked gate, advanced a few steps on the wrong side, hearts thumping, willing him to come thundering towards us, but he affected disinterest, his tail fly-twitching as he lowered his ringed nose to snuffle at the grass. 'They kill you by trampling,' said Cormac. 'So you'd be dead when he started to gore you.' The bull raised his head and we scrambled screaming back over the gate and Estelle kept up the screeching for all she was worth, a high-pitched glorying as we sped downhill.

Tom hangs a sharp left into a parking space called The Hollies. The clouds part on the far horizon to reveal a weak hint of sunlight as I step out of the car on to ground that is pocked and pooled with last night's rain. Out on the eastern bridle path a horsewoman proceeds at a leisurely pace. A spaniel dashes about in huge sweeps near a battered Volvo where a woman in a woollen hat with a red tassel laces up her walking boots, the kind that I should have now instead of these lightweight trainers. Tom takes his wellies out of the car and exchanges his raincoat for the Barbour.

I have not walked the Forest for years but I remember a path not far from here and a summer long ago when the ground was burnt dry and we had cycled for ages in the heat with just one bottle of water between the three of us. Cormac singing up ahead, Estelle in the middle so I could shout at her when she swerved out into the road.

'Excuse me, where exactly is the Forest?' asked an Australian couple.

'This *is* the Forest,' Estelle giggled.

'But there are no trees?'

Estelle pointed behind us and they turned round to a cluster of straggly conifers. 'Right,' said the girl smiling uncertainly as if she suspected some tourist prank. Estelle could not contain herself, her howls of laughter burned my cheeks and I gave her a shove but she was doubled over now.

'They used to call any open land a forest if it was used for hunting,' I explained. 'But there are really good views if you continue along this way.' I was anxious to save them from Estelle's mocking, anxious to make it OK and it comes to me now that this impulse to *make it OK* for everyone is in fact some urge to insulate them from injury in the great rush of life. To protect them from being crushed by the wonder and variety of experience, as if it might be preferable to reach death without having lived at all. As if that is what I want for myself: a regular and predictable beat.

We walk in silence, Jack trotting ahead in the middle of the path, stopping every now and again to sniff at cow shit. Tom marks time with his stick, he is a fast walker with a long stride that keeps him a foot or so ahead of me. I can imagine him leading Scout patrols across mud trenches in torrential rain, although I notice he sticks to the narrow tracks that deer and cattle and dogs have worn into the scrubby fringes of the heather. He bends his head to scan the uneven surface, on the lookout for a pothole that could unseat him, a fall that would leave him with a smashed hip or a broken ankle, some injury that would never entirely heal.

At the crest of the slope the land falls away in dappled sunlight to reveal a picture-book winter scene, the hills dipping and rising, the odd splodge of grazing sheep, a distant horse picking its way up a steep slope, clusters of birch and pine hiding the stream that cuts through the valley floor below. The track is growing soggy underfoot and clumps of bog cotton bob on spindly stalks, their white tufts like Tom's old man's hair, dry and matt to the touch.

'My trainers.' I look down at the churned and sodden slope that lies ahead.

'Yes, they might not survive this outing,' he says and moves ahead prodding the ground with his stick while I take a fussy circuitous route, stepping as much as I can on the clumps of heather, but the slick grey mud seeps ever higher and dampness finds its way into the sock on my right foot. Tom's swinging stick annoys me, and his perfect outdoor clothing, and I wonder why on earth I have agreed to come. He has me billed as a follower, it is his imperious manner and my outmoded idea of deference due to the aged that made me capitulate to his whim.

'Now, this is a better place to remember, don't you think?' he stops by a low circular stone wall with a small wooden gate. Someone has been here ahead of us for there are a couple of fresh wreaths lying on the flagstones. Tom takes a poppy from his pocket and places it at the foot of a brass plaque erected by the mother of Sgt E.M. Sutton, who, along with the six other soldiers of Bomber Squadron 142, was shot down by enemy fire on this spot on 31 July 1941.

'"To live in the hearts of those who are left behind is not to die",' I read aloud from the plaque. This is of course the problem. The dead won't release their grip. I try to visualise that summer night, a huge fireball erupting in this quiet spot, the wreckage of the plane in all this beauty.

'So what do you think of when you come here?' I turn to Tom who is looking over to the east where a thicket of furze comes to an abrupt end at the top of the hill.

'The terror,' he says, staring straight ahead. 'The plane reaming down ablaze in the dead of night. The certain end.

Perhaps one or two already dead, bleeding from the mouth. The others struggling with parachutes. I think of the flames rocketing in the darkness. The German pilot looking down at the kill. The smouldering wreckage in the morning. The surviving debris. The grim knock on the door. The mother on the threshold. So many had nothing to bury.'

His skin is very pale, showing no sign of the walk's exertion. 'And what do you think of when you look?' he turns towards me.

'The waste.'

'What is most of life but one sort of waste versus another?'

'That's a pretty bleak view.'

He pulls back from the wall and swings around to face the valley. 'I used to take Charlie here on Remembrance Sunday.'

'He must have enjoyed that.'

'Actually, it bored him rigid.'

'I thought a boy would like all this war stuff, all the stories?'

'I wasn't much of a storyteller back then. And Charlie sulked because he wanted to go to the parade with the Scouts instead. But I wouldn't let him.'

'Why not?'

He shrugs. 'You are not a parent.'

'No.'

'It was not my finest hour. I was unnecessarily capricious. These days you'd say my own father was not such a great role model but by and large I left it to Beth to run Charlie. I kept my distance like men often do. Hard to find a way in when mothers are so damn competent.'

He pokes the ground at his feet as if testing the soil. Jack comes over and starts to scrabble in the soft earth. 'I intervened to lay down the law. I policed. And tried and failed to be a different kind of father to my own.'

This is not the remembrance conversation I had antici-pated, out here with a wet foot and an old man grubbing over regrets. I turn my face up to the sky and feel my cheeks warmed in the sun that has parted a large blue gap in the clouds.

'Beth was a great mum. You've never seen a boy so loved. She spent hours playing in the sand pits, taught Charlie the names of all the birds and the trees, made up stories and wrote them down for him, she even taught him to read before he started school. They were always laughing and giggling, had a ball together, they were the best of friends. In fact I used to think he'd grow up to be a bit of a mummy's boy.'

'And did he?'

'Not a bit of it. Captained the local rugby team, had his teeth knocked out in a game once. Not a bother on him.'

'You must have enjoyed the sports?'

'I never saw him play.'

'Why not?'

'I never went. If you were to ask me back then, I would have said it was because I was waiting to be invited.' He leans forward on the wall and studies his open palms as if they might reveal some new information.

'And Charlie never asked?'

'Beth went along, that was enough for him.'

'You think?'

'Oh, he had a happy time. All down to her really, she encouraged him all the way. They say that's what kids need, plenty of boosting.'

'You don't agree.'

'Oh, these day fathers are all in vogue. I see them at the weekends pushing prams, carrying little ones on their backs. Maybe it's a fad, I don't know. Maybe they'll lose interest.'

'Isn't it a good thing for the kids? Especially for little boys?'

'I was busy with the grind of working. Didn't really see how I was needed for Charlie. He was brought up pretty much the way I was – close to my own mother, afraid of my father.' He straightens up, adjusts his muffler. 'But it was war time, they had their difficulties. And there were complications and my mother changed. Things were never the same again.'

I let my finger untwist itself from the strand of hair that I have wound, a habit from long ago, a thing that straight-haired girls do.

'Now that's exactly what Beth used to do,' Tom snaps. 'Always fiddling with her hair. And then she had it cut off when Charlie was still a little boy. "Not practical," she said one evening, standing in front of the mirror by the kitchen sink twirling a strand looking over her shoulder at me. "Maybe I should have it all cut off." "It'll stop all that fiddling," I said but it occurs to me now that she might have wanted me to dissuade her. When she came home from the hairdresser's the next day, she looked like she was wearing a swimming cap. Even I could tell it was a hatchet job. Charlie cried his eyes out, he was three or four maybe so she wound a coloured scarf round her head to distract him. "I'm a pirate," she said and he was all smiles again. In fact she looked like the cancer victim she ended up becoming years later. Only then she learnt to do one of those turban-style arrangements. Someone told her it looked elegant and mysterious but I thought it made her look exactly like the terminal patient she was.'

Tom's head bobs up and down as if he has lost control of the musculature. At these close quarters the veinous texture of his right cheek is pronounced or perhaps it is this mean wintry light. Old skin does not bear close scrutiny. He is gaunt and I wonder if he has lost a little weight again, the Barbour hangs loose on his shoulders.

'Have you ever seen someone die?' he whips around with a fierce glare, the scarf tight as a noose round his neck.

'Yes. My father.'

'So you know they are often asleep.'

'He had a heart attack at the kitchen table when I was twelve.'

He swings away, somehow infuriated by my response. 'Charlie came for the end. I called him to say time was running out. He brought Laura with him, Beth loved that girl, said she was just the sweetest thing. And do you know, they stayed at the hotel up by the church even though the house is just down the road. Charlie brought Laura round to see it while I was out – oh, he made no secret of how much he disliked being around me. Though he's always polite, Charlie. Impeccable manners, never says anything.'

I reach out and touch his sleeve. 'It is getting cold. We should be going.'

'I don't expect he'll visit ever again,' he adds peevishly. 'Beth used to go out to Melbourne twice a year and stay for three weeks each time. Badgered me to go but I knew neither of them really wanted that.'

'Why are you telling me all this?'

'Because it needs to be said.'

'But not to me. Surely you should be talking to your son?'

'He is ten thousand miles away. We do not speak.'

'Maybe you should start.'

'And you are the kind of person people talk to.'

'Or offload on. Depending how you look at it.' Shedding some burden that does not concern me, or perhaps to hear how it sounds when shabby little truths hits the airspace.

'You invite others to invade, Caroline. It is your way of remaining private. You don't give anything away. That is not always a good habit, you know.'

The cloud shadows roll over the valley and up the slope. The dog is fed up with all this hanging about and starts heading up the hill.

'Let's go back, Tom.' I start to follow Jack and the old man follows me.

10

'YOU SURE YOU WANT TO park your dirty great Jeep there?' I ask as Tom pulls up right in front of the vicar's *Reserved* sign that is propped up by the churchyard wall. The place is deserted, the Remembrance crowds disappeared, but the church door is ajar and I can see a volunteer on a step-ladder securing a flower arrangement in the stone architrave. Hannah trundles round the corner with a wheelie bin, waves at Tom and does a double take at the sight of me in the passenger seat. She smiles coyly and waves again, trundles off behind the church.

'The grapevine will be buzzing tonight,' says Tom. 'Wondering if we are related.' He cuts the engine. 'Or is it something more?'

'What d'you mean?'

'A romantic entanglement.'

'What?'

'Aha,' he laughs and belts the steering wheel. 'That got you going.'

'You're crazy.'

'These things happen, Caroline. Men shacking up with women young enough to be their daughters,' he leans back against the driver's door, delighted at my evident discomfort. 'But don't worry, my dear. I have nothing but the purest of thoughts.'

Jack is warm on my lap and shows no signs of budging. I ease him onto the seat and open the door but he stands staring, refusing to jump, so I lift him down and place him on the ground.

'Come with me to do my flower duty,' says Tom.

'I have to go.'

'It won't take a minute.' He pulls a woolly hat from his pocket, black with a grey stripe that shrinks his face to a long oval and whitens his papery skin, giving him a ghoulish appearance.

'Nice beanie,' I say but he seems not to hear.

A chubby little Cairn terrier on a red lead slinks out through the gate and growls faintly as we pass. Jack spins round. 'Come on, Twister,' the owner tugs on the lead, but the Cairn bares his teeth. 'Twister, leave it, come on,' snaps the woman pulling hard, but this proves the last straw for Jack and he lunges at Twister's neck with open jaws.

'Jack, NO,' I grab his collar but the woman is pulling backwards, screaming, 'Get your dog off.' Tom shouts, 'DROP THE LEAD' and she lets it fall into the chaos of fur and teeth on the ground. Tom bends down to intervene but Jack jerks his head around with a vicious snap, they are no longer dogs, they are snarling killer primitives and this looks like a fight to the death. Jack has Twister pinned on his back between his legs, his snout buried in the terrier's throat and Twister's little legs are wriggling frantically in the air. Tom opens the back of the Jeep and takes out a shotgun. The woman shrieks, hands clasping at her neck, 'NOOOO' but Tom steps forward, swings the barrel round and takes aim. A dog yelps and then both fall silent in the shattered air. Hannah comes running around the side of the church, stops abruptly halfway down the path, one hand covering her mouth. Tom hands me the shotgun and then scoops up Jack, flings him into the front seat of the Jeep and slams the door. Jack hurls himself growling against the windscreen.

The woman stares at the gun in my hand. Twister cringes at her feet, his paws scrabbling at her wellies. His neck fur is tufted with saliva and there is a skinned pink patch on his nose. She crouches down and picks him up. In her arms Twister is another dog entirely, a whimpering nuzzler with a bleeding ear.

'Well,' says Tom, 'that did the trick.' He holds out his hand and I pass him the gun. The woman sucks her lips inwards, she is not at all happy about this and I cannot blame her since Jack's attack was entirely unprovoked, but she is staring at the gun and weighing up the cost of protest.

'Isn't that illegal or something?' I say as he closes the boot.

'It's licensed.'

'So what, you just drive around with a gun in your Jeep and fire it off whenever you want?'

'More or less.'

'That doesn't sound like such a great idea.'

'Don't worry, my dear, you're quite safe,' he says and offers us both a mad grin. The woman steps back.

'Goodbye Madam,' he says. 'I apologise for Jack. He's been under a cloud lately.'

But she is already hurrying away back to her car with Twister squeaking in her arms. She sits behind the wheel with the trembling terrier on her lap, staring malevolently out the window as she pulls away and drives off without looking back.

'Everything all right there, Tom?' Hannah calls out behind us. Tom salutes and she smiles uncertainly, backs away up the slope, disappearing into the church.

Tom leans back against the Jeep, his mouth slightly agape.

'You look terrible,' I say. 'Are you OK?'

He nods, pats his sunken cheek, an odd stab at private encouragement. 'Come on,' he opens the car door and releases Jack who trots off into the churchyard.

'I was just leaving.'

'You are always just leaving, Caroline. Surely you can spare me a moment.' He offers me his crooked arm, I take his elbow and he leads the way. But it is Tom who leans, just a little every now and then as we walk over to his regular spot where he settles on the bench and I stand looking over the wall down into the valley of the estate. The lake water is black from here; there is a huddle of deer on the far horizon. Winter has flattened the bracken and the long grass lies dead and drenched. When I turn to face back into the graveyard, the bench where I normally sit looks child-size. It is definitely a bleaker view from this elevation, a different perspective entirely with the long flank of the church sternly in view. High up just below the spire the two small round windows with wooden slats have the look of an elephant's beady eyes.

A car pulls up to park beside Tom's Jeep and a slender woman in a long belted gabardine stands in the open door fiddling with a flourish of black feathers that protrude from the side of her head like the feathered aftermath of a shoot. Her partner stands off to the side, hands in pockets, looking up at the steeple. She says something to him and he walks over, holds her at arm's length inspecting the hat. He shakes his head, her hand flies up, rips it from her head and throws it into the passenger seat. She ruffles her hair, a short red crop, her head looking lost above the collar like a new girl in her school coat. And there is traffic approaching, a convoy of sports cars in various stages of parking. A woman with a fur-trimmed wrap steps out of a Mercedes and opens the back door, lifts out a baby wrapped in a soft fleece blanket. A man comes round from the driver's side and leans down and kisses the bundle. The vicar emerges in full regalia from the entrance and the woman makes her way daintily towards him along the tarmac road.

'Isn't there some chap knocking about?' says Tom. 'Some boyfriend or whatever? You don't want to end up like me, sitting here on a bench with only a stranger to talk to.'

'Will I too develop eccentric hobbies?'

'You already have. Spending your weekends with the dead. Befriending old men.'

'Why don't you patch things up with Charlie?'

'Why don't you get yourself a boyfriend?'

'You could at least write him a letter.'

'Don't you want to have a family?' says Tom. 'You haven't got all the time in the world, you know.'

I think of Cormac's strawberry blond children digging on a beach. Of Estelle and me shivering at sundown in wet swimsuits, standing at the water's edge with our ankles sinking into the dark cold sand.

'You might make a good mother,' he chuckles as if the prospect amuses him.

'You might make a good father. It's not too late.'

'You are full of good advice for the elderly.'

'And you are full of advice for me.'

'I am not looking for a surrogate child.'

'Nor I for a surrogate parent.'

'I don't believe you.'

'This is… schmaltz. Like a bad movie.'

'In the bad movie the old man dies happily after a reconciliation with his son,' he says.

'And in the other ending?'

'He dies alone, while the son broods over a beer on the other side of the world.'

Tom rustles the flowers by his side. 'Today is Beth's anniversary. You see? I have a bigger than usual bunch of yellow carnations,' he lifts up the bouquet tied with a gold ribbon and points to the little card tucked inside the wrapper. 'Do you know I sat at the kitchen table for an hour and couldn't for the life of me think what to say.'

'So what did you write?'

'My name,' he slaps the flowers down on the bench.

'Beth won't mind.'

'It's the thought that counts,' he says in a high-pitched voice. 'Must you always try to smooth troubled waters?'

'Why don't you take me to see her grave? I don't even know where it is.'

He shifts forward on the bench and stretches out his arm. 'Give me a hand there.' I take his elbow in both hands and hoist but he is surprisingly light. I follow him back along the path towards the older section of the graveyard.

'My parents are buried here too,' he holds out the bouquet. 'You put it down for me,' and I kneel down, place it on the white gravel and read the dark grey headstone.

Ellen Warren	**Harold T. Warren**
Beloved mother and wife	Died 3 March 1975
Died 22 January 1974	

Beth Warren
Beloved mother and wife
Died November 9 2006

'Beth was sixty-four, such a saveable age, you would think. They operated, but I knew all along what the result would be and so did she. She was fading away even before they told her. Bloody hospitals and waiting and shuffling around in dressing gowns. The curtains on the window by her bed had come loose from the hooks and just hung there flapping, didn't close properly. I saw her frowning at them, Beth was very particular about that kind of thing so I got up on a chair to try and fix them but the holes were torn as if they had been pulled at. Said it to the nurses, they looked at me as if I was mad. Your wife is riddled with cancer and all you do is whinge about curtains. But I knew they would bother her. I could see her watching them and I knew she wouldn't sleep. Told her not to worry and she'd nod. I suppose she had learnt by then that there was no point in complaining to a man who never listened. So I came in the next day with some safety pins and was able to bodge it. They were crooked but at least they weren't flapping. She laughed. We both did. It took her dying to make us have a laugh together after all those years.'

'That was kind.'

'It would have been kinder not to have married her. To have let her find someone who would care better.'

I look away. Grief as regret, the prize only revealed in the loss. Paying her all this consideration now that she is six feet under.

'I didn't love her. Oh, who can tell after forty years what it becomes. Habit, I suppose. Beth was a good woman and I was not such a good man. She didn't interest me, she was very small somehow. And it was always her and Charlie from the time he was born. Then a whole series of miscarriages. She longed for another one and I longed for it to stop. The midnight bleeding and cramps. Tea in bed with her staring into space. More waiting rooms, consultants. She lost one at six months.'

'I'm sorry.'

'So we stopped. *I* stopped letting her try. It was too much. "You have Charlie," that's what I said to her. You have Charlie. Make the most of it.'

The wind picks up and hustles a few leaves along the ground. Tom's sad story crowds in amongst all the others in this place. Jack sits in front of us by the graveside, he has his own doggy version of this story. He too was Beth's, all the hearts belonged to her and not this cussed old man.

The small christening crowd emerges from the church and hurries back to their cars. The vicar follows behind, stooping slightly to lend his ear to an old lady who hobbles along beside him leaning heavily on her cane.

'I didn't honour any of Beth's dying wishes,' says Tom. 'Except for him,' he points his thumb at Jack who is watching the vicar's passage down the slope with unusual interest. He stands alert, ears twitching and I am suddenly worried that he might hurl himself at the old lady's stick and topple the pair to the ground.

'Jack,' I whisper and he turns his head sharply and hurries over, waiting for the punch line.

'Yes. Him I kept.' Jack glances up at Tom and then back at me as if to express his impatience with whatever kind of foolishness we are engaged in. He scurries over all business to the vicar and the old lady and parks himself directly in front of them. The old lady leans over supported by the vicar who casts a wary glance around and waves with his free hand. Tom salutes him.

'You know him?'

'He buried Beth.'

The vicar nods and smiles in return while the old lady talks to Jack in that sing-song voice that people use for pets and little children and he sits before her like a model dog, lapping it up. The vicar straightens her up. Jack steps to one side. The old lady adjusts her hat which has slipped forward a little in the proceedings and they resume their walk down to the gates with Jack keeping time. He stands to attention as the vicar helps her into the car where she sinks down in the passenger seat, her hat just visible above the dashboard. Jack watches to make sure the vicar executes the job to his satisfaction, the car follows the others towards the hotel and Jack shakes himself and trots back over to us.

'What was all that about?' I say but the dog ignores me as if any explanation would be beyond my comprehension. He is not suffering fools today.

I should make my excuses and leave but the prospect of the drive back requires a concentration I cannot muster at the moment. I close my eyes and tip my head back but it doesn't work. I can see Tom even behind closed lids, standing stiffly beside me.

'When Beth was a little girl she had an aunt who read her a story about being buried alive. Edgar Allan Poe's "The Premature Burial". Lord, it made such an impression on her. She told me it was her biggest fear, that she was absolutely terrified it might happen to her. I read it after she'd gone – very grim, although the ending is a real howler. Why on earth an aunt would think it a good story to read to a little girl I don't know.' He laughs. 'I suppose the story could be Poe himself, I gather he was something of an oddball. In any case the narrator has catalepsy – where you look as if you are unconscious and the muscles don't move. One night he dreams he's woken by a ghost, a sort of spectre of death who lifts the lids off all the graves of mankind to see the decay and the shrouded bodies and the worms. But the worst thing of all is that they are *moving*: "a feeble struggling, a general and sad unrest; and from out of the depths of the countless pits there came a melancholy rustling from the garments of the buried."'

'What did he do?'

'Well, our man goes berserk. Persuades all his friends to make absolutely sure when his time comes that he is actually dead. Of course he doesn't trust them so he goes to the family vault and puts springs on the lid of the coffin and a lever that will open the vault doors and he stores some food and water and a rope attached to a bell. In the end of the story our man is overnighting on a shooting expedition and has fallen asleep in a narrow little cabin on board a boat. He's crammed into a tiny bunk and when he wakes up in the middle of the night he thinks he's in a coffin, but there are no springs and no lever and he starts howling and the crew wake up and he realises where he is. That cures him. He starts to live after that, stops obsessing about death, goes travelling.'

'And Beth?'

'She made me swear I would double check. That I would pinch her really hard, prick her with a needle. If you are dead the blood won't flow.'

'On the last day she was asleep, semi-conscious maybe. Her eyes were closed and she was breathing but she didn't move. All this waiting, sitting in the room with Charlie and myself, like the preamble to a dogfight, so I went out for a walk along the sea front. Sat down by the World War Two tank on the promenade at Eastbourne, watched the oldies wandering about eating ice cream, taking their constitutionals. Clinging on while Beth was letting go. When I came back I knew by the nurse's face. And when I went into the room Beth looked dead. But she had been looking dead for some days by then.'

He frowns up at the sky, a low grubby grey.

'Laura hugged me. A big warm hug that I think she meant. Charlie and I, we didn't touch. And then the whole funeral business kicked into gear. Her friends doing flowers and bringing round food and offering to walk Jack who of course wouldn't budge. There was nothing at all for me to do. At the service Charlie sat in the opposite pew which confused the hell out of the vicar. He was very jittery. At the graveside he stood away from me, held Laura's hand. He cried, big tears rolling down his cheeks for everyone to see while I just stood staring straight ahead. I vetoed drinks at the house, didn't want all Beth's friends crowding about. Charlie didn't come to the hotel reception. That miserable event was over in less than an hour.

'The next morning I took Jack for his walk and when I came back Charlie's rented car was parked on the drive. And there he was standing on the big flat rock outside the front door looking down over the lawn. I sat in the Jeep, didn't bother to get out. Actually I couldn't, my legs had turned to jelly. Never happened before or since. He walked over to the window, his face was all hard edges, the effort of holding something in or the effort of release. But I could see it was fear as well and that was the worst of it. He couldn't look me in the eye, after all these years he was still afraid of me. And I knew that feeling so well, remembering how I had been afraid of my own father. Not of being hit – although he clipped me often enough. Afraid of the power of my own rage, how much of a taboo, how big the defiance and how great the loss. How hard it is to square up to your old man and tell him what an utter bastard he is. So I saved him the trouble. I said, "Charlie you've probably come to say you won't ever be back now your mother is gone." That shook him up a bit, stole his thunder. Of course it would have been the moment to ditch my pride and fall on my sword, to try, as Beth always wanted me to. A good man, a brave man would have done that, even if the son wouldn't listen. A spineless, craven, cold-hearted man would have done what I did. Which was to sit like a stone in the car and let him walk away.

'You know, Laura still writes to me every month, sends me pictures of my baby granddaughter. I don't know if Charlie knows. But I do know that he is a better man than I have ever been.'

His clenched fists fly up to his forehead and bang hard against the skull as if there is something inside that must be shaken loose. 'Aack' he says and staggers away from the grave and I go to help him but he flaps me away with his arm and heads off down to the path back to his bench, his upright carriage collapsed, leaning hard on the stick now, his head bowed. Jack falls into line behind him keeping a steady distance a couple of inches from his heels.

I look over at the church, there is a marked austerity in this light, the steeple sharp and pointy and not at all conciliatory. And it is growing late, the afternoon will soon be spent and I long to push off but I cannot leave like this without at least saying goodbye.

'Tom. I really have to go. And you should leave too,' I say, rubbing my hands together but he swats my question aside with a glove.

'Do you know I had a call from one of Beth's friends yesterday reminding me of her anniversary. Bloody cheek.'

'Maybe they were trying to be helpful.'

'Hnnh. I asked her who would know if I missed it. After all, the party girl herself is dead.'

'You said that?'

'Of course I said that. Women are always butting in, trying to take over. Taking charge of events as if men were incompetent. Everything has to be a celebration or a ritual – anniversaries, christenings, weddings, Beth was always writing cards, sending little notes to people. The grandchildren of friends. "They barely know who you are," I'd say but she'd just give me that bland glazed look, the kind of smile you might give an imbecile. Placatory, not really listening. Thinking back now I'm sure she didn't pay a blind bit of notice to anything I said.'

His thin lips are working as if the nerve endings are in spasm and they cannot decide where to settle. Something has rattled his cage – the anniversary, the end of the dead year and the prospect of more to come. Him and Jack rattling around in the silent house and this snorting 'Hnnh' is a new development, a nervous tic accompanied by a rapid flutter of his hand on his knee.

'I have no idea what Beth thought about her life. She seemed happy enough, I suppose. But what would I know? I haven't got a clue.

'Before the body was even cold her friends were muscling in with their advice. Fussing over details, hymns, funeral notices. Apparently she despised carnations. Hnnh. Apparently she loved red roses. They knew all these things about her. Beth would want to be wearing such and such an outfit, some pink suit that she wore to Charlie's graduation, Brenda fussing about it being a bit loose. For Chrissake, I said, no one will see her where she's going. Does it really matter if dead people's clothes don't fit?

'All these little intimacies that women share. The kind of casket Beth wanted, for example. Do you know they talk about these things at their coffee mornings, all their little preferences, right down to which music? She wanted Bach's "Christmas Oratorio" if you can believe that – I didn't even know she *liked* music. I found the cassette at home so I just got a new version and gave it to the funeral directors. A very catchy, overlapping sort of choral piece, very regal, dignified. Charlie knew it well, was pleased as Punch at the choice. Brenda told me he'd remember it, that Beth often played it for him when he was very young and he used to march around in time. All the things you find out after someone has gone.

'She left a letter with the solicitor to be passed on to Charlie on her death. I never knew what it said. A declaration of love, I suppose, as if the boy could have been in any doubt. Or maybe an apology for his inadequate father. She didn't leave anything for me. I was miffed about that I can tell you. Oh yes, I suppose I'd been jealous all those years of what she had with Charlie.

'I had decided on burial. Didn't consider any alternatives until Brenda called round. Burial would be a mistake, she said. Beth wouldn't want to be a bother to me in later years. Who would tend to the grave? With Charlie away, who would look after it when I couldn't do it any more? And visiting would become a burden if I was sick, Beth wouldn't like that, wouldn't want to make extra work for the volunteers. "You might very well say burial now, Tom,"' – he mimics a hectoring female voice – '"but just think about the years to come." I hadn't thought about that, hadn't factored in the business of tending to a grave, spending time here. At first I came because it seemed like the decent thing, to not leave her alone. But Jack needs his walk anyway, so it's just a little shift in routine.'

He winces, a twist of his lips as if he had been jabbed with a sharp object. And I am exhausted, hijacked by this outpouring.

'Sometimes when I sit here I even forget she's dead.'

'So now that Beth is dead she's got your attention. Death has finally brought her into focus.'

'I suppose I come here to pay respect to the person I ignored all my life. Maybe it's a sort of atonement.'

'And what will that achieve?'

'It might earn me a place in heaven,' he shoves his hands deep in his pockets with a mean laugh.

'So selfish reasons again.'

'Isn't that the motivation behind most of what we do? To make us feel better.'

'Beth is dead, she doesn't know.' I imagine Estelle's snigger. She knows better. 'So you are busy redeeming yourself.'

'And you?'

I shrug.

'You come to what – to remember? To regret? Or because you have nowhere else to go?'

The light is disappearing, the church shrouded in a mist that sinks weighted to the ground. The dead, the ghosts are hard to see in these conditions but Estelle will be listening and curious about the answer to this question: to know why it is that I keep coming.

'Leaving little presents for a corpse. Hnnh. You have to wonder how long you will keep this up.'

'I could say exactly the same to you. It's a guilty conscience that brings you back here.' I should know better than to prolong this bickering, but I cannot let it go, a childish insistence on having the last word.

'I am an old man. It does not matter how old men waste their time. But you are like Miss Havisham. The clock has stopped and you are stuck.'

'I do other things. When I leave here I go back to my life.'

'You go back to work you mean. Is there anyone at home? Even *I* have Jack. Is there time in all your self-absorption for a man?'

I stand up with such suddenness that I lose balance and stumble backwards. The fog has thickened even in the last minute and now only the dark outline of the church door is visible.

'Going back to your life?' he asks with a leer.

'You are not a kind man.'

'That we know. But there is no kind way to deliver truths.'

'My life is none of your business. You don't even know me.'

'Then you shouldn't talk to strangers.'

'FUCK YOU,' I shout with all my might, and turn away and head for the invisible gates. Jack appears by my ankle as I lift the latch; if he runs through I will not retrieve him or call out. He might just be lucky enough to find another owner.

11

THE FOG GLOWS YELLOW in my headlights as I inch blindly forwards onto the road; there may be other cars about but I cannot tell in near-zero visibility. A green light shimmers to the left and I move slowly across the junction, steer the car across the bypass and pull up at the top of my mother's road, by a field away from the houses. I rest my forehead in an arm cradle on the wheel, tears seep through my closed lids, a flood that will not stop, as if Tom's barb has ruptured an old wound that cannot be staunched. A useless unspent regret for all that followed from that morning two years ago when I woke from a dream about my favourite dress, brown velvet clinging like a skin you never want to shed. Four other women were at the dinner table, all with loose wavy hair in various shades from auburn to black and each of us wearing satin gloves to match our dresses and there was white décolletage on show. A woman in red wore a huge ruby ring on her gloved finger. A cloud of cigarette smoke clung to the chandeliers, there was jazz piano somewhere behind us and the background suggestion of dark-suited men, an oblique view of a curved zinc bar. I noticed scarlet lipstick stains on someone's teeth and ran my tongue over my own. A woman beside me with a green bow in her chestnut hair coughed delicately and as I turned my head she lifted the napkin to her mouth and discreetly vomited a steaming heap of food into the napkin. She folded the cloth and smiled sweetly at me from beneath long lashes. We all applauded and said, 'Well done,' the muffled clap of satin hands.

When I awoke I got up from bed and opened the wardrobe to find the favourite dress, remembering how perfectly it had flattered, with its snug bodice and the little ruche of velvet around the tummy. I whipped hangers along the rail, trying to remember if that dinner was the last time I wore it, unzipped a row of suit bags in the guest room and then began to worry that it might be languishing in the dry cleaner's. But how is it possible to lose a dress? I must have spilled something. The cleaners must have it still and of course would keep it – but wasn't there something about disposing of uncollected items after three months? Don't they have my phone number? Surely they could tell that it was a very expensive dress, a work of art in fact, although I could not recall where I had bought it and how much it had cost.

Half an hour later, squashed up behind someone's news-print on the Tube to work, I am still struggling to piece together the sequence of events and the lost dress, when it comes to me that I did not know any of those women at the table. I had never been in that restaurant, never worn long satin gloves, and the beautiful brown dress, like the whole rich scene, was just a dream. As the train shoots through the darkness, I cling to the strap with both hands, terrorised by the idea that I have no firm grip on reality, that I am no longer able to distinguish between the actual and the imaginary, that some unspeakable fusion has taken place and I am falling backwards through a deep dark chasm, the air hissing out of me as if a valve has been unscrewed in my chest. My hands fly to my constricted throat and I lose balance, smashing through the newspaper into the dark.

MIND THE GAP! MIND THE GAP!

Rush-hour shoes are wedged heel-to-toe shuffling towards the exit. I am bent double, staring at my navy pumps. They have pointed toes. I recognise them. I remember buying them. I know that the left one is slightly loose in the heel. And I know exactly where I am, I am sitting on a wooden bench on the platform at Bank. When I press down I can feel my elbows dig into my thighs. 'This is now,' I whisper. This has happened to me before, it is a panic attack.

A gentle squeeze on my right arm. A pair of shiny brown brogues on the ground beside me and I swing my head upwards.

'Whoa, take it easy.' A man, a dark blue pinstriped suit, white shirt, smiles at me with straight white teeth, brown eyes. Tiny grey elephants march across a blue tie. His free hand, the one that is not steadying me, raised in approbation. 'No sudden movements.'

'Who are you?'

'I am Luke.'

I flinch, an involuntary spasm, my floppy muscles recovering some purpose.

'Matthew, Mark, Luke and John,' I mutter.

'But I am not an apostle,' he smiles.

'How're you doin'?' A guard materialises in front of us, bends down to peer into my face. 'I call a ambulance for you?' I can smell her chewing gum.

'No thanks. I'm OK.'

Behind her crowds rubberneck as they drift past, checking me over. Any minute now someone from the office could recognise me. I do not know how I got from the Tube to here, just exactly how undignified was my removal from train to bench.

'White as a sheet,' she shakes her head.

'You should see me on a good day,' I say straightening up, tugging at my jacket.

'You sit right here and I call the doc.'

'There's no need. Honestly.' I turn in appeal for back-up to Luke who is still sitting head cocked, faint smile. 'I just didn't eat breakfast. Low blood sugar.'

'I dunno…' she purses her lips.

'I work just round the corner, there's a doctor there. I'll be fine.'

'You know this lady?' she frowns at the man beside me.

'He's Luke,' I say, patting his arm.

'Well, Luke, you goin' to be her knight in shining armour,' she says slapping her hands on her thighs.

'I'll deliver her right to her desk.'

I stand up. Luke holds my elbow and slots my handbag over my shoulder. My fingers clutch at the soft felt of his camel coat.

'You be sure and eat some breakfast tomorrow, girl. I don' wan' to find you sprawled all over my platform again.'

'Was I sprawled?' I say to Luke as he positions me on the escalator step above him.

'An elegant sprawl. More of a swoon really. You came crashing through my newspaper and flung yourself at me. Out cold.'

I sneeze. And look away, deep breaths.

'Of course I normally have this effect on women at rush hour.'

A burst of pigeons flap up in front of us as we walk past the Royal Exchange and Luke is still holding my arm. 'I'm OK. Really. You don't have to do this.'

'I work just there,' he jerks his head towards Threadneedle Street. 'Anyway I promised I'd take you all the way.'

I don't argue. This is better than being responsible for my own deliverance and my knees still wobble a little as if they might give out.

'You look better,' he steps forward and bends down to

look at me. 'Actually you look lovely.'

I do not speak, I concentrate on placing one foot forwards and on what is real. The wet pavement, the rumble of passing taxis, the clicking of high heels that hurry past us, the blast of bus exhaust, the steady crook of his elbow. I could walk all day like this. When we stop at the traffic lights by Fenchurch Street I allow myself to lean a little on him and Luke tells me a story of his own humiliation, how he smacked his head on a stationary side mirror cycling along Moorgate last summer. Waving away help and then blacking out in the middle of the road. He gave up the bike after that, there are easier ways to stay fit and breathe in clean air. And then he stops talking and we proceed in silence with the sounds of the working city all around us: the car screeches, the vibrations deep below the pavements, the snatches of passing chatter. And it seems to me now that we were gliding like an invisible ship cutting through rough waters. A slow, almost leisurely walk through the Square Mile, the warm press of Luke's sleeve under my fingers and the way he stood upright and smiled by the pedestrian crossing.

'Whatever happened to Luke?' said Nicola, it was months later and we were stepping into the lift. 'He was *so* gorgeous. Remember I bumped into you both that time walking along the street one evening? You looked so good together.'

I turned away, shrugged at the tinted mirror.

'You blew him out, didn't you? Oh Caro, what am I going to do with you,' she sighed, jabbed at the button, shook her head all the way up to the fifteenth floor.

When Luke said we should move in together, I knew it marked the point at which I would withdraw. I could not put him in front of the memory of Cormac no matter how hard I tried. He looked at me in the half-light, elbow crushed into the pillow. 'What are you worried about? I love you.' But it was as if my capacity for intensity had gone, fled. He stroked my temple, slow light fingers along the hairline and I closed my eyes on our future. A can't is always a won't. Dressing up refusal to make it more palatable.

But it was that unhurried procession along Cornhill that I remembered best of all when I saw him leave for the very last time, whitefaced and bony, his shoes heavy away across the tarmac, all his features sharpened in the streetlight as he turned his head back towards me for one final look, and the sound of my door closing on him and a possible future that I had crumpled in my hand.

My phone rings and I lift my head from the steering wheel. I lean forward to fish it out of my back pocket. The LED shows Mum and I snatch it open.

'Are you all right?'

'Of course I'm all right,' her voice is a little muffled as if she is holding the receiver away from her mouth. 'Why do you ask?'

'Because you never call,' I say. Misty streaks stream over the bonnet, the fog is lightening but my mother would not see my car from the house even if she was looking out the window, which she is not.

'I have a message for you.'

'What?'

'Are you driving, Caroline? Shall I call back?'

'No, no, it's OK.' I straighten up in the seat. 'What is it?'

'Hold on.' I hear the flick of her lighter and an exhalation.

'He called here last week.'

'Who?'

'Cormac,' she sighs. 'Who else would call here looking for you?'

I squeeze the steering wheel. It is now twenty years since that morning when he waved to me and I have not seen or spoken to him since. I have spent all of my adult life without him.

'Caroline?'

'What?'

'He wants to see you. He left an address and a date. Do you have a pen?'

'Yes. No. Somewhere in the car.'

'Oh well, you can call me back later,' and her voice drifts away as if she is about to hang up.

'NO, WAIT. Wait. When is it?'

'First of December. Seven p.m.'

'But that's very soon.'

'Are you going away?'

'No.'

'Well then.'

'Did he say anything else?'

'He was his usual self.'

'You haven't spoken to him in twenty years!'

'He sounded just the same.'

'What did he say?'

'Asked how I was, how you were.'

'What did you say?'

'That you were fine.'

'What else did he say?'

'He said tell Caro it's been far too long.'

'Did he say that?'

'Yes.'

'Did he leave a number?'

'Yes. Yes he did. Only –'

'Only what?'

'I seem to have lost it.'

'You LOST it?'

'It was a different scrap of paper. Probably stuck in some book. I have been looking for it but –'

'I don't believe it.'

'But I have the date. The address. The time.'

'I need his number.'

'For what?'

'To say if I am coming.'

'He said no excuses.'

'He said that?'

'Yes.'

'Exactly what?'

'He said tell Caro no excuses.'

Silence. I can hear her rustling with paper.

'Caroline?'

'What is it? Is there something else? Did he say something else?'

'No.'

'Sure?'

'No. There is nothing else.'

Part **two**

12

ALL THIS WEEK I HAVE HAD difficulty with the most basic physical tasks. On Tuesday I stood staring into a shopping trolley and it wasn't until the woman at the checkout shouted 'EXCUSE ME' that I registered the queue of tired faces stretched out behind me and remembered where I was. On Thursday morning I arrived late for an appointment with the owner of a warehouse development that had been burgled, the owner tapping his fingernails on the desk while I rummaged in my briefcase for the paperwork that was clearly not there but lying on my desk on the other side of town.

'Are you with us, Caro?' Nicola touched my wrist at our monthly meeting on Friday. But I was not there, I was editing one version of the reunions with Cormac that I have scripted over the years. I have choreographed many alternatives but the setting has always been a city centre café in mid-morning. Somewhere like Truc Vert, with its studied casualness: a generous square of supportive oak to lean on, natural substance instead of artifice and veneer.

Cormac orders a coffee, probably a triple espresso. I order peppermint tea. I may smoke but this is not certain. A cigarette would be a useful prop, something to busy myself with, something to impair my breathing and slow down the torrent that could gush from my mouth. But it has been years since

I smoked and I do not think I could start convincingly again now. I will have to concentrate on trying to look nonchalant as Cormac leans in over the table, so close that I can see the little striation in his left iris. He will fix me with a direct gaze, it is a sort of nakedness that he has perfected but I know it to be illusory. Or the mark of a true heartlessness. It will remind me of our last encounter in the flesh, that day outside his bedroom door when he crouched down so that his eyes were level with mine and told me he was leaving. I remember everything, the carpet by his threshold coming loose from the gripper, the dent in the skirting board from a golf club that one of his brothers had whacked years before, a woodlouse trundling along the floor. The smell of bleach from the loo door behind me. The skull and crossbones drawing tacked to the top of the door that Cormac drew in Year 2, chalk with red paint on black paper, torn in one corner. A full-size poster of Springsteen below – the album cover of *Born to Run* that Cormac had blagged from the record shop in town. Marker scribbles along the bottom of his door, possibly some of them mine and Estelle's for the house was scarred with traces of our childhoods.

Cormac will ask what I do now with my life. And I wish I could say that I have scaled Everest or performed open-heart surgery or painted a picture that graces a gallery wall, rather than the dull truth. For years I have thought through tactics of opening and disclosure but I know that being close to him again will cause any strategy to crumble. The people around us in the café will try not to stare, the staff will nudge each other. Of course a public place is a trap for him and we might be overwhelmed within minutes, autograph hunters or passers-by taking pictures on their phones, paparazzi rushing to the scene.

. . . . .

I made a furtive visit to the address my mother gave me on Wednesday lunchtime, looking my anonymous self in sunglasses and a beret. It is a grand townhouse with white pillars, just a stone's throw from the park, and there was no sign of its occupants. A video phone on the door. Security cameras trained on all entrances. A well-stocked window box at ground and first floor where large French windows overlook the street. His London residence, I assume. So at least I will not have to sit in a restaurant like a grinning fool while the glow of fame pulses all around us.

I am trying not to worry about what Cormac will see. We are both twenty years older and I have watched him grow up on screen but he has not seen me since I was fifteen. There are fine lines radiating from the corners of my eyes. On close inspection in the magnified side of the mirror my irises seem grey, almost grubby. My skin is a little pigmented along the right cheekbone and I am less soft, more bony, with a steely side profile that I sometimes catch in the mirror. My lips in repose are less full than I remember. 'Your natural expression is really rather stern,' Nicola once said. But perhaps it has always been so, perhaps that will not be a surprise to Cormac. I close my eyes and imagine the sea. It was only a half-hour drive to the cluttered coastline where Estelle's mother used to take us on picnics. Later we made the slow bus ride alone, swaying on the top deck with sandwiches and ginger nuts and money to buy a 99 from the Mr Whippy van in the car park at Cuckmere. There were pill boxes dug into the hillsides, black-and-white sheep nibbling in the heat, herds of static Friesians dotted like ornaments on the grassy slope. 'A crocodile,' Estelle shrieked at a stagnant log adrift in the sea-bound river. We sat on the banks and threw pebbles at its snout, poked at the grey mudbank that was dried and cracked like animal hide.

On the beach we piled stones into cairns under the glare of the crumbling chalk cliffs. We were lying underneath a blue Newhaven sky when I caught Cormac staring at my breasts for the first time. Estelle was wandering nearby looking for cuttlefish. He leaned over me, his head blocking the sun so that it seemed his curls were burning and I felt that first lurch of desire, a prickling river running down the back of my neck. His finger touched my bare shoulder and it was as if the world was concentrated in that very point, he had found the whole axis of my being. And at the same time a heart-stopping fear of the desolate vista that lay up ahead, this trembling like a taster, a warning of the complexities of passion. And in that exact moment my body stirred and was forever altered, flinging me headlong into the unknown. I could smell change on the horizon. It was the end of childhood.

Estelle came clattering towards us across the stones with a cuttlefish in her hand, her voice small and distant although she was closing in. The beach was almost empty, gulls swooping down on scraps left by picnickers who were heading back over the ridge for the long trek back to the car park. Cormac slid his hand inside my T-shirt and rolled it up. Estelle flopped down on her knees beside us, her mouth half-open in a rare and quiet concentration. We both watched as Cormac dipped his head and pressed his lips against my breast. The wind roar dropped and in the sudden silence I heard a harsh sigh, like the gasp of the wounded. It seemed as if I had stumbled on a new way of breathing and I closed my eyes, discovered a need to arch my back into the stones, to grip his hair. I felt a pressure on my arm as it was pulled gently outwards until my hand came to rest on soft flesh and I opened my eyes just as Estelle spread my fingers over her breast. Cormac turned his head. I did not pull my hand away. And I see this freeze-framed tableau, sunset on the beach with me on my back and Cormac's head laid sideways on my bare chest, Estelle kneeling beside us as if she is caressing the hand of a dying maiden.

I chivvy my thoughts away from those times. It feels excruciating, almost pornographic to remember. All that is behind us and it would be different now. And I, inspecting myself in the bath last night, do not look bad at all. My thighs are soft and smooth to the touch. The pink nipple sits proud on my white round breast. It might even be better now. There has been plenty of time to wonder.

Oh but if Cormac touches me I may be speechless, immobilised by loss and desire. He used to fold his hand round my wrist when we lay on his bed, pressing his thumb against my pulse. *Feel the beat, Caro. I will always remember our beat.* And I have wondered if this promise cast into the future was already a reference to some planned departure. If he was already leaving then, if he knew and if I should have been more prepared. But how to do that? How to configure your heart at fifteen, as if you could just steer into safer waters by an act of will?

The crossroad marks the western perimeter of the hotel's estate. These traffic lights were put up a couple of years ago when this quiet junction became a rat run for the train station. I am less than a mile from where I grew up and I remember this road well for its darkness, the tree roots clearly visible in the high banks that border both sides. They have grown more dense now to form a natural arbour so the road is cast in permanent shade even in summer. I round a bend and break suddenly into light as the vegetation gives way onto an unfarmed field bounded by flimsy fencing which is regularly trampled by deer. As I slow to a crawl I see the nameplate mounted on two thick slabs of wood. The house is not visible behind the trees but I know this must be correct. I turn into the mouth of the drive and pause, engine running.

I do not have to make this call. I have no responsibility to an old man who may very well consider an unannounced visit to be a major imposition. And I do not intend to apologise. The simple fact of age does not entitle Tom to be so careless with my feelings but he has wheedled his way into my routine and I spent this morning's churchyard visit sitting on my bench distracted by his absence. Imagining him dead, or dying. I will call just this once while it is still light, if I linger much longer the day will be lost. And I am tired, jangling at the approach of December One, trapped in an endless cycle of imaginings that keep me hovering on the borderland of sleep and dream. It was sleeplessness drove me out early when the spider webs in the graveyard were still lit with dew and I sat remembering how Estelle would wake me in the winter dark, it was a feature that she always woke at dawn and sometimes would get straight out of bed and hurl a handful of clay at my bedroom window, pyjama legs flapping in the wet grass. 'Ever since you were a little one,' her mum would yawn by the back door, hands muffled inside the sleeves of her dressing gown, the cat snaking around her slippers.

The drive rises steeply up from the road, a straight strip of stippled concrete that is heavily mossed in places and flanked on both sides by a copper beech hedge. There is a Manderley aspect to the wrought-iron gates with thick ivy clinging to the posts. A sharp bend winds through a thicket of holly, laurel and rhododendrons and every now and again the pale flash of silver birch. Twigs and large sticks litter the drive, leaves brush up against the body of the car and giant strands of dead bracken stick out from the side. Up and up we twist and wind, I am peering over the steering wheel into a fortress of vegetation on all sides with no sign of a house until I round a bend and the foliage gives way to high rocky banks topped with brown heather. There is a tunnel on my left that seems to be carved out of the grey stone. The ground underneath has been levelled and there sits Tom's Jeep, its number plate almost completely obscured by mud.

I nudge forward and the house comes slowly into view: a long two-storey rectangle of rough-hewn sandstone and a flat castellated roof that lends it a baronial air. As I open the car door I hear yapping from inside the house. So Jack at least is alive, or perhaps he has already started nibbling at his dead owner's legs, and here he comes now barrelling around the corner, barking furiously all the while and I hope that my out-of-context presence will not overrule his memory of my scent. He stops at my feet and dance-hops a little pirouette that I have never seen him do before, wagging his stumpy tail. Clearly visitors are a rare event.

Set deep underneath the arch of a wide porch is a massive oak door with beaten iron hinges, like the dark entrance to a brooding castle. Jack starts up a savage scrabbling at the bottom which I take as a sign that Tom is alive and well and quite capable of opening up. Although it is possible that the dog escaped through a flap somewhere round the back and is now ravenous and desperate for me to get us in so he can tuck into a sack of dog food. A hand whips back a curtain that covers a small side window and Tom's white face appears behind the leaded panes with a look of frowning annoyance. The door opens and Jack scuttles off barking into the bowels of the house.

He is wearing a grey hoodie with *University of Melbourne* in big white letters across the chest. The front is stained with small flecks of green and white paint. He seems thin and quite bloodless, his lips almost indistinguishable in colour from the skin of his face. Perhaps I have disturbed a nap.

'So this is where you live.'

'Obviously.'

'I just wondered –'

'If I was lying dead at the bottom of the stairs?' But there is a play of a smile about his lips and I cannot but grin.

'Well maybe. I haven't seen you for a while.'

'I have been – away. One cannot devote all one's time to the service of the dead.'

'Not your usual get-up,' I point at the hoodie.

'Charlie left it behind on his last trip. I wear it when I do not expect to be interrupted.'

Jack returns with a red rubber ball in his mouth and parks himself at my feet looking up expectantly.

'I didn't know he had toys.'

'We never bring them out. He prefers to keep them for home entertainment.'

'It's a very impressive place you have here,' I spread my arms wide. 'Almost magical, hidden away at the top of the hill.'

'When my father built it there were wonderful views but that's all blocked out now by those trees. I don't like to cut them down, although some of them are dangerously close,' he points at a Scots pine that towers over the house.

'Well, seeing as I'm here, any chance of a coffee?'

He looks out behind me, hand resting on the latch. This is not a simple request, he is weighing up the pros and cons of granting permission to intrude. I assume it is his sensitivity to my seeing his old man's home. The dispassionate eye that will spot all the domestic shortcomings to which the owner has become inured: the dog hair on the sofa, the lime-scaled kettle, the neglect that settles on every surface like a fine dust; a chipped teacup, a broken door handle, a spent bulb, the small advertisements of decline left untreated now that Beth is gone. Or maybe the house is littered with empty bottles of booze and he has shipped in a simpering under-age maid to massage him through his old age, some slender sex slave with only a few words of English. Maybe he hasn't tidied away the stash of porn that he drools over on his long lonely nights in the living room.

Tom steps aside and I pass into a narrow hallway with smooth grey flagstones and heavy oak beams above my head. I follow him down the corridor into the kitchen with walls of limed cabinets and a pinkish expanse of worktop – a farm-house style that was popular in the eighties and has been very well maintained. A fat kettle gleams on the hob and the oak floor is polished to a high shine. There is clearly someone who takes charge of the domestics. Jack slops at a water bowl in the corner, the red ball between his feet.

'There is no coffee,' says Tom opening a cupboard.

'Herbal tea?'

He snorts and takes out a packet of Earl Grey.

'So you've been away. Anywhere nice?'

But Tom busies himself with the kettle, ignoring the question. There is a shadowy look to his face and a turkey-ing effect to the exposed neck that is normally muffled, or perhaps it's just grubby stubble, it is not always easy to tell when old men are unshaven. His brows are untrimmed and a coil of nose hair protrudes at a wild angle. The loose folds of the hoodie are incongruous against his frame and add to his dishevelled appearance. His chest is concave and bony and the slippers encourage a shuffling gait about the kitchen. I decide it must be contextual. Tom does not come out well of an indoor viewing. Old age needs rigorous grooming to achieve presentability, after all it is the window to our own incipient decrepitude. No wonder I look away.

Jack trots over with the ball wedged in his jaws but when I bend down and put out my hand he growls and backs away, biting down hard on the rubber.

'He won't give it to you.'

'So how does he play?'

'He tosses it in the air and then races to catch it. He always wins. It's a performance rather than a game.'

'And if I try to catch it?'

'I imagine he will bite you.'

'Has he ever actually bitten anyone?'

'There's been a couple of incidents. A delivery man kicked him. A friend of Charlie's took his food away. Provoked attacks.'

'Has he ever bitten you?'

'No, but his predecessor did.'

'Why?'

He sighs, rests his hands on the worktop. 'I hit someone. It was no more than I deserved.'

I stand at the patio door in the kitchen conservatory looking out onto a large irregular-shaped blue pool edged with slabs of grey stone.

'My father tacked the swimming pool on in 1951,' says Tom. 'He was running out of projects by then and had done just about everything else around here. My mother was dead set against it, she hated water and only on sufferance would she sit on the steps.'

'Must have been fun for you?'

'I had left school by then and was at university up in London so I didn't come home much. My father would make a point of noisily splashing a few lengths every morning all year round, just to prove a point. But it's only five feet deep and not very wide so makes for a rather frustrating swimming experience. He gave up eventually and stopped chlorinating – too much to maintain. Each spring ducks would nest there in the box hedge and the ducklings would lunge off the wall into the water. My mother loved that, it did make her laugh. She wrote in a letter to me that maybe the wretched pool was worth it just for the privilege of watching the ducklings take their very first swim.'

He sets a slim white ceramic pot down on the scrubbed pine table. Two china cups and saucers, a dish and strainer for the tea, milk and sugar in matching jug and bowl.

'Proper service.'

'Beth always said make the effort for visitors. Good discipline. I don't have cause to do it too often.'

'So tell me about the house.'

'You would really like to know?'

'Why do you ask?'

'You shouldn't fall into the habit of indulging old people.'

'I'm not.'

He moves the tea cup to one side and leans forward, placing both elbows on the table. 'My father, Harry Warren, was a master builder from a family of master builders and stonemasons. That was a tradition that ended with me, his only son and heir. Since you grew up around here you know that there are lots of sandstone deposits – this site was originally a quarry that my father inherited from his father. When he'd mined all the sand and built all the houses you saw along the road, he started on this one. This house was Harry Warren's labour of love.

'He broke ground with a pickaxe on New Year's Day 1933 just a few months before I was born. My father was a real craftsman but he was also something of a tyrant. He once made a bricklayer – a man much older than himself and very experienced – take down that entire back wall there,' Tom points over my shoulder, 'and start again. He wasn't at all popular with his workers and he never listened to advice, which explains some of the flaws in the design. For example, everyone warned him about the flat roof – they're notoriously difficult and expensive to maintain and we've always had a problem with recurring leaks – but Harry was stubborn and paid no heed. The house is full of oak beams – I'll show you in a minute – he salvaged them from old ships and some of them in the living room are beautifully curved. There are lots of quirky little details, like the latches on all the internal doors, tiny wooden alcoves embedded in the walls, handmade panelled wardrobes, a lavish display cabinet which my father carved. He even installed an intercom system for the wireless and put in pipes running along the exterior which collected rain water and fed it down to the flower beds. He was obsessive about detail and order.

'While he was supervising the building we lived in the closest of the cottages – the white one you would have passed as you came through the gate. On the day we moved in my father insisted on chauffeuring me and my mother up the drive in the car. My mother was wearing a fox stole and her best white gloves and she covered my eyes as she walked me up the stairs. 'Your new bedroom, Tommy!' she said and there I was in this enormous room that made my little bed look tiny.

'If you look out there you'll see the magnolia he planted that day. He promised my mother white blossoms.' Tom points out the window to a tree that is reminiscent of a large rubber plant with thick leaves of yellowish green. 'The flowers are magnificent in a rather sinister way – huge white blossoms that crash to the ground while still completely fresh, as if the weight is too much for the tree to bear. I can remember lying in bed at night in late spring and hearing the soft thud as they hit the stone and in the morning the patio would be littered with petals.'

Tom shifts his chair around, positioning himself at a side angle to me and facing the pool. The water is greenish grey and dead with a small heap of black leaves submerged in the corner.

'On our first day here, my father stood out there on a ladder with a workman holding it steady and carved his name and the date into the stone lintel above the patio doors. There was clapping and glasses of sherry. It was February 1939 and I was six years old.'

'What a place to grow up in. These gardens,' I say, looking out beyond the grey stone into the clumps of rhododendron that border the pool and behind them a wall of Scots pine.

'There used to be a lovely view down this side over open farmland when I was a child but most of the land around the plot has been subdivided, sold off. The neighbours are a lot closer than you might think here tucked away behind all this greenery.'

'So go on, you moved in here in 1939 –'

'All that spring and summer I roamed the garden. Eleven acres of woodland with enormous sandstone cliffs and caves, a paradise of danger and excitement. I had a couple of play-mates from the houses along the road and we built rope ladders, abseiled off the cliffs. My father levelled the quarry bed and had huge amounts of topsoil brought in and turned it into a lawn. We played football, it was a great summer. My father was very proud and my mother was very happy. But of course all the time there was the ticking backdrop of war. I don't remember much of the build-up. The radio was always turned up very loud, booming through the house. We would hear the news every morning and every evening. And then the war itself. And my father opening the letter that would change everything.'

Jack nudges my leg underneath the table and then sits down on my foot, his bottom firmly resting on my toes. 'Look at that, eh?' Tom tips back in his chair to peer under the table.

'So he likes me after all.'

'Not necessarily. That's dominant behaviour. He's showing you who's boss.'

I study Jack's head, glassy black with a coppery vein zig-zagging across his skull and down his neck where it disappears in the fur frill around his collar. I slide my foot out from underneath him and cross one leg over the other. He stands up and clamps one paw down on my shoe again. The old man laughs.

'He's got your number.'

'Does he do this to everyone who comes round?'

'He doesn't try it with the woman who does for me. Gives her a wide berth.'

'So why me?'

'Maybe he thinks you need to know your place in the pecking order. Maybe he's worried you're going to move in and kick him out. Who knows what plots Jack may be hatching?'

Tom stands up with a sudden surge of animation and claps his hands together. 'Come now and I'll show you the roof before the light goes. And tell you the rest of the story.'

13

THE WIDE OAK STAIRCASE IS dusted and polished and heavy velvet drapes frame an enormous picture window to the front of the house, a sunless northern aspect and a heathery view. At the end of a long corridor a steep wooden stairway is cut into the corner. 'He can't quite manage the climb,' says Tom scooping up Jack and placing him on the top step. Pressing both hands flat against a hatch above his head, Tom strains so hard that for a moment it seems as if the lid will slam down on his skull but it swings back on a pulley and we emerge into a burst of sunshine. The roof surface is striped with patchmarks and coated in a silver paint that glitters in the light. It is a long empty rectangle except for a large squat water tank with weathered board sides. Tom walks to the edge and stands right by the castellated wall that barely reaches his knees. I keep a few feet back from the vertiginous drop. Jack sniffs around the corners of the tank, hops up suddenly onto a rock shelf and I scream.

'For Christ's sake, girl!' Tom spins round.

'I thought he was going to jump off. It's not safe, right there on the edge. It must be a forty-foot drop at least.'

'Jack likes heights.'

'He's a dog.'

'He can take care of himself,' and Jack swings his head

round from his rooftop perch to fix me with a sardonic leer, his mouth open, his tongue pink and mocking.

'Seven months after we moved in, the house was requisitioned by the Army. So in December 1939 we had to move back into the cottage down the road. I was very cross, brattish about it in the way of children. My mother was stoical, told me it was our big contribution to the war effort. My father was furious, although less about the house and more about the fact that he couldn't sign up. He'd been injured in the Great War – shrapnel embedded in the leg that left him with a slight limp, but in any case he was too old, so he volunteered for the Home Guard. I can still see him fuming in front of the mirror in the hallway – in the beginning they were issued with denim overalls the colour of cow dung, they looked like farm clothes. Some time later they were given proper serge uniforms but he used to wear his old greatcoat from the First War though it was stiff and heavy as board.

'Here,' he crouches down in the centre of the roof where a square brass plaque is mounted on a low stone plinth.

Royal Regiment of Canada,
Canadian 4th Infantry Brigade
1939–1942

'The Royals were billeted here in the house. Detailed with defending the south coast against enemy invasion. That was the big fear at the time, we are so close to the Continent, it would surely be the likely point of attack. You can see this is the highest point for miles and the Army wanted the flat roof for an anti-aircraft gun. This is exactly where it stood,' he taps the plaque with his finger. 'A Bofors 40mm. Weighed nearly five thousand pounds so they had to reinforce the whole roof and widen that hatch.'

'Must have been very exciting for a little boy having soldiers next door.'

'I remember the day the Canadians arrived in their jeeps and trucks, a cold wet morning in January 1940. They smiled and waved as they rolled up the drive – one of the cars stalled on that sharp bend by the gates.

'The gun was assembled on the roof – the whole thing had to be dismantled and taken up in pieces and put together again. We were allowed up here to see it at close quarters. My father walked round studying it from every angle, as if he was conducting a formal inspection. My mother stayed close to the hatch, she didn't like heights and didn't want me anywhere near the gun but the sergeant took me by the hand and walked me over. It was camouflaged with nets and greenery. "Go on, touch it, Tommy," he said. Through the netting, the metal was ice cold. I had imagined it gleaming, not dark and grubby. "Why don't you polish it?" I said. "You don't want to do that, kiddo," said the gunner, "you don't want anything shining up at Jerry giving your position away."'

'Did it get used much?'

'In fact it was only ever fired the once – shot down a V1, diverted it into the hotel estate across the road. Lots of doodle-bugs and rockets crashed in the forest – you can still see the craters everywhere. The invasion that never came.'

Tom bends down and wipes the plaque with his sleeve. Jack sits on the ledge looking out to the south where clouds are gathering about the sinking sun.

'Within a couple of weeks a wooden sentry box was erected just inside our gates. A tiny thing with barely enough space for a man to stand up. The house and garden were out of bounds to me but I used to stand halfway down the drive and one day I crept closer and out popped this head. A young soldier with fair hair and a chisel in his hand. Jimmy – Private

James McGarrigle. He was a carpenter by trade and he carved the most wonderful swirls and figures inside his little box.

'Jimmy wore wire-rimmed glasses and told me about a man he knew who'd sawed off his own frostbitten toes. He had stories about ice-fishing in the frozen wastes, polar bears twice the size of a man, moose that could overturn a tractor. And he was full of practical advice – for example, how to handle a grizzly bear – did you know the best thing you can do is to play dead? I told the boys at school and we used to practise that in the playground at lunchtime. He showed me rope tricks, card tricks, new rules for marbles; he had a Davy Crockett raccoon hat that he brought all the way from home as a memento and he let me wear it dashing about with my stick guns. He told me where all the soldiers were from, exotic names like Vancouver and Winnipeg and Saskatchewan so I could look them all up in my atlas. He cut down a storm-damaged birch and fashioned hockey sticks and we used a cricket ball to play on the sunken lawn that was once the quarry floor. He showed me pictures of his sweetheart, a black-and-white smiling head and shoulders of Alice with thick curls down to her shoulders. "Oh Tommy," he'd say, kissing the photo, "just you wait."'

He shoves his hands inside the hoodie pouch and frowns down at the plaque.

'You don't know anything about the history of this area in the War, do you?'

'No, not really.'

'Aren't you at all curious?' he swings his head towards me, lips tight with disapproval.

'My parents were born after the War. I guess it just always felt remote.'

'This whole area was transformed,' he sweeps his hands wide with sudden energy. 'It was crawling with mobilised soldiers and Home Guard. There were roadblocks, all the signposts were blacked out, rolls of barbed wire all along the beaches, the church bells were silenced and only rang to warn of air attacks –'

I am nodding but my listening interest seems to irritate him for he stops mid-flow and turns away.

'So you were telling me about Jimmy and the soldiers?' I prompt.

'By 1942 there were about twenty thousand Canadian forces in the south-east who had never seen action. The history books say the Canadian soldiers were cooped up in quarters, bored and restless and homesick, but that's not what I remember. They were happy as sandboys.'

He swings around, smiling now in recollection. 'The War Office distributed leaflets telling us how to behave when we met Allied soldiers. I can remember it vividly. "When you meet Americans don't make fun of their accent or vocabulary. Your accent and words probably seem just as odd to them. Take care not to snub an American. Don't talk about Chicago gangsters as if they represented 90 per cent of the population of America. Be a little more friendly than you normally would. Remember the British people have a reputation in America for being standoffish."

'The Canadians were impossibly glamorous and cheer-ful. Everyone loved them. When rations allowed, my mother would bake a Madeira cake and get me to take it up to Jimmy. Christmas Night 1940 we went up to the house in our best clothes and my parents drank sherry out of small glasses. The officers sang carols at full volume out there on the patio in the crisp night and shook my father's hand and offered him rye whisky. He inspected the label and spoke of the Great War while they stood by the fireplace smoking pipes. Unlike them, my father had seen combat in the trenches and they listened very respectfully, but he was a ponderous storyteller, actually not a storyteller at all. He was a list man, a facts man who managed to erase the human content. And even though I was just a child I could see that he was not at all the tough confident man he was with his builders. He cleared his throat all the time and his face was very red. The officers topped up his glass, nodded politely and there was a moment's silence when he reached the tally of all those in his company who never made it home.

'I was responsible for adding logs to the crackling fire that was roaring away in the front room. The Christmas tree was decked out with thin strips of paper and red berries from the holly in the garden. Jimmy gave me a present wrapped in newspaper – a carving of a grizzly about six inches high standing upright with his mouth open in a fierce roar and the tiny sharp teeth clearly visible and painted white. My mother was practically in tears, it was such a beautiful piece of workmanship. I could barely speak. I stood there amongst the circle of soldiers in a haze of pipe smoke and all I could think was that I never wanted this war to end.

'I used to dream of Canada, of walking out the door to face a snowdrift towering over me.'

Tom steps over to the roof's edge just as the clouds slip over the sun and cast us into shadow. Jack approaches from the opposite end to stand in the middle, watching his owner who shakes his head at something on the darkening horizon, or more likely his own folly in resurrecting a past that still aches and a story that seems to have diminished him in the telling. For he seems smaller, the tracksuit flaps loosely about his bony calves and shoulder blades, the hood ruffles round his neck, the whole ensemble lends him the air of a decrepit boxer who has lost all condition.

'Did the Canadians stay here all through the war?'

'Towards the end of 1941 my father insisted that I be evac-uated to Somerset. My mother didn't want me to go, she was dreadfully lonely. And I hated it, stuck with a farming family down in the Quantocks who clearly only took me in out of duty. I wrote miserable letters begging to be allowed home and after a few months my mother managed to persuade my father. But when I came back to the cottage in the spring of 1942 everything had changed. My father was very angry and shouting all the time, banging his fist on the table if food wasn't served on the dot, finding fault with everything. My mother was tearful and suddenly skin and bone. When I came home from school I'd find her lying in her room with the curtains drawn. I had no idea what was going on. Eventually I got cross, frustrated I suppose and I wrenched them open.' He sighs. 'I'm afraid I wasn't very kind to her.'

A sharp evening wind is picking up from the north and I shove my hands into my pockets. I feel a prickling in the back of my neck, Tom is uncomfortably close to the edge, his hands are tucked back inside the pouch and one good gust could topple him. Still he has left the story hanging and a nagging curiosity keeps me here, coupled with the desire to entice him back from the edge.

'Were the soldiers still here when you came back?'

'Oh yes, they were all still here. But my father forbade me from visiting the house. He wouldn't say why, I fought and whined about it but my mother warned me to do as I was told. I managed to sneak up to Jimmy in the sentry box when I could be sure my father wouldn't catch me. I asked him if he knew why the house was out of bounds for me. But he just said, "Listen to your father, Tommy, and don't upset your mom. Don't make trouble for yourself."'

Down on the lawn dusk is in its final throes, a couple of rabbits snacking on the grass. The drive back home will be long and slow in Sunday traffic.

'Before you go,' says Tom, 'come and see the end of the story.'

Back down in the house the radiators are cold. I follow him through the kitchen out into a stone hallway with an oak door at the other end. An old wireless radio sits in an alcove carved into the side. 'My father's Lee Enfield from the Great War,' he points to a mounted rifle above the door. 'It has a rather beautifully engraved plate. And his certificate there beside it, signed by King George.'

In the years when our country was in mortal danger Harold Warren who served from 1940 to Dec 1944 gave generously of his time and powers to make himself ready for her defence by force of arms and with his life if need be.

Tom opens the door and ushers me into the gloom, reaches up to pull on a cord attached to a metal lamp suspended from the ceiling. Light pools on a large table in the centre and reveals a model landscape about six feet long and four feet wide. It is a relief map of a coastline, a ridged blue sea that abuts a brown landcurve. A promenade runs all along the wide flat beach and, directly behind it, a town clusters around the mouth of a river. There is an extraordinary amount of detail – little grey ships dot the sea and smaller flat craft follow arrowed routes towards the sheer cliffs that rise at intervals either side of the main beach. There are coloured flags marking the beaches up and down the coast – tiny cloth triangles of blue, green, red, white, orange and yellow embedded in little hollows of sand. Miniature sections of barbed wire line the base of the cliffs and the promenade. Streets are blocked by slivers of cement, round pillboxes with tiny slits are dotted around the cliffside and four long-barrelled guns squat camouflaged on the highest points. At the front, painted in careful black calligraphy on the ocean blue is:

Dieppe, August 19th 1942

'You made this?'

'I was just touching up some paintwork here when you called.' Tom points to a jam jar with a small brush in white spirit and a little paint pot with green drips around the edge.

'Sometime in May 1942 I sneaked round to see Jimmy. He was so excited, he told me the Royals were going off on some special training exercise – he didn't know where but I found out later it was the Isle of Wight. "You never know, Tommy," he said, "this could be our lucky day. Maybe they're going to let us get stuck in."

'They were gone for six weeks or so and then on the way home from school one day I saw that they were back. Jimmy was bitterly disappointed. All he would say is that they'd been all packed up and ready somewhere on the coast and then everything was called off, they were sent back home and now he didn't think they'd ever see any bloody action and he'd spend the whole goddam war sitting on his ass in bloody England.

'School broke up at the end of July and I saw him only briefly then. In the second week of August I called round and there was a new sentry. He asked if I was Tommy and said he had a message from Jimmy, gave me a piece of paper tucked in behind a slat in the roof of the sentry box. "Dear Tommy, This time it's the real deal. I'll be back soon to tell you all about it."'

Tom stares down at his battlefield, runs a finger along the sea blue. 'On the 19th of August my father told me and my mother to assemble in the living room after supper and turned the wireless up very loud. Allied forces had been sent to northern France on a special raid. The announcer said that they had acquitted themselves very heroically on the beaches at Dieppe. My father stood with his hands behind his back and told us that the Royals were amongst them but that he didn't know what had happened to them. The next day I sneaked up to ask the new sentry but he didn't know either. Another day passed. That evening my father came out to the garden at the front of the cottage where I was kneeling beside my mother helping her weed. The newspaper was rolled up like a baton in his hand and he had his back to the sun so I couldn't see his face. His voice was very clear and strong. He said, "I thought you would both want to know right away. Your Canadians were all killed at Dieppe. May the Lord have mercy on their souls."'

'So you've been working on this for years.'

'I started when Beth and I moved in here after my parents died. I finished it when Charlie was leaving for university.'

'He must have loved helping with this.'

'Not really. In fact not at all.'

'I would have thought –'

'Charlie would always rather be out kicking a ball than cooped up inside. He was never much of a child for models and building and I suppose I made it a bit of a chore for him, insisting he do it every Sunday afternoon. He'd stand there sighing, being deliberately sloppy with the brush, dripping the sea onto the land, that sort of thing. Drove me mad and so I lost my temper one day when he was about ten or eleven. I shouted at him and he dropped the glass jar and spilled the white spirit all over the town. Right there –' he points to the little streets leading away from the promenade on the main beach.

'I hit him. It was the first and only time, a great big backhander right across the face.' He reaches out and picks up the jar, shakes the little brush against the rim with small tapping movements. 'That was when the old dog bit me. On the ankle. And Beth, oh, I'd never seen her angry before. You don't much with women, I don't know where you put it all. Into being upset, I suppose. I remember how she glared up at me, her face all flushed, the pinch of her fingers digging into my wrist and said if I ever laid a finger on him again she'd pack her bags and leave and I would never see either of them again. She never forgave me. Nor did Charlie.'

'Did you patch it up?'

'I never apologised to him if that's what you mean. I was his father. It's not what I believed in doing. There were worse things done by fathers to sons, you know.

'I sent Charlie away to Lancing College. Beth was distraught, although the school is less than an hour's drive away. I wonder now that she didn't kill me. Charlie and I barely spoke after that and I didn't visit, Beth went down on her own. So we rarely met except in the holidays. It never got fixed up. He stayed very close to Beth and behaved as if I didn't exist.'

'He was just a child.'

Tom sighs, places the brush in an empty jar. 'I too was once a child and it was not much different. We repeat the sins of our fathers. A cliché, but there it is.'

'It's never too late to say sorry.'

'That is something young people prefer to believe,' he raises a hand to switch out the light and the room is plunged into darkness. 'Sometimes it is too late. Too late. Too far away. Enough.'

He leads me along the corridor to the front door and puts on the outside lantern.

'So now you know almost everything.' Tom lingers on the threshold looking for some solace, searching my face to see if I think less of him now that he has been revealed as a child hitter. But I am anxious to be gone now, from his past, his war, his empty house and the litany of disappointment and failure.

'Thank you for the tea.'

He does not reply but draws himself up with a deep

breath as if an extension to his full height might restore some dignity.

'Drive safely now,' he says looking down his beaked nose at me but the effect is curiously ironic and I wonder if he intends this as a joke. I turn and crunch down the gravel. Jack scampers alongside and then stops halfway down the slope. I reach the end of the light pool from the house and tread more slowly on the uneven ground where the drive is cracked and broken. Jack sits watching as I start the engine and make my way slowly down the dark narrow drive.

14

NICOLA STEPS INTO MY OFFICE and closes the door behind her.

'You've been on my mind all weekend.' She leans back against the door. 'You know me, Caro. I prefer to come at things head on.'

I rise from the chair and she turns towards me, a feverish tint to her cheeks.

On Friday afternoon she had stopped me as I was leaving a meeting in her office and asked, 'Is everything all right?' She was standing by the window so I couldn't see her eyes, just the pursed concern of her lips.

'Fine. Why do you ask?'

'There's something we need to talk about.'

'Anything wrong?' I said and she did not immediately answer, an uncharacteristic hesitancy.

'That depends,' she said looking down and we both stared at her swollen tummy as if there might be something to see through the flesh wall.

'I've got a doctor's appointment,' she checked her watch. 'I guess it can wait till Monday,' and she said goodbye with a new searching look, the kind you might give a worrisome child, wondering if it's safe to leave them unsupervised. I walked the long way back to my room, past the lift doors and the open-plan Friday hum, stopped to rest a hot palm on the water cooler. Unsure how to proceed.

'Oh, sit down, Caro, for God's sake,' Nicola flaps a hand and I sink back into my chair. She sits opposite, slides a plastic file towards me that I do not recognise.

'I don't like uncertainty. I like to know what's going on.' She smacks her hand on the file, but without opening it, I know.

'Pure fluke that it came up at all. I was round my brother's for dinner on Thursday and of course Michele was there. Yakking on about her time in the office, how loss adjusting was much more interesting than she'd expected, how much she enjoyed going to the meeting with you, how nice you were, etcetera, etcetera. So of course I'm listening with only half an ear and then she starts telling this story about the girl with the nasty boyfriend and the lost video camera. How this Anna Murray was in tears, how you asked Michele to step out of the room to get a glass of water and when she came back, the camera was miraculously found. Right in the middle of a meeting.' She flings her hands up in the air, shakes her head at me and looks away.

'Maybe I'm a bit over-sensitive at the moment. I don't know but I lay in bed that night thinking it over. I'm not sleeping very well anyway at the moment, can't get comfortable now so close to the end. Something about the story just bothered me. I've never had any reason to doubt your professionalism before, Caro. So I checked the file on Friday and it's all in order. Claimant cancelled. Your report confirms the missing camera was found.' She shrugs, fixes me with a frank stare. Studies my face as if there was something she needed to commit to memory or something that she could not decode. 'So why do I have a problem?'

I cannot hold her gaze but look away out the window at my jagged edge and a silent rain dribbling down the glass.

'Caro,' she raps the desk. 'Believe me, now is not the time to do your silent act. You have to give me something here. You have to open up. Otherwise I think the worst.'

I nod, fumble with the idea of lying and then let it go. 'OK.'

'Did Anna Murray make a false claim?'

'Yes.'

'And you didn't refer it.'

'She cancelled the claim.'

'At your suggestion?'

'No. I didn't tell her what to do. I told her that sometimes people cancel their claims because things get found.'

'Her claim was false and she admitted that to you.'

'Yes.'

'And the correct procedure is that you report this to Claims and they take it from there.'

'Yes.'

'So you cut a corner. Bent the rules. You didn't report it. You let her bury it.'

'Yes.'

'*Why?*'

'I don't know.'

'Not good enough,' she snaps. 'Have you done this before?'

'No. Never.'

'Have you been playing God?'

'*No.*'

Nicola lowers her head, brooding, turning over this burden of knowledge. Moves her hand slowly over the bump as if she is scanning for a signal. I imagine the child snug and warm and dozing to the steady thump of her heart.

'I really do not need this right now. I'm going in a few

weeks, supposed to be leaving you at the wheel. There is no room for you to become a liability, Caro. I need a caretaker I can trust.'

'You can.'

She grips the chair arms with both hands and pushes herself up, walks over to the window, shaking her head at the darkening view. 'I still don't know how you stand this bloody office. That *thing* cutting into your light.'

'I'm used to it now.'

'It's got bad karma or something,' she mutters and turns to face me, hands by her side.

'Look, the rule break is a trivial thing in itself, Caro. But what really concerns me is *why*? Why would you do that? What does it *mean*? I'm not going to ask you to explain, I know you won't tell me what's going on. You never do give anything away, do you?'

'It was a one-off, Nicola.'

'I know.'

'I – have had a lot on my mind, I guess. I mean, outside of work.'

'I guessed, you've been preoccupied. Distant. You know you can always talk to me? I'm always here for you.'

I nod. She approaches the desk. The flush is gone now, her face white with greenish half-moons under her eyes.

'When you were a little girl, did you ever play that game where you fall backwards and trust your friend will be there to catch you?'

She stands, waiting. This is the moment for me to freefall but I am caught looking down at an unscalable height. I fold my hands, one palm on top of the other. There is too much and too little to say and my eyes sting with tears that cannot fall.

'Maybe you've got someone else you can talk to,' she says, with a rueful smile. 'But there is something you need to deal with. I want you to take a couple of days off.'

'I don't need to.'

'Take them anyway,' Nicola picks up the file.

'What are you going to do with that?'

She slips out the pages and holds them out to me. 'You know I felt like such a sneak checking up on you.' I stand up and take them and move round to her side of the desk.

'Bin them,' she grips me by the shoulders. 'And try to go easy on yourself,' she pats my cheek. 'You know where I am.'

15

WHEN I PICKED HIM UP at 5 a.m. this morning he was standing at the foot of his drive. I could see him peering into my headlights as I turned onto the road, flagging me down, as if it would have been possible not to recognise this tall figure with a battered leather satchel on the deserted road. Tom had dressed for the trip: a felt trilby for the occasion that sat too low as if his head had shrunk and which, together with the long belted overcoat in a dull brown, gave him the look of a secret agent adrift after the Cold War.

'I would have driven straight up to the house, you know,' I said as he opened the door and placed the satchel on the back seat. 'You didn't need to stand out here in the dark.'

'It's a tricky turning.'

'I did it before, remember?'

'Cars often stall on that sharp bend.'

'You manage it well enough in the Jeep.'

We set off for Newhaven in silence.

'Where's Jack?'

'My domestic.'

'Will she walk him?'

'She doesn't walk. She will let him out in the garden.'

'I'm sure he'll be fine.'

'He wouldn't eat breakfast this morning.'

I imagine Jack turning his head away in disgust at some unscheduled break in the routine that might herald disaster. The door closing that might never open again.

'He'll eat it later. Don't worry.'

'I'm not at all worried. Jack may do as he pleases. It's all the same to me.'

'You don't mean that.'

'Drive, girl. It's too early for chit-chat.'

And he settled back in the seat with a grim twist of his lips as if he was being press-ganged into this journey that he had apparently always wanted to make.

'I suppose you've been to visit the war graves,' I'd said the last time I saw him and was intrigued to find he hadn't. 'Dieppe is only a day trip from Newhaven, you know. People your age go on booze cruises all the time.'

But this outing has all the insanity of a drunken promise, it is my misplaced spontaneity that has the two of us teamed up for a cross-channel nostalgia jaunt to visit the war graves of Dieppe. Or perhaps it is a desperate attempt to distract myself from the crippling hysteria that has gripped me as I count down to next week's meeting with Cormac. And now here we are, the two of us flung together like mismatched gloves, off on the high seas on an ill-fated adventure chasing Tom's childhood heroes. A cold winter day with a querulous old stranger who should be at home with his cranky terrier or playing with his war model or beached in front of the TV or whatever it is that a bitter old man does when he is finally left with nothing to do but contemplate the ruin of his own life: a dead wife, a son and a dog who despise him.

The drive to the coast takes just thirty minutes and even as we join the queue for the ferry he sits with his hat still on, staring straight ahead at the gaping bow doors. 'Looking forward to it?' I say and cut the engine but there is no sign that he has heard me or perhaps it is simply his usual habit of ignoring questions that he chooses not to answer. So we sit, both of us locked in the darkness, memory spinning like a wheel.

'Let's go, Caro, let's go to France now,' I hear Estelle's whine, head dangling over the railings there to the side watching the cars inch up the ramp. 'Please, please,' she begs, I grab her wrist and drag her away. She scratches at my arm but I hold firm, I am losing patience with her whims in the grip of this new distraction. Since that day on the beach at Newhaven I exist in the twilight of frustration and desire. It is like hypnosis, I feel nothing but Cormac's touch. I turn on the kitchen tap and leave it running, staring out the window. Sitting in class sucking on a biro unaware that ink is spilling into my mouth; lying in bed at night in the darkness, the sound of his strumming flooding through the window as I trace his hands over my body, inching lower. I bake in a sun-streaked delirium at a window seat in double maths. I switch socks for tights and then back again for the press of sticky bare thighs underneath my skirt. My form teacher calls me aside and asks if I am all right. 'Look,' she taps the closing paragraph of an essay that ends mid-sentence, as if I had lost concentration – which of course I had. Completely. Slumped dreaming on the page. 'Try to stay focused, Caroline. You've always been an A student.'

It takes some weeks before anything happens. I do not believe all the sad stories girls tell – that the first time is like going to first aid class. Technical failure. Mechanical incompetence. Biological ignorance. Not knowing where things are. Dryness. Premature ejaculation. Jaw ache. Numbed lips. The spectre of pregnancy, the constant fear of adult intrusion as you bungle your way towards release. There was one thing I knew for sure: that sperm made you pregnant. But how close you could get to it without risk was uncertain. Disinformation was traded in giggled conversations at school; if it got on your knickers and somehow travelled; if you swallowed it by accident; if you didn't wash your hands it could stay alive like a virus, even a drop could give you twins. But to fall pregnant was such an outlandish concept that it did not seem at all real to me. The risk of being found out and separated was far more likely.

Early one Saturday in June I slip away while Estelle's mother is cutting her hair in the kitchen, take a bus to town and buy a bra so that I can look in the changing-room mirror and see the shape of a woman in the contour of an A cup. I sweep up my hair and imagine a ball gown with spaghetti straps. Back home I parade my tingling new body around the bedroom, listening through the open window for the sound of Cormac's mother leaving for the shops, his brothers off playing matches. Flying down the stairs, cutting through the hedge, waving to his father who was wheezing the hand mower along the lawn. I slip off my sweatshirt behind the closed bedroom door. Cormac likes the bra, it bestows an air of knowing adulthood, he tugs at the strap with his teeth, mock-biting, fiddles with the hook until he becomes expert and can do it one-handed. There is a pause in the mowing, his father's muffled greeting, the snap of flip-flops on the porch. When I make to get up from the lower bunk, Cormac says 'Wait.'

The door bursts open. Estelle's angry face in the middle of the room, hands thrust in the pockets of her shorts. 'You went out without me,' she stamps her foot. Snatches up the bra from the floor and dangles it accusingly in front of us.

'Lock the door, Estelle,' Cormac says in a new commanding tone, the voice of a captain who steers his crew to safety. She smiles, pleased to be entrusted with this responsibility.

'Sit down,' he says and she settles cross-legged on the floor. Cormac lowers me back down on the pillow. Kisses the skin, the slope down from neck to nipple, his tongue flicking around the astonishing hardness. He breathes in snatches, we breathe together, I feel Estelle creeping closer, hear her sigh and then I hear no more.

I come so easily to his touch.

I discover that desire lays a scent that boys can sniff out. Johnny Pullen licking his lips at me in Geography, the tip of his slow tongue sliding between his lips like a plump worm. Freddy Pitt twangs my bra strap from the seat behind me in RS and is despatched grinning like a hero to the headmaster. A bus stop gang pushes Denis Mackin towards me so that he trips on the kerb and bangs into my arm. 'Sorry, sorry,' his hands flapping, the boys whooping, 'He fancies ya,' his head whipping round 'FUCK OFF' as the bus bears down on us. On the top deck I loll against the glass and count the minutes till I will see Cormac.

Desire leaks from my body, infecting my movements, adjusting my dress. I wear an old school blouse that's a size too small flicked open over my belly button. I buy a second-hand uniform skirt from a classmate's older sister that is two inches shorter than mine and tight around the hips. The next day I am wolf-whistled by the driver of a passing van on my way to school. But this body is like a siren, attracting far too much attention and I must learn not to advertise it on the home front. If my own mother is oblivious, Estelle's mother isn't, nor is the postmistress.

'Growing up so fast, aren't we,' says Mrs Harris with a new tight smile, eyes travelling over my bare shoulders. I run home, throw a jumper over the halter-neck top. And start to dress in layers, loose sweatshirts that I can peel off when we are alone, jeans with lacy knickers underneath.

But we are rarely alone, it is impossible to exclude Estelle without causing a fuss. I lie in bed twisting the corner of the sheet trying to figure a way that the three can be unmade. But any insistence on exclusivity means that Estelle could betray us. 'And they will stop us being together, Caro,' says Cormac, sitting on a stool restringing his guitar. It is true. A trinity is the perfect defence. And so Estelle is almost always there because she is almost always with us. Except for Wednesday afternoons when she has special classes and is never home till eight, but Cormac's house is overrun with older brothers who slam footballs down the hall and barge into the bedroom with their cereal bowls, looking for tapes, scratching their chests, arm-wrestling and catching each other in headlocks.

I lay out homework as cover. We sit side by side, his hand up my skirt, my legs spread, his fingers slipping inside my knickers, when the door is kicked open and his eldest brother strolls in, only missing Cormac's hand slipping away because he is towelling his hair. If we lock the door they will smell a rat. If we start going to my house this change in behaviour could put the adults on high alert and then there would be curfew and monitoring. So we borrow time, fighting disclosure. In our last summer as the weather warms we go to the fields on Wednesday evenings, way down the valley where we lie in the long reeds and do all that we want. Stroll home with bruised lips.

But one evening we arrive just as Estelle climbs out of her mother's car. She stands in the middle of the road watching our approach with a dangerous scowl. 'I know what you've been doing,' she snaps, loud enough for her mother to hear. But her mum is distracted by Harry's mewling, his ice lolly spattered on the pavement, one of her sisters running down the garden shouting that Nan is on the phone. 'I'm telling,' says Estelle. The post office door opens across the street and Mrs Harris steps out, waves and begins to sweep the path in front of the entrance.

'I'm telling Mrs Harris,' says Estelle, hands on hips.

'Stella, Stella,' Cormac murmurs, stepping closer and lifting her hair, whispering something in her ear. Her face brightens into a smile and she stares at me with her chin tilted upwards, her eyes the clearest emptiest blue. And for a moment I see a flash of how she will age. Coldly, dangerously, the blue yellowing into an unseeing white. 'But, Stella,' he says, backing into his front garden, 'sshhhhh.' She reaches out and plucks a grass seed from my jumper, drapes my arm around her shoulders. Mrs Harris leans on her brush and smiles as I follow Estelle into her house.

It rains hard for the next two Wednesdays. On the third I lie on the floor while Estelle flops on her tummy on a beanbag, rolling marbles towards the skirting board. Cormac sits on the edge of the desk practising a blues scale. His eldest brother is singing in the bath down the hall. Their mum and dad are at a PTA meeting and his other brothers are out. Estelle crawls over on all fours in dog play and straddles my legs, pressing her nail-sharp knees onto my thighs. 'Oww, that hurts,' she switches position to sit heavily astride my legs, pushes up my sweatshirt and drags her long hair over my stomach. 'Stop, that tickles,' I say as she traces her fingertip around my face, over the chin, down the throat. 'Get off, Estelle,' I swallow on a confusion of sensations even as I turn to glance at Cormac who is watching, fingers working their way up along the fret, nodding his assent to the proceedings or the music as she pushes my shirt ever higher, slides the pockets of my bra down, my nipples hardening in the cool air or the drift of her fingers. 'I said get *off*, Estelle,' but my voice is weak and hoarse, the music stops, the guitar clatters on the ground and Cormac kneels behind me. 'Sshh now, Caro. Sshh,' he slips the sweatshirt over my head, folds my arms back, runs his hands along the inside, laying them out splayed cruciform, Estelle's tongue licking harder now, her knees pressing down on my thighs and I say 'No,' but Cormac covers my mouth with his. I keep my eyes closed tight and he holds my arms wide and I am wet and Estelle is whimpering and then his mouth leaves mine and I open my eyes to see Cormac jerking forwards in a quick rhythm, hand thrust inside his jeans as he stares not at me but at Estelle's hand inside her shorts. They kneel like statues frozen in each other's gaze. I sit up and push her off, grab my top. The bath is draining, water gurgling down the pipes as his brother crosses the hallway into his room and the door slams behind me.

'Bloody tourists,' Tom casts about scowling. The café on the middle deck is warm with chatter and full of senior citizens who look as if this is a home from home. At the table to our right three women are tucking in to full breakfasts while a fourth sits with a cup of tea, clutching her handbag on her lap, pale and silent and faintly disapproving as if there was a bad smell. Sea sickness perhaps, or nausea brought on by all this eating. Behind me there is talk of wine and cheese.

'So would it be better if they were all having a miserable time?'

'Pah,' spits Tom. 'The last generation to bear witness. The last ones to appreciate the debt we owe. And look at them, like pigs with their heads in a trough.'

'This is a booze cruise, not a pilgrimage.'

He looks away, pinching his thin lips. This sour mood was evident as soon as we came to a halt on the car deck and he'd started fussing with his satchel, whether or not it would be safe to leave in the car. Already there was a heaving to the grey water.

'What's in it?' I asked him.

'Items,' he snapped, fiddling with the straps. 'Maps, binoculars.'

'Are you on a special mission?' I had to suppress the urge to giggle but it was the wrong thing to say. He froze in the open door and glared at me.

'Lighten up, Tom,' I said. 'It's only a day trip.'

'Actually,' I push my coffee to one side, 'I was going to buy a book to bone up on Dieppe. But I thought why bother, seeing as I have an expert guide.'

'You mean you didn't even look it up on the internet?'

I laugh but it is a thin wavering noise that doesn't fool him for a second. He stares at me shrewdly from underneath sprouting brows.

'OK, I admit, I did look it up. A quick five minutes before I left the office.'

'And?'

'Dieppe: August 19th 1942. Of the 6,000 Allied troops who landed only 1,128 made it back to England. Most of those killed were Canadian soldiers. The RAF lost more planes that day than on any other day in the whole of the Second World War. Variously described as tragic, disastrous, controversial. In short, a fiasco. I am already expecting a story of bungling and mismanagement. Have I missed anything?'

'Your generation thrives on soundbites and misinformation.'

'Oh, here we go.'

'You have been everywhere on your computers. You know it all and you know nothing.'

'You're very full of yourself for someone who spends all his time playing war games.'

I hold my breath, watching the grim press of his lips.

'Touché,' he says and I exhale.

'I'm sorry. That was rude.'

'Why do you always worry about insulting me?'

'Because,' I shrug, twisting the mug.

'Because I am an old man. And you think you should let me say what I want and then go off and roll your eyes behind my back.'

'It feels – inappropriate.'

'You think seventy-three years of survival doesn't bring resilience? You think the prize for surviving should be the kind of indulgence you would lavish on babies and tod-dlers?'

'I hadn't thought of it that way.'

'Well, perhaps now you will, Caroline. And you will under-stand how dull it is to be treated like an emotional cripple.'

'I consider myself rebuked.'

Tom nods, all business. But the telling-off has revived him. He has perked up, a touch of colour steals across his cheeks.

'Well then,' he slaps both hands on the tabletop. 'I will tell you the story of Dieppe. It will be my little contribution to the war effort – keeping the history alive.' He dons his trilby and picks up his gloves. 'Of course I suppose you've seen the movie?'

'What movie?'

And he bursts out laughing, a great crack of merriment that turns the heads of the women at the table across the way.

'To the upper deck,' he cries. 'Ladies,' he spins round and gallantly doffs his hat, bowing at the delighted foursome who giggle and smile as he makes his way towards the exit.

Dawn steals across the rolling sea. High up a lone star spar-kles in the graduated blue that bleeds into a peach horizon. And there are no breakers now, the water glitters with the promise of a clear crisp day. We find a sheltered spot at the rear upper deck by the funnel and watch the lights of England recede from view.

'This would have been the last view for the British Commandos and the Cameron Highlanders,' Tom points at the vanishing coastline. 'Little groups of twenty-five men packed into wooden assault craft called Eurekas. August 19th 1942. A warm summer's night and a very choppy and uncomfortable ride. They would have felt every buffeting wave but at least it was quicker and it took them straight to the beaches. But this was not the route Jimmy took. The Royals sailed out of Portsmouth on the *Queen Emma* and the *Princess Astrid* – old passenger ships that were used for troop transport. Six thousand men in a flotilla under cover of darkness, all heading for northern France, following the sea path cut for them by the minesweepers. All set to land on different beaches in and around Dieppe and all to link up in the end. At least that was the plan.'

I look back to England, hold up my thumb and erase a whole country. The sky is lightening, glowing pink now at the water's edge. Tom beckons me to the side and peers over the rail, one hand holding onto his hat. The wind whips about our heads and jangles some distant bell, the swell is steady, wave after advancing wave folding into one another on the rising tide.

'I can picture Jimmy holding his breath as they sail through the German minefields at 2 a.m. The shadow of the destroyers, the silence, the excitement, the rush. There is no moon. Perfect weather conditions with high tide at 0403, visibility 700 metres, wind velocity 2 south-south-east. Everything is going so well. The engines throb beneath him and Jimmy is dreaming of the headlines back home, Alice reading the *Toronto Globe*, scanning the pictures, for there would be photos. The first Canadians to see action in France. His grandmother had given him a little silver cross that he sewed inside the breast pocket of his tunic. I often think of that.'

A strip of streaked cloud breaks away from the grey blanket that squats on the eastern horizon, just enough to block the first glimpse of the sun. I look up at the guiding star that the wise kings followed, it is growing fainter now but I will watch it and see where it leads.

'The attack was supposed to happen at nautical twilight. "A little darkness, a lot of surprise." That meant no night bombing in advance. Once the landings were under way the RAF would provide air cover and take out some of the big guns in and around Dieppe. The 554 men in the Royals, including Jimmy – together with the Black Watch and a few Commandos – were heading for Blue Beach which was one mile to the east of the town. A flank attack that would pave the way for the main assault on the town beaches. They would sail into silence and darkness and take out "Rommel", the big gun battery high up on the cliffs a mile east of the town.

'At 0320 the *Queen Emma* is ten miles off the shoreline and our boys start to lower the landing craft into the water. Lieutenant Colonel Catto is in charge. It's dark, the men move as quickly as they can, but they are carrying fifty or sixty pounds on their backs and it takes time to get everything in position. So they are running late, all the unloading is taking longer than expected. The landing craft are lining up and Catto is edgy, he checks his watch, he checks the sky, it is getting lighter by the second. They are due to land at 0450 and they are behind schedule.'

Tom turns his back on the water and leans against the railing, frowning at the lifeboats hoisted above our heads as if he has spotted some irregularity in the configuration. He takes off his hat and turns it about in his hand examining the band, wisps of white hair blowing about his skull.

'The last part is a cock-up. The landing craft follow the wrong gunboat, so they have to turn around to regroup and then they take a route into shore that brings them in sight of the enemy on the main beaches. They are sixteen minutes late. *Officially*. According to an account given later by Lieutenant Catto they were actually thirty-five minutes late. An enemy destroyer had already stumbled on some Commandos in the flotilla an hour earlier and the Germans were on high alert. The attacks on the other beaches have already begun, it is almost daylight by the time they reach Blue Beach and the enemy is expecting them.

'The firing starts before the Royals even get off the craft. There are trenches with heavy guns dug in at the bottom of cliffs that are over a hundred feet high. There are pillboxes with machine-gun nests halfway up the cliff face and at the very top is a big white house with guns blasting out through the windows. Bodies pile up on the ramps. Out of 150 men in the first wave, only fifteen make it to the sea wall. Catto watches the disaster unfold.

'Jimmy is in the second wave. He jumps down over the side on the double, takes his place at the starboard side. Catto is there too, he's in the craft with Jimmy looking out at the bloodbath that awaits them. His bodyguard shouts that they should get the hell out of here, but orders are orders and they plough on. The landing craft are open at the front and there is no overhead shelter so if you're sitting in the centre you have no protection. There is steel decking just above Jimmy's head and he shrinks beneath it under a crush of comrades. Their machine guns have a range of 500 yards but they are no match for the German guns that can fire 1,200 rounds a minute. That's twenty bullets every second – ten times faster than the Allies' Brens! Jimmy would have seen bullets shatter the steel helmets, men collapsing all around him as they bump against the shore. One fellow has his eye blown clean out of its socket, another grabs at his stomach trying to push his guts back in. They sprawl and fold in front of him. The lucky ones are killed instantly. Die on the boats without ever setting foot on French soil.'

Tom turns away again and looks down over the rail, holding the hat with both hands. I knead my fingers in the lining of my gloves and stamp my feet, hear him mutter something swallowed by wind and water. I lean in closer, he is singing in a thin tuneless voice.

For when the dawn comes up,
There'll be bluebirds over the white cliffs of Dover, Tomorrow
just you wait and see,
There'll be love and laughter and peace ever after,
Tomorrow when the world is free.

He clamps the hat down low on his head and peers down at my face, his nose whipped red.

'Good Lord, have I set you off?'

'It's just the wind.'

'Beth always used to cry at the cinema. I used to pass her my handkerchief and then I refused to take her any more. Go with your girlfriends, I'd say, if there's going to be tears.' Tom slips his arm through mine and leads us across the deck. 'It's a form of theft, you know, crying over other people's stories. Very Keatsian. Very silly. Hnnh. But I am learning to tolerate emotional display. A little late perhaps.'

16

HE COUGHS AND WHEN HE IS NOT coughing he is wheezing and sighing at my driving as we round a bend on this interminable coast road that might as well be England, apart from the signs. When he thinks I am going too slow Tom sucks the air through his teeth. When it is too fast he presses his fingers hard against the dashboard and shoots me sidelong glances of disapproval that I ignore. The Channel broods sluggish and malevolent below us on the right. He has the map on his knee while I jut my jaw against the windscreen.

It is Puys he wants to see, site of the Blue Beach landing. He is impatient now, straining against the seat belt and glaring through the windscreen as if there is something offensive about the surroundings. He fiddles with the radio controls, twiddles the tuner until a burst of French blares through the static and he switches it off. When we finally landed he was fidgety and crabby, all the good humour fled. I insisted on stopping for a decent coffee and he sat at the café table like a rod-backed general, shook his head at a croissant. A young girl arrived with the offer of more tea.

'Why do you refuse to speak a single word of French?' I asked while he scowled at his cup.

'I don't speak the language.'

'You could say *merci*. You could say *s'il vous plaît*. It's not that difficult.'

He shrugged.

'You just don't like the French,' I jibed. 'Your generation think they threw in the towel, don't you?' But this needling did not produce the desired effect and he fixed me with a contemptuous stare, the blue eyes bulging.

'What do you know about what I think? Your generation believes it has it all worked out.'

Despite the shirt collar and tie and the V-neck there is something tatty about his appearance. His hair is limp against his skull and sometimes he appears to wince for no apparent reason. Through the corner of my eye I notice a palsied nodding which he seems unable to control and which lends him a new air of fragility, as if his head is about to snap at the neck. Little signs of slippage, of old age squeezing him in a firm embrace. Tom might be into the home run or perhaps it is his sudden distaste for my charity mission, perhaps I come over like a volunteer who bothers friendless old people with witless chat, little gestures of cold cheer driven by an urge to disguise the discomfort of pity.

'Here, here,' he shouts as I cruise past a turning. 'It was there,' he twists and points. 'You've missed it.'

'All right, all right. Keep your shirt on. I'll turn round when I can.'

'Let's come here early tomorrow,' he says as I pull into the car park. 'Very early in the morning, just like it would have been.' He flings the seat belt back unleashing a new vigour.

'You mean a sort of re-enactment?'

'Exactly.' He grips my hand, the leather glove is soft and sleepy. A flush blooms along his cheekbones.

'But it's the wrong time of year.'

'Yes yes,' he shakes his head dismissively. 'We can adjust for all that. Sunrise will be about 7.30.'

'The light will be all wrong. It was August. And we'd have to stay over.' I'm not sure about this caper, not at all convinced about the therapeutic value of reconstructions. It is something I come across at work when the client wanders back to the scene and their distress rises all over again. Some new detail recovered with each repetition – the way the fire brigade gave a badge to their little boy, the way the neighbours came out with mugs of tea, the tattoo they swore they saw on the side of the perpetrator's neck, the glint of the ring when they opened the box.

'You don't have to if you don't want to,' he withdraws his hand like a petulant child. 'I'll stay by myself.'

'You haven't got a car.'

'They have taxis in France,' he says and jerks open the door.

'Let me take your photo,' I suggest. Tom stops still, frowns. 'Come on, it'll be a souvenir for you. Stand there, see?' He sidles over to the cemetery gate, takes off a glove and puts it on again. He is gamely trying to pose without knowing where to look.

'Look into the camera,' I say and he spins towards me, a mild panic transforming his features into decrepitude in the viewfinder. This is not how he will want to remember himself. 'No, actually. Turn your head a little bit away. Look at the plaque and I'll do a side profile.' This relaxes him, he can concentrate on reading the engraved script. The wind blows back his hair and whitens his face, lends the shot a certain dignity in the viewfinder. I switch on the flash.

A busload of teenage schoolchildren is assembling into some sort of formation inside the entrance to the cemetery. They are quiet, none of the usual jockeying, and their backpacks carry a red maple leaf and the words Victoria County

Choir. A teacher steps in front and raises his hand and they burst into song that stops us in our tracks. It is the Canadian anthem, I can tell by Tom's sudden rigid bearing. There is a furious blinking among the boys and the conductor battles bravely on against a trembling lip. Beside us a little girl in a navy coat holds an older woman's hand and watches curiously. She points and speaks into the old woman's lowered ear. The woman pats her cheek. Two sopranos wobble tearfully on the high notes. At the end the stillness roars in our ears and the choir collapses into one another's arms. A fat girl with long hair and a visible roll of midriff beneath her fleece clings to a tall boy with enormous trainers. The choir starts piling into the bus.

Tom is rooted to the spot, clutching his satchel. I touch his elbow and he turns his head slowly and steps forward. We walk without stopping, threading through the V formation of white crosses, row upon row of numbered markers that stretch out across this garden of death. I try to imagine a thousand bodies blown to bits. A few rows at Wembley mown down. Half the contents of a Tube train. The population of my secondary school. I have seen these numbers assembled. When I try to picture this graveyard as the battlefield it once was, all the screen footage rolls into one – the shells, the whistling, the flashes, the body parts catapulted into the air – but it is really just the lines of crosses that I see.

We are getting closer to the sea, the waves audible now and the wind whipping up. A couple of plucky palm trees stand like misplaced props in the mouth of the cliff path and I follow Tom down. I stay close, tracking each of his careful steps, a slow sideways progress down the bumpy track. When we finally make it to the beach, he stands twisting his binoculars, the satchel at his feet, while I walk along the water's edge. It is a low mean heave, a listless sea that hasn't the heart to swell a decent breaker and shrinks back from the shore leaving a stinking tangle of seaweed on the stones: a lifeless crab, a flip-flop, a plastic bottle, a frayed length of rope. It is the unidentifiable objects that stop you in your tracks: the stiff fingers of a rubber glove protruding from the sand, the lumpen bundle of clothing that looks from a certain distance like a small corpse, the dripping bin liner that might be stuffed with body parts, the voluptuous curve of a bloodstained hip that turns out to be a piece of driftwood. It is dog walkers who find the really gory stuff, mad border collies unearthing gruesome discoveries left by the receding tide. A huddle of seabirds chatter on the stones up ahead and bobbing further out is the black S-curve of a cormorant. As I edge closer an alert ripples through the flock and the birds rise away from me, a brown ascent with a startling white flash as they cut a collective dip.

I remember a beach trip from years ago, a holiday for Estelle's family with me as add-on. Bird prints littered the damp morning sand, cinder-coloured crags jutted over a proliferation of rock pools. Clusters of baby mussels clung fast to the rocks, their indigo shells glinting in the sun. We found sea anemones like glistening plums and I showed Estelle how to press close to the centre spy hole and deflate the plump jelly till a thin jet of water spurted out. 'That dries them out, you know. Kills them,' warned a passing fisherman, a wading suit buttoned over his shoulders like a babygro. 'So what?' Estelle squared up to him in her shiny green swimsuit, pale and scrawny as a dried fish, her face belligerent in shadow and he backed away, sensing what people sometimes did – her indefinable difference, a petulance that would quickly degenerate into an extraordinary rage rarely seen in someone so young.

Dune grass spiked our calves as we ran. A red kite bobbed overhead as we lay scissor-legged on dry sand, pricking little twigs of driftwood between our fingers. Forget-me-nots grew in crevices and Estelle plucked, methodically deflowering every one she could find until the green stalks stood denuded. 'He loves me, he loves me not, he loves me, he loves me not.'

'Leave them there,' I said. 'They look pretty.'

'No. I want them all.'

How did I ever learn to acquiesce? To deflect, and, like a boxer, to take the blows. To submit, like a trained puppy.

That evening on the emptying beach we stood with our backs to the sea staring at what seemed to be a girl lying on her stomach at the foot of the dunes, long blonde hair flopped forwards over a bent head. 'Look, look,' Estelle shouted, running ahead, pointing with her spade at what was in fact a bale of straw blackened by sea water with a tuft of golden stalks dangling like a ponytail over the edge. She kicked and it tumbled forwards. We ran seawards across the evening shore, sand ridges pressed hard under my feet, and we stopped to stare at a stranded jellyfish. Hunkered down to study its transparency, its coloured heart glowing in the fading light.

'Is it dead?' Estelle bent down, hair skimming my cheek.

'I don't know. Maybe it's waiting for the tide to come in.'

She edged a toe closer.

'Don't!' I warned. 'They can sting really badly,' but in a single movement she whacked her metal spade into its sapphire heart. The jelly wobbled, sand flew up and covered its split form.

'What d'you do that for?'

She straightened up. Her eyes a clear guiltless blue. Shrugged a shoulder, the strap of her swimsuit slipping down.

'I hate you,' I said. 'You're so mean for no reason.'

The smile disappeared, her smooth white forehead folded into a deep frown.

'You do horrible things,' I sniffed, as tears sprang hot on

my face. I turned away, wiped my nose with the back of my hand just as the spade whipped through the air. My screams brought adults and eventually Estelle's mother who wrapped my hand in a towel and drove me to the hospital, clutching the steering wheel, every now and again patting my bare leg with a stifled sob. Blood seeped through the yellow towel and onto my shorts, trickled onto the car seat. 'You're very brave, Caroline.' Estelle sat humming in the back seat, oblivious to her mother's vicious stares in the rear-view mirror.

They gave me tetanus injections in Casualty. I sucked on glucose sweets while the nurse stroked my hair. I heard Estelle shout a protest in the waiting area, running footsteps and the curtain snatched back. 'Caro. I want to see.' Her mother's restraining hand.

'It's OK,' I said.

'Hold still now,' said the doctor without moving his head. Estelle leaned forward on the plastic chair, a concentrated smile of wonder on her lips.

'They just sew you up again,' she murmured.

The doctor slowly stitched the hand that saved my face. A faint scar still snakes across the back all the way up my ring finger knuckle.

This was not the day they had back in 1942. A cloud mass on the horizon is breaking now into some hideous apparition, a side profile of a monstrous jaw that could eat the chilly sun. Frosted sand crystals cling to the shadowed stone, here where the sun never reaches, where the soldiers crouched, clutching at the cliff base. It is clear the beach is a death trap, just 250 yards long with towering cliffs. And there is nowhere to hide. A twelve-foot high sea wall spans the entire length and Tom has told me that the only two exits were mined and blocked with huge coils of barbed wire. I stand facing

the swell, imagine the bow doors opening and Jimmy falling
out, ducking into six feet of water. There are bodies lying on
the shoreline. When he surfaces he looks back and already
the ramp of the landing craft is filled with the dead. There
is only one option, to wade forward and run, so that is what
he does. He runs and drops and runs and drops just like he
was trained and somehow grace is with him. Bullets rico-
chet off the stones at his feet but Jimmy slips unhurt through
a strafe of machine-gun fire, leaping over pulverised bodies
and limbs. He veers off to the right, to the side exit from
the beach. He doesn't go for the sea wall at the base of the
cliffs, he had decided this before they even landed. Gunners
in pillboxes have the whole wall covered and they are picking
off the soldiers one by one. The snipers are ordered to take
out officers and radio operators. Jimmy reaches the barbed
wire coiled at the base of the steps and flings himself down
on the ground. Piles of dead on top of each other, shredded
limbs dangling on the wire. He knows his only chance is to
get off the beach.

But Jimmy needs to blow the wire – you set a charge and
detonate, but he doesn't have one, or it doesn't work. Either
way he is trapped. If he moves he will be gunned down like
that fellow with his face impaled on the spikes. He sneaks a
look behind him, his head low on the ground. There is movement in the smoke. He decides to play dead until a better
alternative presents itself. He will lie still here amongst the
dead and the dying and not listen to their screams and maybe,
just maybe, the Germans will not guess he is alive. They are
running along the cliff edges now, dropping grenades on
survivors. Then minutes later men fling themselves down
around him. It is Catto and a few others and Jimmy is overjoyed, there is some hope, now that he is not alone. He sees
that Catto is wounded, blood drips from his sleeve, but the
men have a charge or they have something that will do the

job and within minutes there is a blast and a breach in the wire and Catto waves them through a barrage of gunfire: one, two, three, four men. Jimmy scrambles to his feet to follow but is flung face forward, pinned spreadeagled on the wire. Through the smoke he sees Catto and the men slipping ahead up the steps but Jimmy cannot move, his chest is ripped open by a hail of bullets, his cheeks are stuck on the wire so that he cannot even look down at the blood spilling out of him. He catches a final glimpse of Catto and the men who will make it – they are climbing quickly upward, they will battle on to the top and take cover and hours later be captured.

But for the moment Jimmy does not know that. He only knows that Alice is still fast asleep now in the dark Canadian night and dreaming, she reaches out to touch him but Jimmy is already gone.

I look about for Tom and see him scrambling up the steps in a harsh wind. The weather is changing, a sharp drop in temperature and a menacing cluster of grey cloud above us. 'Be careful,' I call out but my warning is lost in the wind. I remember a guy at work who told me he took his grandfather to see Spielberg's version of the Normandy landings. His grandfather said the real thing was much worse than the movie, but he still cried. He was crying for the blokes he remembered, he said. He remembered one of them shitting himself, the smell of shit as they rocked towards the shore. My colleague said he wouldn't take an old man to see a war movie ever again. Like maybe I shouldn't take an old man on a grave hunt. Who knows what Tom's heart rate is hitting now.

He has clearly forgotten I am here. He is bareheaded, the trilby crushed in his hand, a bald patch on the back of his skull that I have never noticed before. I follow behind him to where a pillbox clings like a limpet to the rock. He pauses, looks inside and I approach, bend down behind him and see the square of sea framed in the lookout, the view as they picked them off, training their gun sights on the arriving craft. Out on the steely horizon a tanker plods its way like a fat slug across a straight path. I will not step inside, it is the fear of unspeakables. When I look up Tom is gone, off again like a hobbled goat down the slope, gathering pace until he accelerates and trips over on the beach. Oh Jesus, he is down and pushing on his hand against the stones. He picks up the satchel and braces himself against the wind. I hurry after, closing the gap as he travels more carefully now, struggling to keep his balance. The back of his coat dusted with sand.

I wrap the scarf balaclava-style around my head and neck. Tom presses on, his long lean body slanted into the wind with the stubbornness of a child. He is looking for the end and the beginning of things at the water's edge, waves seething at his feet. The hat is off again, thin hair fuzzing, white-lipped and blanched. He is replaying the landing in his head: the dark towers, the coiled beast of barbed wire, the certain annihilation that faced them at dawn. I stand a little off to the side and he is back blown now, the oversized coat bunched in front of him, one hand deep in the pocket as he steadies himself against the wind. I would like to hurry back to my car and hit the nearest bar rather than crunch along this massacre site. He turns and takes a few wild steps to the right and starts to walk slowly along the shore.

Dieppe 1942: even the sound is final. The little I read sums it up as a botched job. Like sending on the dancing girls to distract the audience from the real plot.

Tom told me it was all over by 11 a.m. Landing craft dispatched to scan Blue Beach reported no signs of life and an hour later the carriers sailed for home. The Germans would not allow captured soldiers to return to the beach to gather up the wounded, so fearful were they of an air attack. And so the wounded and the dying lay here on the stones listening to each others' groans as the noonday sun blazed and the afternoon tide crept in and out and the bloody water inched closer. The sea lapped at their feet, tugged at their legs, seeped into their battledress, bubbles hissing and fizzing. Those who were able tried to drag themselves further up, those entangled on barbed wire drifted in and out of wakefulness, stung by the slap of cold water that would numb them eventually, shifting the bodies that lay on the ground, lurching against the sharp stones until they found themselves weightless. Perhaps they too saw the beginnings of a star guiding them towards an end. But I do not think so. I do not think they saw anything as the water flooded their nostrils and they flapped their butchered limbs, choking on their own blood and the blood of others and the salt water that closed over and dragged them weighted down into the blackness. Corpses bob heavily, staining the tide. I have seen this on screen.

Up overhead my star has disappeared now, swallowed up by the grubby shade that this November sky has settled for. I do not remember what the wise men did when the star vanished.

Two black birds chase each other across the water. Another larger one soars overhead and dives down to ride the waves, scanning for something only they can see. Beyond the white crests the sea is deathly grey and only a final glow of light separates it from the sky. This is not like any other sea, this is one to cure you of all previous impressions of majesty and beauty. A white snowflake drifts down and lands on the stones at my feet. I look around and sure enough a snow shower is thickening all about my head. The flakes are large and unevenly sized and they are suddenly cascading down. The wind shifts and it is transformed into a slanted storm and visibility has dropped. All above me there are no cloud breaks, how quickly this shutdown has come upon us. I look over to the sea wall but Tom has disappeared. I start to run, imagine him fallen and unfindable, hidden by some rocks fading into the grey. The sea keeps up its constant angry roar, all this noise rising to a menacing climax with each breaking wave.

He is slumped against the side of the car. I am breathless and busy admonishing him as I open the door but Tom lets this flow round him like a man finally defeated by events. His face is pale and wretched beneath the hat, his fingers fail to engage the handle so I reach in front of him and he levers himself with a new difficulty into the passenger seat. I watch through the corner of my eye as he fumbles with the belt, his hands trembling inside thick leather gloves. I start the engine and turn the heater up to full blast. What he needs is a restorative drink. I will take him to some warm café for a reviving cognac to banish the chill. At a glance I see that his chin is sunk down into his scarf and his eyes almost closed. There will be no dawn reveille tomorrow.

'Let's go for a drink,' I say brightly. 'I'll find a nice bar.'

He shakes his head.

'It'll warm us up.'

'No,' he says, soft and slow and final. A tour bus with a GB sticker grinds past and sways down the hill. The snow spatter melts in rivers down the windscreen and I switch on the wipers.

'Would do you good.'

His hands lie limp on his lap. I reach out and touch his forearm, am shocked to feel the sharp spike of bone like a rod inside the padded sleeve.

'Or perhaps we could just go home.'

He nods and finally closes his eyes.

. . . . .

Rain streams across the windscreen when we disembark at Newhaven. Tom's head lolls in the rest. The passing beams of cars cast his side profile in a sickly glow. He could expire right here in my passenger seat and I would not know. His muffler remains intact, his hands are folded on his lap and his coat is buttoned despite the heater. He sleeps intermittently, chin sunk into his breastbone, but when I pull up outside his house at 1 a.m. he begins to speak without opening his eyes.

'I must finish the story and tell you the end. I was thinking of the day we moved back into the house after the War. My mother and my father and myself. August 13th 1945. I was due to go away to school the next week. Just like the very first time, my father took us up the drive in the car. But this time my mother just sat quietly in the front with a forced smile. My father carried in a few bags and then told us to come down onto the lawn. "What for?" I asked but he snapped his fingers and said come along.

'We stood on the edge of the grass and watched my father come out of the shed with an axe in his hand. "Stand over there," he said and we moved to the spot he indicated, a little further down the drive just before the big bend at the gate. He walked over to the sentry box and with one almighty swing he split the side right open. "NO!" I shouted out and lunged forward but my mother grabbed my arm. My father stopped and glared at her, his face was very red. "This is for you, my dear," he said in a strangled sort of shout.

'She stood very still staring into the middle distance as if there was something invisible that she could see. Her fingers gripped my shoulder so hard they dug right into the bone but I didn't dare make a move in case she too would shatter. My father carried on hacking and chopping, the wood clattering to the ground, Jimmy's craftsmanship destroyed. His face purpled with the effort, he had his jacket off and he was grunting, wiping sweat on his sleeve. When he had finished and the sentry box was completely levelled, he stood there gasping with the mountain of splintered wood all round him, the axe hanging limp in his hand. "You may go back to the house now," he said and my mother released her grip and turned away. I went to follow her but he roared after me. "Tom, you come back here and build the bonfire." "Do as you are told now," my mother whispered without turning her head. And so I did.

'We piled the wood behind the big rock and it burned, a huge inferno that threatened to get out of hand, the flame reaching all the way to the top of the rock and singeing the heather. Later that night in the dark you could still see the embers glowing in the soil. The smoke hung for days, there was no wind.

'The next morning my father got me to hold a ladder up against the big rock and he climbed up to the dovecote. There were only a few pigeons, since Jimmy had gone there was no one to train them. My father only had to shout at the birds and they flew off, landed on some branches nearby. He nailed chicken wire over all the openings. After he'd gone I sat and watched as two or three of the birds swooped down on the rocks at their little opening. Batting their wings to stay aloft but finding no purchase, they flew off again. One of them made three attempts. And then no more. When my father died, which was not long after my mother – both of cancer and both relatively quickly – Beth and I moved into the house. On the first day I climbed up and took down the wire that blocked the dovecote nesting. But no birds ever came back. I tried everything, put little bits of food in but never since that day have I seen a single bird there. It is as if the place is cursed. As if even the birds can sense the father in the son.

'I went off to boarding school. I wrote to my mother and

she wrote back. Big long newsy letters in her scrawly print. She had terrible handwriting, it was as if she was uncertain how to form the letters. We had good times together during the holidays while my father lurked in the background, worked late, went out in the evening – God knows where, because he was never a drinker. And then I went off to university, worked away during the summers, eventually got a real job. My mother would visit me in London one Saturday a month and I'd take her out to lunch in an Italian restaurant in Kensington called "Il Portico". She loved it, the staff made a fuss of her. She would always get dressed up, laughing and relaxed the way she never was at home. And she cried each time I took her back to Victoria to catch the train. Standing on the platform dabbing at her eyes with a little handkerchief. She didn't like tissues, said they reddened your nose. We never spoke about my father. And when I said I felt guilty about not coming down more she said, "You must live your own life, Tom. No one asks to be born. You must live your own life now, find a girl, someone you love and make her happy."

'My mother was dying when she finally told me her own story. But you know I think I'd guessed without ever actually realising. It was Jimmy that she had fallen for, even though he was so much younger. "Such a silly thing to do," she said, "but I loved him." Said she'd never stopped loving him and that was what my father had guessed and it had made him an angry man for the rest of his life. Said she was sorry, even apologised to me for ruining my childhood, turning him into the punishing father he became. I said I thought he'd had plenty of time to forgive.

'And so it was all this I was thinking of today on Blue Beach. Lost love, missed opportunity.'

17

I STOP THE CAB DRIVER on the corner of Green
Street so that I can walk the last few feet and calm this thudding heart. I over-tip wildly and stand for a moment beneath a
streetlight, breathing in the cool night air. After twenty years
of waiting I have forced myself to be five minutes late. But
Cormac will know this is totally out of character and he will
smile. The new dress rubs unfamiliar against my thighs and
I remind myself how beautiful it looked when I stood in front
of the dressing-room mirror, staring into the silk ripples of
sea. My finger reaches out for the silver button on the intercom. I count to thirty, press again. A sudden panic – what
will I do if Katarina answers? But the lock clicks and I push
gently, the door swings open onto a shiny mosaic floor and
ahead of me is Cormac, he is bounding down a long curved
staircase taking the last three steps at a leap, arms spread
wide in welcome. 'At last,' he whispers. I look up into his face,
his arms fold around me and I am home.

But instead on the corner of Green Street the cab driver slides
back the glass partition and says, 'You'll have to walk from
here, love, or sit in the traffic for God knows how long.'

Rivers of rain surge across the windscreen and we haven't

moved for some time. I look down at my delicate turquoise slingbacks. When I open the door a gash of rain swipes the back of my head and the smell of hairspray rises into the air. Holding the brolly down in front of my face I take rapid tiptoe steps along the pavement. Cormac will see the funny side of this, of course; I will kick off my soaked shoes and we will laugh. There are feet everywhere, a forest of legs blocking the pavement. 'Excuse me,' I say to a thicket of dripping anoraks but no one answers, they are packed tight. I force my way sideways holding the umbrella high above my head and step down from the pavement and try to scurry round the edges of the crowd that spills out onto the road. A man in uniform jumps out of the driver's seat of a rain-slicked limo and opens the rear door. The crowd lurches forwards, a slender white leg appears in the doorway followed by a head of golden curls and a red-lipped smile. The men cheer and shout 'Jerry, Jerry. Over here, love, over here.' The woman stands underneath a black awning and waves into a burst of flashes, rearranges her pose on the red carpet and glides forwards through a hail of shutter clicks. I push further out onto the road and a hand grips my shoulder.

'Hold your horses.' A black face inside a hooded black cape with a plastic wire snaking behind his ear. I am pressed up so close I have to lean back to avoid jabbing him with the spokes of my brolly.

'I need to get to number 22.'

'Yeah, you and a million others,' he says, head cocked to one side.

'I need to get to Cormac.'

'You're all wet. Where's your car?'

'I got out.'

'You got an invite?' He leans forward, peers into my face.

'I never got one.'

'You never got one.'

'I mean he called. *Cormac* called. I am – his friend.'

'We-ell, if you ain't on the list here...' his hand slips inside the cape and draws out a long thin clipboard. 'Name?'

'Caro.'

'You got a surname?' he shakes his head, moving a pen up and down a list. 'No, no, no, wait, *wait*. Here we are. Caro, just like you said.' And he frowns at my face, searching for recognition. 'I like that. Caro. OK.' He bends down, lifts the heavy red rope. 'OK guys, make way.' I step underneath the awning and the rain stops pelting down, his voice behind me shouts 'Iiiiiit's Caro,' like a circus master announcing the next act. I watch my drenched blue shoes take one foot in front of the other.

'You can put the brolly down now, love,' a voice roars and there is a snort of laughter, but I need the brolly to shield my face. I follow the carpet up the steps, across a threshold where the umbrella is snatched from my hand by a girl in a black catsuit who shakes it crossly and ushers me off to the side. Another girl with scraped-back hair appears from behind a screen to remove my coat and hands me a small glass disc with the number 86 inscribed in gold. She gestures to a man in a sharkskin suit standing behind a narrow table. 'Bag please, ma'am,' he pokes about the interior with a long wooden probe and takes out my mobile. 'No pictures,' he slips my phone into a small net bag. 'You're all set,' he says and hands me a black metal dog tag with a number.

I emerge to the beat of 'Playground Chains' and straight into the path of a tall fair-haired boy, unsmiling and beautiful and balancing a lacquered tray of pink champagne. High above me a glittering chandelier spills splinters of light on a stuccoed ceiling. A dark wide staircase sweeps down from the landing where a man in a black suit and T-shirt stands scanning the crowd and talking into his shoulder. A woman with raven hair drifts past in a dress that seems to be made of metal pieces and sparkles when she moves. Two girls wearing halter-neck minis and high thick wedges, their bare arms linked, clop past me like skittish ponies. A man with a lined face and long brown hair in a pair of ripped jeans and a black jacket with an upturned collar steps into their path, takes one of their elbows and says, 'Hey baby.' His face is so familiar that I cannot match it with a name. He leans up to kiss the cheek of one and the other snaps her head away as if someone had just called her name. He strokes the first girl's long white arm with his finger and strains to whisper something in her ear. She flashes shiny white teeth. The boy with the tray returns and stops unbidden by my side, holding it aloft by my shoulder. But he is not offering me another drink, he knows I am not one of them, he is looking behind me into the crowd of people who are someone.

I swing round to a flurry of activity and there, fifteen feet away, hugging and backslapping his way through the guests, is Cormac. His smile is whiter, his hair more perfectly tousled than I had imagined. He glad-hands his way through the crush. I step forward. A woman in a satin tuxedo follows closely behind him, wearing lime green glasses and a glossy black ponytail that flicks as she turns her head. A small thin wire coils down behind a huge glittery earring and disappears underneath her lapel. Her hand appears on Cormac's shoulder every few seconds as she propels him forwards with little nudges, bestowing professional smiles on all those around her. This is Penelope Fisher, Cormac's right-hand woman, and she is looking ahead, scanning the crowd and directing him to left and right. Cormac stops to embrace the man in the ripped jeans and they mock-punch each other and then hug bear-style while everyone watches. Cormac leans over the man's shoulder, his eyes flicker past my face and then return.

He pulls back, releases the man and shouts, 'IT'S CARO.'

Heads swivel. The boy with the tray turns his head to stare down at me. I feel my lips twitch into a smile or a grimace as Cormac pushes forward and holds me out in front of him with both arms, looks me up and down like you might inspect a lost child.

'Caro. Finally. I'm so glad you came,' and he wraps me in a hug, a hug like the one he just gave the man in the ripped jeans, a familiar buddy hug, as if we spent our time arm-wrestling and building Lego. His smell is an adult version of what he was underneath.

'How *adorable*, it's the childhood sweetheart,' announces Penelope Fisher, prising him loose. I am mineswept up and down by large black lashes. 'So lovely to meet you. I am Penelope,' a cool dry hand slips through mine. She smells faintly of burnt lemon. 'How cute. Isn't she cute?' she barks at the assembled onlookers and clicks her fingers high in the air. A man with two cameras dangling around his neck elbows his way forward and Cormac's hand slips around my waist. Penelope flicks my hair behind my shoulder, plucks something from my dress and steps back when the photographer moves into position. Penelope does a biting motion behind his head which I understand to mean I should loosen my locked jaw.

'Tell me, darling. Was Cormac your very first love?' she shouts.

'Ooooh,' a blonde woman in silver jeans presses her hands together.

'Caro was the girl next door,' says Cormac. 'Weren't you, Caro?' He cinches my waist and I wobble.

'Aaaah,' sighs the crowd. I look down at my shoes, the turquoise silk is stained with rainwater. They are probably beyond repair.

'She was my very first girl, weren't you, Caro? And I

haven't seen her for twenty years.' He pulls my head in and plants a kiss on my mouth. His lips are dry and light and gone in an instant. The crowd whoops and claps. 'AND,' says Cormac, raising his free hand, 'she never returned my call!'

They shriek with laughter and I laugh too, at the very idea, at the sheer stupidity of that.

'So what d'you think about your old boyfriend's success?' roars the man in the ripped jeans.

There is a second where the track ends and everyone holds their breath and my mouth flops open, but I cannot speak.

'She thought I was bloody rubbish, didn't you?' says Cormac and they howl again and he grabs me, dips me backwards salsa style over his knee and the crowd Ooohs as I almost skid on the slender heel, my other leg flails uselessly in the air and my dress rides up my thigh. There is a ripple of blinding flashes. He pulls me upright and then Penelope is in between us saying, 'Lovely, darling, lovely.' The group is disintegrating, the photo call is over and she inclines her head, mutters something into her earpiece as she clasps Cormac's shoulder and steers him to the right. I reach out but my hand falls short of his sleeve, he is slipping away from me, Penelope has a firm grip on his elbow now and is steering him through the crowd. He turns his head, shrugs with a helpless grin and calls out, 'Hey, Caro, keep in touch. Don't disappear again,' and is borne away by his escort. Penelope whispers in his ear. And then he is gone.

The blond boy stands in front of me. With a little bow and a new deference he formally presents the tray but I am looking not at him but behind him at the bodies that have swallowed Cormac's head.

I have waited twenty years for a three-minute encounter.

'Hi.' A hand squeezes my shoulder and I realise that it has

been there for some time. It squeezes again and I turn towards a face that I have seen so many times.

'I'm –'

'I know who you are.'

A girl appears by our side with a square tumbler on a tray and Katarina takes a water glass, her nails are short, square-tipped and high gloss.

'Perhaps you want something a little stronger after that,' she clicks her fingers and the blond boy reappears but my trembling hand cannot reach for the slender glass, I might topple all of them and heads will turn and I will once again become the focus of attention.

'Champagne it is then,' Katarina plucks out a drink and hands it to me.

I drink but it is not this delicate fizz in a flute that I need but a real hit, a giant tumbler of neat vodka that I could drain and smash against the wall.

'There is something I would like you to see,' says Katarina. 'Would you come with me?'

But I cannot answer, I appear to have lost the ability to produce sound, maybe it will never return or maybe if I open my mouth to speak a bloodcurdling roar will emerge. Katarina takes my silence as assent and slips her hand over my wrist, it is a soft and silky grip and her chunky bangle knocks against my knuckles. The crowd parts, she murmurs acknowledgements to some passing faces, a confetti of smiles follows as she leads me away. The lights are dimmed now with coloured projections shimmering on the walls. Two men in black stand guard at the bottom of the staircase, heels planted on the lower steps. They step apart in synch like a dance move and check me over, professionally recording my likeness.

'People forget that this is our home,' says Katarina. 'They wander.'

We rise in a slow curve up a sweep of white marble.

Pinprick spots embedded in the wall cast a sliver of shade on each step.

'I sometimes prefer to enjoy the party from up here.' She stops level with the chandelier and I lean on the banister and look down at the crowds moving below me in the spot-lit darkness like coloured fish in dusky water.

We walk past many closed doors until she opens one at the very end and steps aside to reveal a large white room with black floors and a double-height ceiling. She closes the door behind us and the air compresses with a soundproofed sigh. 'This is a very private place,' she points to a low-slung armchair that faces a large flat screen. 'No one is allowed in here except us and the kids.'

My hand rests on a control pad built into the arm of the chair while Katarina fiddles with a glass drawer embedded in the wall. She slips a CD into the drive and a collage of hundreds of photos appears. A cursor clicks and Estelle's front garden explodes onto the screen, we are both lying in the grass in our T-shirts and bikini bottoms, Estelle's arms are flung wide and her mouth is open in laughter, her pink tongue clearly visible. I am staring straight into the lens at Cormac, like I always looked up at him, in the clearest open expression of love.

Katarina sits on a chair at right angles to me and crosses legs that are a perfect shade of honey.

'It was very sad. Your friend.'

'I don't want to talk about it.'

'Yes, of course. I'm sorry. I just wanted you to know that Cormac remembers.'

'I don't belong here.'

'You know *this*,' she gestures vaguely to the door behind her, 'is just so much stuff. I think that Cormac is pretty much what he was when you knew him as a kid. You mustn't think –'

'What? What must I not think?' and even as I spit out

the words I am incredulous that I am being angry with this woman, this Katarina who is trying so hard to be kind.

'That Cormac is not still the same person underneath it all.'

I look away from the screen. 'I wouldn't know.'

'Why did you come along tonight? After so many years?'

'Because Cormac asked me. I didn't know it was going to be a big party.'

'But the invite?'

'I never got one.'

'Penelope is usually very efficient.'

'She may have sent it to my mother's address.'

'So you thought it was – you and him?' I nod. She looks away with a sympathetic cluck of her tongue. 'Oh dear. I'm so sorry. Sometimes Cormac is –'

'I know what he is.'

She flicks a button and the screen dies. 'You still love him,' she says, one arm stroking the other as if it needed consoling. 'Everyone loves Cormac,' she nods sadly and I could bludgeon her now, I stand up so quickly I am dizzy and stumble towards her but something in my face alarms her. She takes a step back, her hand flutters by her side and she glances sideways at the exit and then back to me.

'It's OK. I'm leaving anyway,' and I press down on the handle and the door opens soundlessly. Katarina follows behind me across the landing but something about her manner alerts the man on the stairs who bounds up and is between us in an instant. He takes hold of my elbow in a way that seems like it is assisting my descent but is actually a vice grip and we hurry down through the gauntlet of everyone staring at who is with Katarina.

He steers me to the screened area by the entrance. I put the glass disc and the black dog tag into his hand and he gives them to the girl in the catsuit and waits beside me without a word, still holding my elbow in his steely fingers. When

I turn towards him, he looks back at me with unreadable good looks and all the charm of a hired assassin who remains stylish and unruffled in the grimmest of circumstances. But there is something oddly comforting about this silent professional taking charge of my inappropriateness. As long as I am in his care I will be safe from harm, he is shielding me from the onset of something that lurks on the other side of this numbness. And my coordination is poor, I appear to be temporarily incapacitated, my legs jellied, the phone slipping from my hand. He lets the girl pick it up and put it inside my clutch bag and both of them help me into my coat and loop my brolly on my wrist. He leads me down some steps, around a corner and into a narrow corridor with a black-and-white tiled floor and red walls. There is a door at the other end and another suited man standing by its side who slides back a bar lock, turns some keys and the door opens out onto the night and the rain and a basement exit with steps leading up to the street. My escort removes the umbrella from my wrist, opens it and puts it in my hand, tucks my bag under my other elbow and guides me up the steps where he opens a black gate and ushers me through, pointing to the mouth of an alleyway a few feet away. He sweeps both palms forwards as one might encourage a small child or shoo away a puppy but I remain rooted to the spot. He steps back and locks the gate – he is setting me free but I would much prefer to remain in his custody rather than proceed alone into whatever awaits.

'Goodbye,' he says and his voice is unexpectedly soft and accentless. I look towards the alley where there are lights and passing traffic on the other side. The rain spills over the sides of the umbrella, my blue shoes are bruised and sodden. I turn back but my guide has vanished, the door below me is locked and lightless and I find myself alone and shivering in the back street, the tall backs of buildings towering over me and above my head a small patch of city sky.

18

WHEN CORMAC'S FIRST BABY was born I went to see my doctor.

'You can see the nurse for contraceptive advice, you know,' he said, scanning the notes on the back of my file. 'You don't need to come to me unless there's a problem.' He waited, tapping the folder with his biro. 'So you've been on Trinordiol for a few years now. Any problems?'

I shook my head, fishing about for the words.

'Well then.'

I said I wanted something more permanent. He mentioned the coil. 'Are you in a regular sexual relationship?'

'Actually I want to be sterilised.'

He leaned back in his chair. The clock on the mantelpiece behind him ticked loudly. Someone coughed in the waiting room. 'You are –' he looked down at my file.

'Twenty-seven.'

'And you have –'

'No children.'

'No children,' he repeated, staring directly at me now as if some vital information might be gleaned from my expression. 'Sterilisation is completely inappropriate at your age. In your circumstances. For one thing, it is extremely difficult to reverse.'

'I want it to be final.'

'People change their minds.'

'I don't.'

'It's not an option.'

'Can I have it somewhere else?'

'Can you tell me why it is so important to you?'

'I have decided that it is what I want.'

He pushed the folder to one side and asked, with a quick modulation in tone, if something had happened to make me feel that way. He said he could arrange for me to see someone who could help me talk through this. I said I didn't want a therapist. He said that sometimes people make decisions in haste and in any case this was not one that he would deliver.

'Then I'll go somewhere else.'

'You will get the same answer.'

And he was right. The answer was the same. But I tried. A silent gesture that no one would ever see. Cormac would never know.

I am driving into the moon. Speeding towards a stark silvery white suspended just below the sunshield. The clouds began to clear as soon as I fled the city, the night glow slipping away in the rear view. And when I swung onto the back roads the rain disappeared and the temperature dropped as if I had arrived in some dry and frozen tundra. Frosted fields glitter in the moonlight and it is now a mackerel night sky with clusters of cotton cloud massing along the horizon in case a soft landing might be necessary should this full fat moon suddenly crash to earth. The road ahead is inky blue tarmac that rushes under my wheels and the smallest tug to the left has the hedgerows whipping the side of the car. A thick mist swarms unexpectedly smothering the view and I decelerate. Fog banks cling to the night like smokescreens hiding an otherworld, a neverwhere from which I might not emerge.

I press the button and the window opens onto the thick air. There is a texture to this vapour, like eating tasteless candyfloss. At the crest of a steep hill I kill the lights, switch off the engine. Keep my foot on the brake and listen to the silent night. Below me the road winds like a ribbon flung carelessly across the sparkling fields, darkly gleaming in the moonlight with the promise of some alluring but fatal thrill, the possibility of leaping beyond loss, of putting all the chips on the black: double or quits, a final solution that might herald a certain peace. And it is difficult not to take the chance, not to burst forward in a spontaneous assent to something unarticulated, or maybe it is towards annihilation. So I release the brake and let the car roll. The tyres squeeze on the icy tarmac, the hissing accelerates into an engineless scream and I am overtaken by recklessness, a longing to flirt with danger, to capitulate to a random outcome. Is this abandon or simply fatigue? Is it the thrill of freewheeling downhill in zero visibility with the windows open? Or is it just relief? Definitely oblivion. My eyes snap open just as the wheels spin, I feel the steering shudder and then the soft crunch and side lurch to a halt in the ditch.

My hands come to rest on the bottle clamped between my thighs, reassuringly solid. There are still some materials that are shatterproof, that can withstand a lot of pressure. I manage to twist off the cap in the dark and slurp but miss my mouth and the liquid sloshes down my front to puddle in the lap of my beautiful blue dress.

Whenever I lay my hand over his screen heart, I am searching for the wound that didn't hurt, the pain never felt. The crowd swoons at his feet, straining to touch his hand and in the tearful wailing of the fans I see my own face. Mine was the first adulation Cormac witnessed, a precursor to all this – and what a powerful aphrodisiac to be so adored, so desired without condition. But doesn't the desired become the desirer? Isn't this the charm that breaks down defences, the very basis of seduction? So what was it then that Cormac loved about me? For he said he did, insisted he did and would still insist right now and be mystified that I could even question this. But I suspect him of loving everyone – the human condition, its majesty, which of course he has made a career out of trying to unpick. And how can you possibly criticise someone for an absence of exclusivity? For a democratic love? Doesn't it mean that they are the better person? Cormac loves them all because he has always been the object of a splurged affection. Next to him I was radiant, without him the colours bled, I faded and dissolved into shadow. I tried so hard to keep him close. His head lay in my lap on summer afternoons in the long grass as I stroked his curls, lightly, careful not to snag as he drifted off to sleep or lay blinking against the grand vision of a future that was never in doubt. But it was not of me that he dreamed, I knew that even then, and I do not think for a second now that my presence lingered in absence.

Oh, how I have lied to myself, huge distorting untruths. I deceive even myself in the skews of remembrance where the past is morphed into a pulp romance, a shoddy tale of heartbreak. The stubborn affections of a silly girl spinning the web of a grand fiction. The small plain fact is that I was there. And available. And I, like everyone else, was spellbound. The truth is I could have been anyone. Moving on did not cost Cormac a thought. My life has been predicated on a fabricated lie, a feverish hallucination, clinging to the conviction that something dreamt was something real.

In the beginning we let her watch. This is what I remember

as I sit here clutching the wheel with my moonlit fingers. It would be unfair to say that it was always Cormac's idea. He presented it as more than just cover for us, but as a sort of solution for Estelle, a pre-emptive strike. He said that it could help to protect her to learn about sex with people she trusted. In safe pairs of hands. I laugh aloud now at the horrific distortion of logic and I wonder at the macabre suggestion, if it was what he really intended. I was initially reluctant for the obvious selfish reason: I did not want to share him. Not even with Estelle. But it mattered that I did not disappoint, it mattered that I did what he desired. Mostly, it mattered that I had him close. Someone had to be watching and I, the reliable audience, was lost in my own moment. Child turned seductress in a heartbeat. None of it seemed strange like it does now in the remembering. Instead it has the stuttering hesitancy of a story that has never been told.

19

I WAKE TO AN URGENT SCREECHING in the window. It is the pre-dawn chorus, the shrill twittering of a hidden multitude limbering up for another day. My neck is stiff and I am cold to aching stalled at an angle here in the ditch. It is not yet light but I can see that the car came to rest just inches from a gate and I'm lucky not to have been spotted already by some farmer or worse still, a passing patrol car and a policeman who would have clocked the vodka bottle on the floor by the passenger seat, the turquoise party dress, the smeared make-up and the little drowned shoes. Inside my rucksack on the back seat is an old tracksuit pricked with grass seeds and walking socks that smell musty and are faintly damp. The dress peels off like dead skin and crumples in a soft ball on my lap. The engine starts, the wheels skid in reverse but the car lurches backwards up the incline and I swing out onto the road.

A couple of miles of trees and vegetation with no recognisable landmarks and then a signpost for a village I recognise that means I am about fifteen miles off course. I must have taken the wrong exit from the motorway on my drunken midnight jaunt. But where to find a service station on a Sunday at 6 a.m? I could sneak into my mother's house but she will be dozing in the kitchen armchair. I could call round to Tom's, he is likely an early riser but I am in no humour for the questioning that would greet me. And he does not have coffee. Although it is water that I crave, a long cold drink that will soothe this throbbing head and wet the cracked pit of my mouth. And then I remember where I should go.

The churchyard tap is stiff so I slip the tracksuit sleeve over my hand to gain some purchase until finally there is a sputter and the water splatters into the dog bowl and onto my walking boots. I slurp from cupped hands until they are numb. This small solution to my immediate crisis is oddly pleasing, the rehydration is transformational, my limbs flood with purging liquid, an ice river courses through my veins. I press a knuckle hard against each temple: I will poleaxe this ache. I will walk it away, it is vigorous exercise I need to sober up and face the approaching day.

In the graveyard all is still but for the blistering screech of the birds. Shreds of vapour hang over some headstones in the centre of one row as if there has been some airborne disturbance. But the departed are asleep, I picture each one lying in blackout repose beneath the frosted stones. I move towards the rear and open the gate onto the fields. I will go back now to where it all ended.

It was September twenty years ago when I last did this walk and the Canada geese were congregating on the grass picking over their travel plans. The air was heavy with dying bracken, a sickly stench of decay as the summer expired all around us. The bracken is blackened now and collapsed and soon this path will be almost impassable, a deep mud trench where we used to lose our wellies and stand on one leg kicking a socked foot in the air, laughing and shrieking and trying not to fall over. From where I stand at the highest point I can see the faint outline of the estate in the denuded winter, the sweep down to the lake and the valley floor, the pale and mottled fields of camouflaged deer, a few village rooftops barely visible. And beyond, where I force myself to look, the trees line up like a dark army on the awakening horizon.

A pair of stone greyhounds guard the posts of what was once the hotel's grand entrance. The black gates are chained shut with heavy coiled locks so that the stately old gravel drive cuts a long straight line through manicured lawns only to terminate abruptly in this muddy and uneven hillside. The hotel's walled garden is in the process of being restored, the huge square beds are filled with rows of stiff lavender and some cabbagey plant whose floppy leaves and serrated edges lend it a vaguely tropical air. And all along the perimeter wall is a line of pleached willows that have been savagely pruned. There are mounds of gnarled stubble where all the major branches have been hacked off by some machete-wielding zealot and the slender new growth trained sideways to form fragile links between the trees. It is a horticultural experiment of staggering deformity, some landscape gardener tinkering with nature, forcing an unnatural lateral growth. From this distance, it looms like a monstrous sculpture in the winter greylight, a homage to some grotesque horror: a row of mutilated torsos twisted in agony, their stunted heads thrust skywards, straining for relief.

I follow the curve of the lake onto a wide tree-covered path. There are not so many gaps in the bank now as there were when we played here. The hawthorn trees have flourished, the reeds have grown dense and the mooring space has been swallowed by vegetation. Spike used to run ahead of us here and startle the orange-beaked geese, scramble them into a clumsy acceleration from the grass with a loud squawking, their flippered feet thudding loudly against the ground before they finally lurched into a state of airborne grace. He hunted in wide irregular loops around this spot, disappearing off on a scent, leaping up through bracken before flopping down in the shade.

A decapitated vole lies on its back in the middle of the path, its long thin tail curved in a loop, its little belly round and full as if it had been made less agile by some large snack. There is a gash of dried blood where the head should be, although the little creature looks curiously complete in its headless state. Beside the body is a small neat pinkish-green mound of regurgitated food, left perhaps by the killer who found the vole's head not to its taste. This is the work of a fox or an owl who was disturbed and fled the scene, maybe even a tomcat prowling around the churchyard and lured here by the promise of easy pickings close to the hotel. Spike used to unearth these little corpses from time to time but it always seemed to distress him, he would nudge gently with his nose as if trying to revive them and then look up at me with a pleading whine, insisting that some action be taken before some other dog came and made a messy meal of it.

Estelle liked dead things. She would hunker down and examine a corpse with dispassionate curiosity and even poke it with her finger. Once she pressed down hard on a fresh kill Spike found by the lakeside while I hovered squeamishly in the background. Blood oozed from some orifice and she whooped in delight. But I have grown braver with the years, or at least developed a hierarchy of distaste, so I do now what Estelle did then: I bend down and pick up the vole by the tail and fling it into the undergrowth.

I make an illegal left turn – that is still how it feels even now after all these years. The arbitrary boundary of child-hood was right here where a small footbridge crosses the river and leads to a second smaller bridge that overlooks the weir. Already in the approach you can hear the roar, both lakes are full to the brim this time of year and water crashes over the edge. We used to lean over the side where it is still clumsily fenced off, pin the brambles down with our feet and throw sticks, watch them bob and resurface in the bubbling water below. Once as a puppy, Spike broke free and jumped in just here, disappeared below the surface. 'There, over there,' Cormac shouted, pointing to his muzzle craning above water, his paws paddling against the current. We ran along the bank, Estelle tripped on a bramble behind me and cried out but I kept on running, shouting encouragement to Spike, 'Good boy, come on, come on, you can do it.' His legs powered towards the side where Cormac and I stood sinking in the muddy shallows ready to receive him and he leapt out, licked my face, shook a great spattering all over us and skittered about in wide circles. 'I thought he was going to drown,' I said and Cormac hugged me, shook his head, curls aglow in the sun. 'No, I knew he wouldn't. Spike's not going to leave us, are you, Spike?' But of course that was not true, like so many other convictions.

A sudden punch in my lower back. It was Estelle, her face scrunched red in fury. 'Look,' she thrust out her bare arms to showcase the long pink scratches on the inside with dots of blood near the elbow. 'Don't you hit me,' I shoved her arm away. 'You ran off and left me,' she whined. 'It's only brambles,' said Cormac inspecting the arm, 'you'll be OK.' 'You ran off, Caro,' she screamed, waving her arm in front of my face. 'Spike nearly drowned, Estelle. I was trying to save his *life*, and all you care about is your stupid scratches.' She caught me with a slap on the side of the cheek and I lunged but Cormac grabbed me, pinned both arms by my side and I struggled while she pranced about laughing and skipped off along the path. Spike ran after her, his near-death experience forgotten, his fur already half-dry in the sun. Cormac loosened his grip and I fled in the opposite direction, over the bridge into the undergrowth and crouched down out of sight at the feet of a massive oak, head cradled in my hands.

Spike came crashing through the bracken, nuzzled my elbow and stood panting in my ear but he could not be still. 'Come back, Caro,' Cormac shouted as Spike darted back and forth between us trying to force reconciliation. I crawled forwards, saw them sitting on a tree trunk by the lake, Estelle holding out her arm and Cormac stroking it, bending his head to lick the blood drops from her white skin.

There are holes in this wooden bridge now, slats missing or broken with gaps big enough to snare an adult foot. I step off onto the forbidden side and the edge of a vast field with clumps of wet grass that is golden and high as wheat in summer. I am standing on the threshold of another country, the African waterhole we imagined in our play, lions and tigers stalking antelope on the savannah, giraffes munching on the distant trees. A long way from roads and adults and any sign of habitation but for the church and the hotel on the hill that we reinvented as a game reserve. We would lie in the heat on a collection of felled oaks conjuring up the chatter of monkeys from the birdcalls, and the distant sound of horse whinnies and the bleating sheep took on an aura of the tropical. Sometimes – and this is how Estelle knew the route – we wandered further, across the stile in search of blackberries, all the way to the shadowy woods where bluebells glowed an indigo bushfire in May and Cormac told stories of witches who whizzed between the branches whining like a thousand mosquitoes, capturing children and coating them in slime. A silent jungle of pine and oak with secret patches of sunlight and a rich smell of moss and damp earth in summer. A black stream rushes clear across twigs and stones and there is a constant rustling from unseen animals – the flash of a speckled deer, the overhead flurry of a squirrel on ropes of tangled ivy. If you made it all the way through the woods you passed beneath a disused railway bridge and emerged close to where the scout hut still stands, weathered brown shingle with blackened bonfire patches all around. And beyond that, the playing fields of the next village.

But Estelle never made it that far. It was high summer twenty years ago when she began her death walk. She would have removed her white sandals as I did when I re-traced her footsteps some weeks later. She would have stopped here at our safari lookout by this cluster of ancient giants, their ivory trunkwood lying incongruously in the middle of the open field. There are traces of more recent visitors – a crumpled box of Marlboro, and an alcopop bottle lies neck down in the ground. From a perch at the highest point of a trunk you could enjoy a 360-degree panorama and, turning northwards now, I see the mist has cleared and the sky has lightened over the distant slope to the hotel. The church spire looks strangely secular at this angle, the absence of a cross hinting at apology, as if it feels such an honour has not been earned. Estelle would have paused here for a while before pressing onwards, following the vanishing deer, straying off the narrow track and into the tall bleached grass. A frazzled forget-me-not wound into her hair, her bare feet dusted with lines of dry earth between the toes, sweat rings under the arms of the blue dress. She may even have danced barefoot, twirling around and singing her favourite song, *Doooooooooo bop-bop-bop-bop, Doooooooooo bop-bop-bop-bop*.

And here is the place where she lay for twenty-seven hours before she was found: a sun-shot copse on the edge of the brooding forest, way beyond our permitted boundary. A birch tree enclosed by a small circle of unexplained deforestation. The charred remains of illicit fire. A crooked branch cracked black like volcanic rock.

No one could account for her absence, it was a confusion of responsibilities never officially assigned, a breakdown in arrangements and logistics, the kind of benign inattention that gets puppies killed or toddlers ending up face down in a paddling pool. Estelle ran off in a fury instead of going home. No one and everyone to blame.

In the middle of September, after the investigation was closed, an impromptu gathering of fathers and teenage sons assembled here one Saturday morning with chainsaws and cutters. They worked all day in a frenzy of clearance and without permission from the authorities, ripping open the hiding places, the camps and the badger setts. With grim and sweaty faces they hacked at brambles and ferns and bushes until the fields lay violated, all hidden pleasures laid bare – mangled beer cans, a broken whisky bottle and even a stash of unopened cider. They uprooted the blackberry bushes by the stile where Estelle's sandal had been found. The police thought she was running but I knew better, she would have climbed up there to check if the berries were ripe. The sound of the frantic activity drew out all the neighbours and there was almost an air of harvest time. Men drank mugs of tea brought to them by wives and girlfriends and daughters and stood around in smoking clusters, feeling that something was being reclaimed. After the paralysis of fear and rage, something was actually being done. Mothers and small children surveyed the defoliation, standing off to the side by a flock of grazing sheep who might have born witness to the chase, whose eyes might have blindly recorded the event.

   This spot was first covered by a white tent inside a perimeter cordoned off by yellow crime-scene tape and patrolled by two dejected policemen. The tent disappeared after a couple of days but the tape remained. Painstaking searches with two dogs were conducted, slow-moving lines of police with sticks parting the vegetation but it was summer, the worst time, everything was high and dense and obscenely abundant. We watched from a distance that shrank for each day that went by and then they packed up and moved away like a circus leaving town and the countryside was restored to a nervous peace. The spot became a no-go zone. Tentative kickabouts were restricted to the playing fields with mothers standing by in an anxious supervision, looking over their shoulders as if they expected all hell to break loose. And then after a few weeks had passed some teenage boys dared each other to lie where Estelle had lain, her body spread out and mangled, the blue dress smeared and torn at the front.

The theory was that she had run, been chased. I told the policeman and the detective that she would have been looking for blackberries, that even though I'd told her it was two weeks to go till they were ripe she wouldn't believe me but would have gone to check herself. I had taught her long ago that the biggest and best were always on the uppermost brambles, that you could only reach the luscious ones if you stood on the stile. *Hold on Estelle or you'll fall right in and get scratched all over.* But they didn't write this down. The detective had a long thin nose that twitched as if he was scenting something. 'I'm sorry,' he said. 'Just tell us anything that might help.'

'Would she have hurt very much?' I asked.

'Yes. Yes, I am afraid she would.'

Cormac and I were called into his living room and told together. His father gripped the back of the armchair with both hands. His mother's face was buried in a soggy handful of tissues. My own mother sat immobile on a dining chair with an unlit cigarette in her hand. Through the net curtains I could see a policewoman talking to a clutch of neighbours out on the road. Cormac stood swaying slightly in front of the mantelpiece until his eldest brother came in and hugged him. The middle ones slouched on the arms of the sofa chewing on their nails. When I slumped in a near-faint, Cormac's dad rushed to catch me. Someone sat me on the floor with a sugary tea. My mother lit her cigarette, accepted a brandy. Cormac's father said we all needed to talk to the police and help them to piece things together. His mother shooed her hand at him. 'Later later, give the poor things a chance.' I stood up under watchful eyes. Cormac and I trooped upstairs to his room.

He picked up his guitar but did not play. I went to speak but he raised his left hand, said 'Sshh, Caro, sshh.' He ran a middle finger up and down the thick bass string as if testing for imperfections while I crouched on the floor swallowing air.

Would we talk to the police now? his father came to the door. Yes, said Cormac and the room was suddenly crowded. The woman detective patted my shoulder, sat beside me on the edge of the bed. Cormac's dad stood on the threshold with his hands in his pockets, eyes shiny with tears. The man detective lifted up a pile of records from the chair by the desk and Cormac told them how Estelle had announced she was dressing up that morning. How she disappeared off to her house and came back here later wearing the blue dress and her white sandals and carrying a make-up bag. She sat in the middle of the floor while I held the mirror. I told her she had too much shadow on the left eye. I helped her with mascara. She used a lot of blusher, she liked the pink spots clownish on her cheeks. The lipstick was called 'Soft Candy' and she slicked it on and kissed the tissue paper and applied again. She tottered about in high heels in the middle of the bedroom floor and I giggled. 'Let's go to the fields,' she said, and when Cormac said 'Not yet' she shouted 'NOW' and he repeated 'Not yet' and she flew into a rage. 'Stormed off in a temper,' said Cormac. The detective scribbled in his note-book. Cormac's dad nodded, his eyes tightly closed. This was so unremarkable as to be scarcely worthy of comment.

Except the truth was a little different. When I laughed, Estelle threw me a cloudy look and took off her sandals. She went to Cormac, put a hand across the fretboard to mute the strings, bent down to find his lips. When he turned his head away, she grabbed his hair. 'No, Stella,' he said and she let go. He started up again, a rich strumming that was the opening chord of a new song. He'd found a place to play in two weeks' time – a pub in the next town where he had lied about his age. Estelle stepped forward, grabbed his face with both hands, squeezed so hard she puckered his lips.

'Do it,' she said and clamped her mouth over his but he chopped her hands away.

'I don't like your lipstick,' he wiped a smudge of pink on the back of his hand. She slapped him on the ear and fled down the stairs. And that was the last we saw of her.

'The truth doesn't help, Caro,' he said. And he was right. The row was an irrelevance and knowing wouldn't help anyone, it was just the full story and even then not the full story, just a thread that would unravel right back to the beginning. He told me nothing would be gained from us coming clean about every little thing. About the story of the Three, which was more than they would ever understand and way more than they needed to know.

'But,' I said, flapping my arms in a gesture of defeat at everything that had gone on in this room.

'Believe me, Caro, they would not understand,' his fingers fluttering a silent scale up the neck of his guitar.

. . . . .

The police retraced Estelle's footsteps in reverse, from the copse where she was found to here: the third lake, so small and hidden that it is not at all well known. In summer it is little more than a sudden and putrid pond with no bankside and no seating spot. We used to make occasional forays here from our African lookout, lured over by frogs complaining in the rushes. Patches of yellow-grey scum cling to the edges, the water is thick with brown-tipped reeds and a faint stink. It was here that Estelle found him: a sullen fisherman sitting on a fold-out chair, waiting for his still rod to arch over the slick green water.

Death is not real until time passes in the absence. Two months after Estelle died and Cormac was gone I was playing her cousin's old records and stumbled on 'Coyote', a track of Joni Mitchell's that I had never heard. A menacing twang of double bass punctuates the open tuning of the twelve-string, a loose chord set adrift like a wild horse gambolling in an open plain. The little girl in 'Big Yellow Taxi' that Estelle so loved had vanished, taking with her the child's triangle and tambourine and the light skipping through sun-filtered years. There's an urgent percussion, a wild harmonic and a sinister drop in key as if the playfulness has fled, the nymphs have tripped away into the shadows and the girl has disappeared, her voice for ever altered, scarred by the knowingness of adulthood, the apple eaten. And there is no way back. You can hear it all in the final transition, an octave drop from child to woman who has seen the dark side of desire and the trouble it will bring. How your body, this wonder that you have always possessed has been transformed into a totem of irresistible allure that can drive men senseless with abandon. It is a song of abject terror with its undulating story of pursuit and possession.

It is the coyote's yellow eyes that I see when I think of
Estelle's last moments. The smell of death must have been all
around her, for death smelt like desire, like the familiar scent
of Cormac's bedroom. And when I think of her last moments
this is what I wonder: if at the beginning she thought it was
the same thing, that it might lead her back to the safe space
where fused arms caress in a soft afternoon and the breathing comes slow. And that even as she fled thrashing through
the undergrowth and the fisherman's breathing grew harsh
and angry and he flung her to the ground, Estelle would not
know that this was desire as annihilation. Until the blue dress
ripped and the knife slipped from his pocket.

A small puncture is all it took. Her blue eyes open to the
blue sky.

Look fear in the face. But there are fears that you cannot con-
front. I feel Estelle's hand tight in mine and it starts to slip
from my grasp, her flesh is already turning cold in my grip,
her fingers dissolving in my clenched palm. I cannot hold her,
I cannot save her and much worse: we led her to that place.
Cormac and myself together in the fatal and heedless complicity of children. We let her watch. We made her familiar
with the animal of desire. It was like teaching her to trust in
strange dogs. Without ever warning her where it could lead:
to the wrong place and the wrong time and a fisherman who
did not know he would become a killer, who surprised even
himself. What are the chances? He had never seen her before,
he said. But he said many things so I do not know if this is
true, if he had in fact been biding his time, looking for a barefoot girl in a blue dress with a daisy in her flaxen hair. He was
denied the excuse of psychiatric defence. He had some previous, minor breaches including an indecent exposure from
years before. Parents untraceable, and an ex-girlfriend keen to

sell his story of impotence and the occasional slap.

It was over two months into the fishing season and empty. There was no one around. And he was unremarkable, undistinguished and prematurely balding at forty-one. But every bald hunched-shouldered man looks like a rapist in black-and-white grain. The story died in the press in the absence of a trial. Estelle's killer pleaded guilty and he spared her family a lifetime praying for hell to rain down on him by dying a year into his prison sentence: one great batter against a wall and a brain haemorrhage that put him in a fatal coma. Estelle would have approved of how he met his end. It was suitably violent and messy and she always believed in vicious retribution.

I do not know how quickly it happened and I try not to worry about things that I do not know. There were bruises on her arms, scratches on her pale skin. The stab wound was well placed and sliced an artery in her neck. I went to a tackle shop and looked at a gutting knife underneath the glass counter – a small, desirable and efficient-looking blade with an elegant curve. But I do not allow myself to think about it. I know well enough that there is nothing to be gained in a reconstruction of her last moments and when I feel myself drifting again along the path she took, I start to follow and I have to turn back.

When they finally found me twenty years ago it was three weeks after Cormac had left and I had fallen asleep, here where Estelle once lay, lipstick dry on my lips. I'd been missing for hours and I was wearing her dress. We had bought them together a month before she died, Estelle's idea sometimes that we wear the same clothes and pose as sisters. All I remember about that day was a numbed drift, as if the end of the journey might reveal a true destination.

There is no greater terror than the random workings of your own mind.

This was the episode the psychiatrist described as pathological grieving. An inappropriate response that was obsessive, neurotic and a number of other descriptions all of which seemed equally irrelevant to me. I was forcibly or compliantly – I can't remember which – medicated into a sluggish inertia, pulled back from the sharp edges of elation and despair into a bleak neutral. I was also exhausted. Sleep had been problematic for a long time. All of this seems to me in hindsight to be a perfectly normal response to violent loss. I was told that it was the morbid re-enactment that precipitated my crisis, that the blue dress, the wandering, were symptoms of post-traumatic stress. I was acting out, over-identifying with the victim. It was an attempt to follow her, the sister I never had. The twin dress. It was a martyrdom wish, a longing for easeful death. There was some suggestion that it had a sexual bias. Did I understand that rape was violent? Would it help to know? And did I feel responsible for my autistic best friend? Did I feel I should have been there to protect Estelle? There was a parade of interested parties. And a whole spectrum of opinion. I was warned not to do this walk again.

My memory of that time is patchy and partially obliterated and it is not a history I care to reconstruct. New words loomed over my bed like prehistoric animals: Largactyl, Diazepam, Priadel, Venlaflexine. I was watched over by blue angels with knowing eyes, psych nurses have seen it all before and can spot trouble on the horizon. But by then I was severely tranquillised, made manageable by a crisp sheet and a thin green bedspread while I sank like a stone into blackwater, faces shimmering far above me and way out of reach. People drifted in and out of my consciousness – a plump psychiatrist with a kindly manner, a matron who stood in homely chat by my bed at 1 a.m., touched my cheek and told me it would pass. An Australian temp with a brace across her front teeth said not to worry. But I no longer knew what worry was in this re-calibration of time. It was a matter of complete indifference to me whether Caroline continued to exist. I was not available to myself. I had no access to any emotion other than deadness. It was a flatlining of the soul.

There was no shortage of professionals who wanted to hear me speak. The chief psychiatrist and his female underlings with concerned faces. A therapist, a group therapist and a host of interested parties. But I kept silent. This was not the result of decision or withholding. I did not have any words. Nothing presented itself for me to say. I was overwhelmed by a crushing exhaustion, as if I had sustained a massive shock to the body. I was not hungry, I could barely eat. And even with medication I would lie awake in bed, listening to the sound of others murmuring.

They kept me on suicide watch for the first few days. They watched me swallow my meds and I took every single pill they gave me, for on the other side of the medicated wall I could smell an ocean of pain. They reduced the tranquillisers and put me on anti-depressants that sealed me in an antechamber of muted sensation. Weeks passed and I was herded into Group where we flopped on yoga mats and attempted the occasional sit-up. Lay beached in tattered sofas, picking at our fingernails. Sometimes people spoke, swapped their dismal tales. A boy on Antabuse who sneaked out one weekend and never came back. A girl who muttered in her armchair without ever raising her head. Another one who jumped off a balcony that wasn't high enough. I wonder still whose idea it was that this could be reinforcing, to sit and marinade in the misery of others; to listen to endless tales of carnage and despair when you are on your knees. Some misguided idea that you are not alone. Except that you are. The trick is learning how to manage it.

My mother visited every day. It was as if she had popped into the library, and appropriated the straight-backed visiting chair, shifted it to a sideways angle to the bed with her back to the window. She did not ask any questions, except the most practical: was there anything I wanted from the house? Would I like a cup of tea? She did not fuss or show any signs of distress, just came each day before lunch and stayed until teatime, a plastic bag of books by her feet and some fruit that she would offer and I would refuse. It was a silent bedside vigil that might have seemed more appropriate for the terminally ill or the comatose, but perhaps she sensed how much I was being badgered by the professionals. Or maybe she wasn't interested in what I had to say. But there was a gentleness about her coming and going, her presence and her reading, the occasional turn of a page. She gave no sign of fear or guilt or concern and it was this baseline conviction that began to suggest that this might be a survivable crisis. The absence of any visible anxiety made me eventually believe that whatever it was would pass, that I might get over it.

One day she began to read aloud from a ragged paperback with a photo of a beach hut embedded in dunes. It was *The Outermost House*, the story of Henry Beston's yearlong experiment with solitude in Cape Cod. And here were things you could name without a quickening of breath, externals that were safe – the detail of a bird wing, the crash and spray of a wave. I could hear the surf, it is still a sound that lulls me to sleep. A reliable thud on the sand, the ebb and flow steady and returning. An experience that will not disintegrate, stripped of the human, a return to the most primitive – aloneness in a natural world, a place without the tangle of relationships.

My mother must have sensed by my reaction that descriptions of the physical world had a calming effect so she began to read from *The Worst Journey in the World*. I could imagine the Adelie penguins huddling in the Antarctic snowdrift, the crackle of ice as the men chipped open the sleeping bags. There was a comfort in these tales of hardship, a painstaking exploration of what can be endured in difficult circumstances. At what temperature will the frost bite toes? How long does it take to melt snow? How many calories do you need to man-haul ten miles? How do you pitch a tent with snow-blindness?

And still she did not ask me anything. Instead, on the day I was leaving hospital, she gave me a book. '*Captain Scott's Last Expedition,*' she said and handed me a small blue hardback. As if this story of heroic failure might be a touchstone. It is the only gift I recall her ever giving me, although she must have done when I was a child. She brought a rucksack for my clothes, stuffed my meds into her handbag and led me out through the heavy door into a sunny street. I wobbled at the light and she tapped my shoulder – I was taller than her already then. 'You're OK now,' she said. 'So let's go.' She handed me a bar of Turkish Delight while we waited at the bus stop. I had grown very thin, the jeans gaped at my hip and I nibbled at the edge, the warm sickly taste easing me back to early childhood.

This experience did not bring us close, but still on a sleepless night it is the sound of her voice and the crash of the surf on the Atlantic shore that will slow my breathing and lead me into sleep.

20

THE CHURCH BELL TOLLS NINE. I hear the sound of skittering paws on the path behind me just before Jack comes to an abrupt halt at my feet. He looks up expectantly, panting urgently as if he has run a long way. I bend down to tickle his fur under the chin.

'I thought you might be here by now,' I say, straightening up, but the laurel obscures my view of Tom.

The vicar emerges from the church entrance and approaches with a professional smile. Jack sits by my feet, one paw commandeering my boot.

'I haven't seen him do that before,' says the vicar looking down. 'He obviously likes you.'

'Apparently it's a sign of dominance rather than affection.'

'Perhaps. But we can't presume to know the mind of a dog. Jack is normally very stand-offish. He must know you well?' he says, the gentlest insistence of a question as his hands settle into a clasp in front of his tummy, a little gesture of repose that seems exclusive to clerics, as if they are limbering up to prayer. His priestly paunch protrudes like a constipated bump that sits oddly on his thin frame, as if he had shoved a rubber ball underneath the black shirt.

'I know his owner.' I had better keep this quizzing short or he will soon be asking me to join the ranks of the volunteers or trying to recruit me into the choir.

'Ah yes, Tom Warren,' he nods, his face folding into a rueful nod.

'In fact I was just looking for him when I saw Jack,' and I glance over at the laurel again, willing Tom to step forwards from his hiding place where he is no doubt amusing himself at this exchange. But there is still no sign, he is keeping well out of sight until the vicar moves on.

'Where is he eh, Jack?'

The vicar coughs, a stifled swallow of the throat, and presses a small plump fist lightly to his lips. Jack backs away off my foot.

'I'm so sorry to have to tell you,' he says. 'But Tom passed away last week.'

He reaches out to touch my wrist, a limp pressure that is meant to offer some clammy solace but feels instead like a fumbling attempt to take my pulse. I step back, look round again at the bush as if this could be verified. But there is no sign, no movement.

'He had of course been very ill. As you might have known.'

Jack slinks away behind a gravestone and buries his snout in a clump of grass as if he cannot bear the endless repetition of this bad news. I shake my head.

'Tom was a very private man. We didn't see him often here, although I knew his wife well. Beth was a regular in the congregation.'

'When?'

'Just three days ago. Cancer, very advanced. He refused all treatment so it went quickly in the end. He held on at home and was only in the hospice for a couple of days.'

Jack returns and I bend down again to touch his bowed head, his nose almost touching the ground.

'I'm so sorry, my dear. Such a shock for you finding out like this,' says the vicar above us. I nod at his feet, his shoes are worn but diligently polished, with thick rubber soles. 'Had you seen Tom recently?'

'Not for a couple of weeks. He wasn't here at the usual time. I should have guessed.'

'Normally all the relatives would have been contacted. Perhaps –'

'We weren't related.'

'A friend of Charlie's?'

'No. We just met here in the graveyard. We used to chat.' And it strikes me as bizarre that I did not even have Tom's phone number when I was the last friend he had left.

'The funeral will be on Wednesday,' he says as a consolation. 'The last one before Christmas.'

'What about him?' I nod at Jack who shifts his weight a little but keeps the pressure firm on my toes. He stares straight ahead as if he is resisting interrogation.

'He's staying with me. A temporary arrangement until we can find someone to take him in. I don't suppose –'

'Impossible.' I shake my head. I know what is coming, how easy it would be to say a quick yes and before I know it Jack would be sitting beside me on the front seat heading back to the city. 'I'm out at work all day.'

The vicar nods, folds his hands in front of him. Jack turns his head away in disgust, but I cannot take you. And you would not like it anyway.

'And he's used to company,' I say, fending off the guilt.

'I'll have to lean on some of the ladies. They're very experienced at arranging the loose ends. Finding homes for the unwanted.'

'You think they'll get something?'

'Oh, round here we are very good at animal rescue. Better than at saving souls I sometimes think.'

And I am furious with Tom for just leaving like that and making no provision for the dog he despised.

'None of the family?'

'Charlie is in Australia of course. So it wouldn't be – practical. There is only a cousin in Aberdeen.' He is looking down now at Jack who shifts again, uncomfortable under this mournful gaze. 'It's always difficult with the pets.'

Jack trots over to a gravestone, lifts his leg and parks himself defiantly on the stone. Growls a low voice of displeasure at the turn things are taking.

'You know they didn't even get on,' I say. 'Jack was Beth's dog. Tom thought he took sides.'

'He wasn't always the easiest –'

'Actually he was a good man.'

'Of course,' he smiles, humouring me.

The small gathering shuffles in the pews, a total of twelve to whom I was introduced by the vicar when I arrived. The Aberdeen cousin is a tiny barrel of a woman with a savagely cut helmet of dyed black hair and a navy blue coat that sweeps the ground as she waddles along on her high heels. Her husband is a portly man with a beard who keeps dabbing his nose with a handkerchief and beside them are two outsize teenage sons who slouch in the pews, the younger one hacking away at his cuticles. These are the only relatives. Amongst the others is an old school friend who lived down the road, but when I ask if he was one of Tom's childhood playmates during the war years he mumbles that they lost touch a long time ago. There are two men of Tom's vintage who know each other, one with a withered hand that he keeps squirreled away like an extra sleeve in his coat pocket. Tom's cleaning lady is called Mrs Curtis and offers me a tight nod but does not shake my hand. Hannah gives me a broad smile which may be warm or may be knowing and introduces me in turn to three women who were friends of Beth's clumped together in the one pew and each of them offers me a limp hand and a curt nod.

There is a definite sense that some unfortunate reputation precedes me, that whatever the vicar may have mentioned has not endeared me to this crew who must suspect me of an ulterior motive. It could be the age gap and the city clothes. Or perhaps Tom had a fortune stashed away, perhaps they think I am some gold-digger who goes about befriending lonely old men in graveyards to see if I can extort a few quid out of them on their deathbeds. Tom would be amused by all of this and it is, of course, no more than he would expect. I take up my position, alone in a pew on the left-hand side after making a big fuss of Jack who remains in custody with the vicar and sits by the entrance where a thick wreath is pinned to the door. The candles are dressed with sprigs of holly and red ribbons veined with gold. Death seems particularly unseemly this time of year and Tom is sandwiched into the Christmas timetable for an early morning slot before a carol concert from the local school choir. The vicar keeps it brief. There is no singing and no eulogy. We are all trying hard to ignore the gaping absence that is Charlie's no-show.

I imagine him nursing his grievance in Melbourne. It is a late summer afternoon there now and he will be out in the garden clutching a beer bottle and watching his little daughter crawl about in the grass, a parent now himself and harnessed to the yoke of unconditional love and perhaps feeling suitably petty that he refused to make the journey. Laura will have tried her best to get him to attend, can sense the regret that will consume him in later life like a bad smell. But Charlie has his old man's stubbornness. He will nurture this new loss, plump it up like a favourite pet grown sleek and fat from overfeeding. He may even perpetuate the paternal experience if he is not careful, although it could be different with a daughter, maybe sometimes familial dysfunction stops repeating itself. Charlie drains the beer bottle, flings it into the bushes. He reassures himself that his non-attendance is an empty gesture. He thinks the dead don't know who shows up.

And it is appropriately bitter. A sharp easterly wind whistles about the entrance as we emerge from the church although there is a break in the leaden cloud and a widening strip of blue that has not yet found the sun. The undertakers roll the coffin down the slope, black suits shiny with wear underneath their raincoats. Jack trots ahead as if he is leading the procession, pauses for a moment by the war memorial to scan for trouble but there is no one about. Just a few scuttering leaves and the sound of a rope flapping against the flagpole that lends the occasion a bizarrely nautical flavour.

Jack stands a few feet away from the graveside, looking airily away as if preoccupied with other more pressing matters. And quite right too, since he is now orphaned and officially homeless. He stares at the gate that leads to the fields, perhaps wondering if he could survive as a feral dog but it is too late, he comes from a long line of pets reared for man's pleasure, his survival instinct has been eroded by easy pickings and comfort and he would wind up being shot for stealing chickens. Dependency is a curse. After a lifetime's grouchiness Jack is without the skills to render himself instantaneously adorable so that some old lady will fall in love with him and take him home to a cosy future of treats and cushions. He might well worry. I do not think that Tom's cousin will bail him out, she does not look like the doggy type and gives him a wide berth. I see her check her watch under the guise of fiddling with her glove. Her features are buried in an accumulation of jowls that fold into her thick black polo neck, a slit of a mouth, lips that barely move when she speaks. The buttons on her coat strain against her bulk. There is no display of grief, just a respectful tolerance of the procedure in this dutiful and joyless gathering. There is nothing of the flavour of the man in the coffin.

The vicar closes his little prayer book and shakes some drops over the open grave. 'In the name of the Father, the Son and the Holy Spirit.' As the ropes slip through the grave-diggers' hands I wonder how Tom feels about being lowered on top of Beth. The cousin steps forward with a single white rose which strikes me as a rather grand touch from someone so distant. Perhaps she expects some inheritance. Beth's friends step forward, doubtless here in her memory rather than his. They throw in a few red roses, and I can hear Tom laugh, that loud sharp crack – I glance round but he is not here, none of the dead are here. I think of him running down the beach cliff at Puys, peering into the pillbox. I see him frowning at the croissant, sketching out the map of Dieppe on the napkin, checking my rear bumper, crouched down over the plaque on his flat roof and I feel a tear, astonishing, slip down my cheek.

Oh Tom, if you were here you would say this miserable send-off is no more than you deserved. A fine mess you made. A lesson for us all.

Jack scurries over to the graveside and peers down at the coffin, wondering perhaps if some histrionics could buy him some time. A mute panic ripples through the assembled group as he inches forwards and dislodges a clump of soil that falls into the grave. The cousin raises a gloved hand to her chest, the undertaker takes one swift step and then freezes in case any further movement might precipitate disaster. The vicar raises his palm in divine intervention, or maybe he is counsel-ling restraint and it seems for a moment as if the whole pro-cedure is about to descend into farce and Jack is going to hurl himself into the grave in a final gesture of defiance. He looks up, his front paws wrist deep in the earth, scans the gathering to make sure he has everyone's attention. He is after all the chief mourner and the one to whom this death matters most, for it has cast his very existence into doubt. He is hanging by a string here, just one step away from a lethal injection and this little stunt is his last-ditch attempt.

'Jack,' I say, my voice surprisingly confident. He pricks his ears, turns around to look at me over his shoulder. 'Come here, Jack,' I say bending down. His bulbous eyes hold my gaze. He is mulling it over, trying to calculate the trade-off and then with one more glance down at the grave he scoots over and hops up unexpectedly into my arms. A little laugh and a murmur of relief through the group. I stand up, he is surprisingly light and I can feel his rapid heartbeat against my chest.

'Well then,' says the vicar looking around with a benevolent smile. The undertaker nods thoughtfully, a little disappointed that the crisis has been averted. Jack sits glaring back at the mourners from his new elevated position. There is a break in the edge of the congregation and a move to drift away.

Behind me I can sense the rising winter sun. Frosted grass sparkles like candied peel, like treasure shavings, and the dead bracken along the edges of the wall glows a rich treacly amber. The iron sky lightens and I turn to see the orange disc embedded in the stubborn grey. It is a universal illumination and it burns with a fire that pains my eye. It rises triumphant, streaks the lightless forest troops and dispels the gloom. Shadows dissolve, melt away and darkness is overcome. A pink jet trail shoots slanting across the sky just skimming my star and I wonder at all this unfolding beauty and death. The sun will struggle to rise any further this time of year but already I can feel weak warmth on the skin of my tipped face.

'I would like to say something.' Heads snap round at my

voice and the shuffling departees stop in their tracks.

'I think something should be said,' I hear my voice again.

The vicar beams encouragingly, delighted that this grim occasion is to be enlivened by a personal touch. The cousin manages a pained smile and her husband puts a tentative arm around her shoulder. I look around the assembled faces but there are no volunteers who have something to say. Jack yawns, lays his head along my right arm and closes his eyes. He has made his contribution with his own dramatics and will not be participating in this performance. But now that I am committed, I scramble – what to say, what do I know? They are leaning forward from the other side of the grave waiting expectantly. This has all the makings of a spectacle just when it was ending so well and then behind me I hear a rustling sound, a sudden gust shivers the wreaths. The cousin's husband raises his hand to steady his hat, reminding me of Tom and his trilby.

I hold Jack with one hand and rummage in my pocket. He grumbles a little at the movement as I walk forward and let the wooden cross and the poppy drop down to clatter faintly on the coffin. Hannah and her friend lean forward frowning, the vicar looks perplexed but when I pull back I can see Tom smile at the gesture. He is over to the side holding Estelle's hand and he laughs out loud, that rare cackle of joy and the others slide out to join them. There is Ellen, Tom's mother, curling around the cenotaph, running a hand over the marble. She turns her head to the west, towards Canada perhaps and thinks of the unlived future with Jimmy in some log cabin on a snow plain. Beth steps forward and pats her shoulder and they stand arm in arm looking out into the world of the living. Tom's father, Harry, appears behind them, mooches about in the background and then turns away, slinks unforgiven into the yew. Ellen nods at Beth as if to say things are just as she expected. Beth lifts her head, whispers something in Ellen's ear and they both giggle.

She smooths Estelle's hair, kisses Tom's vaporous cheek.
Estelle leans down and grabs a flower from a grave, sticks it
behind her ear and Tom nods approvingly. He lays his hand
on Estelle's shoulder and nods to me as if to assure me that
my friend is in good hands now, she will come to no more
harm. And there, streaking up behind them is Spike, speeding
through the air in graceful flight. He has a stick in his mouth
and he stops in front of Tom who takes the stick and hurls
it in slow motion right to the other side of the churchyard.
Spike shoots off to retrieve, his long silver mane ruffling in
the Christmassy air.

And they all turn to face me. Estelle fingers a sliver of her
straw hair and smiles, a secret knowing smile. Beth nudges
her, a little prodding of her ethereal ribs. Tom leans forward
and nods encouragement and then Estelle raises a slow arm
and waves, cartoonish, side-to-side, like another wave I once
witnessed as semaphore and then she blows a kiss, a gesture
that I do not recall from her in life. Beth and Ellen wiggle
their fingers and Tom himself bows and salutes. Spike stands
like a mascot in front of them, sniffing the air. They are all
waving goodbye.

And then they are gone. It is time for me to leave. It has
always been time to leave the past and recover the present.
The vicar looks beseechingly in my direction, the mourners
make to move away and out of the long, long ago, a line comes
back to me from the sing-song chanting of the classroom, it
comes rushing up through the years and I strike out in full
voice, trusting that I will make it to the end:

Remember me when I am gone away,
Gone far away into the silent land;
When you can no more hold me by the hand,
Nor I half turn to go, yet turning stay.

Remember me when no more day by day
You tell me of our future that you planned:
Only remember me; you understand
It will be too late to counsel then or pray.
Yet if you should forget me for a while
And afterwards remember, do not grieve:
For if the darkness and corruption leave
A vestige of the thoughts that once I had,
Better by far you should forget and smile
Than that you should remember and be sad.

21

JACK DOES A THOROUGH INSPECTION of the kitchen, sniffs around each pile of books and, finding nothing of interest, returns to sit staring up at my mother.

'Of course,' she says. 'Some water,' and she pokes about in a cupboard, eventually pulling out Spike's old bowl which she rinses and half fills with water and places on the floor in the corner.

'I can't believe you kept that.'

'A souvenir,' she shrugs. 'I thought it might be needed some day. And I was right.'

Jack turns his head, but he does not drink, just remains looking up at her. 'Something to eat maybe,' she says and steps over to the bread bin, peels off a chunk of crust from a bloomer.

'Here,' she says bending down. Jack takes it very delicately from her hand, trots over to her reading chair and hops into Spike's old bed, positioning the bread right by his nose.

'I'll have to get a new footstool then,' she says and she looks right at me and then away and nods as if some private assessment has been conducted. A gentle smile, knowing, mournful spreads across her face. Of course she has heard. Mrs Harris will not have missed it, will have got her hands on the gossip mags and my humiliation immortalised in the social diary.

. . . . .

'What's all this?' Nicola jabbed at the magazine lying open on her desk. Upside down the photo looked even worse. '"Cormac reunited with his first love!" I can't believe you never ever mentioned it. You even gave me those tickets last year.'

'We were kids. He was just the boy next door.'

She was rubbing her tummy again, the baby is due in three weeks and it was her last day at work. A few cardboard boxes on the floor. The shelves emptied of photos. 'God, you don't give much away, do you? Come, let's get a coffee. I want gory details of the party, the whole works.'

'Between you and me, Caro, I might not come back,' she said as we headed for the lift. 'I've been doing this for long enough, it's time for a different life now. No more dealing with all this –' she gestures at the open-plan, 'all this *loss*.'

The blue-veined, white-skinned girl floated past us and smiled at Nicola's bump.

'I'll miss you,' I said as the sudden truth hit me with some force. I have fallen into the easy habit of her warmth.

'Haven't you had enough too? I mean wouldn't you like to try something else? Something a bit more upbeat?'

'I'm used to it. I'm good at it.'

'You could be good at something else. Easily. You have far more talent than you use. I know that.' She stopped by the elevator. 'You know that too.'

The lift doors closed on us. 'You loved him, didn't you?' and it was a statement of fact rather than a question. A rush of hidden air and my ears popped in the descent. 'Oh, I always guessed there was something way back in the past. That you'd had your fingers burnt, your heart broken, whatever.'

There was nowhere to look except my blurry reflection in the steel doors as we stood facing forwards. 'It's OK,' Nicola patted my arm. 'I'm not prying. Remember I'm the expert on childhood sweethearts.' The doors slid apart and we stepped out into the lobby. 'Wait,' she says, 'he's kicking like mad,' and bent her head, hand smoothing the baby. 'Reminding me to tell you something. To let go.'

My mother manoeuvres herself into the armchair, careful not to disrupt Jack who is curled up tightly in Spike's bed. She puts one foot slowly on the side of the bed and Jack lifts his head, shuffles forward and rests his head squarely on her foot.

'That's a sign of dominance,' I say.

She tilts her head to one side, considering. 'Or maybe it's a gesture of affection?' and it is a question, the first question she seems to have addressed to me for a very long time. Perhaps ever.

'We should talk sometimes,' I say. 'Instead of just reading.'

She nods, strokes Jack with her foot. 'Was there something in particular?'

'No.'

Jack sighs, a soft growling sigh, keeping his lids shut tight in concentrated sleep. I make a small 'thuhh' sound and he opens one bleary eye, raises his head only to let it sink down again on his two front paws.

'Maybe we could start by talking about the books?' she says.

'Yes. We could start with the books.'

Acknowledgements

THE LOSS ADJUSTOR IS ACCOMPANIED by a music video which can be viewed on YouTube. I am extremely grateful to the people who gave up their time to work so enthusiastically on this project. Special thanks to Mac for song writing and art direction as well as ruthless feedback on the first draft of the novel, to Mike Edgerton for drums, keyboard and late nights spent recording and editing the video and to Roy Marshall for lead guitar. Thanks to Rebecca Janes for her patience and energy in bringing Estelle to life on screen and to Paul Donovan for facilitating the guest appearance of Tess all the way from Australia.

This book began unexpectedly at Yaddo in Saratoga Springs in 2007 and I am indebted to staff and benefactors for continuing to provide a place of such inspiration. Thanks to Noreen Heaslip for expert advice on the world of insurance, to Steve Janes on fire investigation and police procedure and to staff at the Imperial War Museum.

As always, thanks to Oscar for great company and conversation on many of the walks through the landscape of this book. And, finally, a very special thanks to the ghosts.

My reading on World War II included *Dieppe 1942*, Ken Ford (Osprey, 2003); *Dieppe: Tragedy to Triumph*, Brigadier General Denis & Shelagh Whitaker (Trans-Atlantic Publications,

1992); *Canada at Dieppe*, T. Murray Hunter, (Balmur, 1982); *The Official History of the Canadian Army in the Second World War*, *Vol. 1* 'Six Years of War', Lt. Col. C.P. Stacey (available online from the Canadian Directorate of History and Heritage); *Ticket to Hell*, A. Robert Prouse (Goodread, 1983); *The Sussex Home Guard*, Paul Crook (Middleton, 1998). The poem on page 241 is Christina Rossetti's 'Remember'. Extracts from Edgar Allan Poe's 'The Premature Burial' in *Tales of Mystery and Imagination* (Wordsworth Editions, 1992) appear on page 122.

The books mentioned on page 231 are: *The Outermost House*, Henry Beston (Henry Holt, 1992), *The Worst Journey in the World*, Apsley Cherry-Garrard (Penguin, 1937) and *Captain Scott's Last Expedition: Extracts from the Personal Journals* (John Murray, 1967). 'The White Cliffs of Dover' on page 183 is the version sung by Vera Lynn, available on YouTube.